Journal of Resistance

Journal of Resistance

MIKIS THEODORAKIS

Translated from the French by Graham Webb

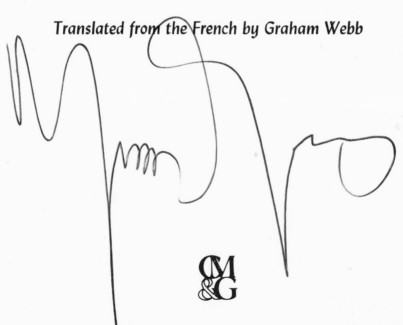

COWARD, McCANN & GEOGHEGAN, INC.

NEW YORK

CONTENTS

ATHENS—The Underground

Friday, 21 April 1967, the day of the military *coup d'état* in Greece, found me under the spell of Federico Garcia Lorca. In fact a month before I had completed my last work, a song cycle on seven of Lorca's poems which had been translated into Greek. (The great Spanish poet had found the closely related voice of Odysseas Elytis to render him in our language.) I spent the first weeks after the putsch in hiding and so was unable to consider composing anything, as this diary shows.

Friday, 21 April 1967

2 a.m.   Closeted in my study at home. Preparing for the Second Week of Popular Music Composition which is to take place on Mount Lycabettus. I have been in touch by telephone with the composers Khristou, Xarkhakos, Loïzos and Leontis. My aim: to present 'metasymphonic' works.

3 a.m.   Just got to bed: telephone call. A friend. She says: 'I've been told there are tanks rolling round Constitution Square. Seems there's been a military putsch.'
   To check this information, I ring Party headquarters. Line dead. I try certain leaders at home. The lines have been cut. I wake Myrto. She is calm. She says:
   'Get dressed! Quickly! I'm going to burn the papers.'
   I ask:
   'Should we wake the children?'

9

'No! Better leave them...It would upset them,' she says.

Before leaving I go into their room. When shall I see them again? A final kiss for Myrto at the door and I disappear into the night. It is beginning to get light. The street is deserted. The district secretary of the Party lives a few steps down the road. I slip into his courtyard. A dog leaps at me and bars the way. A little farther on I spot two policemen in the road. I run to Yannis's. I wake him. 'It's dictatorship. Go quickly and warn the secretary and Kostas (a member of the Executive). Kostas lives opposite a colonel...Be careful!...(the colonel was Papadopoulos!) And tell them to come here!' I am planning the first Resistance cell.

The radio begins broadcasting military marches. I telephone home. The line has not been cut yet. My wife whispers in haste: 'They're here!' and hangs up. The secretary arrives. 'I'm going to look for Kostas,' he says. Time passes. They don't return. Have they been arrested? (Later I learned they had stumbled upon a police patrol which had given chase, but they had got away. Now one of them is on Leros and the other has just been arrested after three years underground.)

The radio is still on. We listen to the text of the Royal Decree:

In pursuance of Article Nine of the Constitution, We, Constantine, King of the Hellenes, take the decision to suspend Articles Five, Six, Eight, Ten, Twelve, Fourteen, Eighteen, Twenty, Ninety-five and Ninety-seven of the Constitution with effect throughout the territory of Greece, because of dangers which threaten the order and security of the country.

Other communiqués follow.

The state of seige is proclaimed.

Arrest and detention are authorised for any person without taking account of the laws which are in force, since at present there is no limit on the length of preventive detention...Any person, without regard to rank or title, can be brought before the military tribunal or a special military commission...Public and private meetings are banned... All gatherings will be broken up by force...Searches can be

10

conducted in public and private premises and dwelling places, without restriction.

We must react. We must go into action. I make contact by telephone with militants who live in those parts of the city where the lines have not yet been cut. They tell me the streets are deserted; the people have not moved an inch! I guess there must have been mass arrests.

Some bits of news worry me. I don't understand anything any more. Antonio G...rings me : 'Arnaoutis (the king's aide-de-camp) lives opposite my place. At the moment soldiers are break-his door down.'

With the help of Thanasis we begin to compose the first appeal.

We wire it to comrades in the struggle and to friends. We ask them to spread the appeal in their districts by all possible means. Yannis's whole family get down to the job of copying it out by hand. Then, with other young people, they distribute the appeal in the district.

TO THE GREEK PEOPLE

Fascism has struck our country. The king, his generals and the CIA believe that our people will be reduced to silence by violence and terror. We call upon all honest officers, soldiers and patriots to stand beside the people, to say 'No to violence', 'No to dictatorship and fascism'.

Greek democrats, this crime will be the beginning of the defeat of the enemies of freedom. Organise yourselves, fight and resist the dictators of the junta.

People of Athens, demonstrate in the streets! Patriots, meet in Constitution Square! Forward to the liquidation of the enemies of the people and the country. Fascism will not be victorious! Long live democracy! Long live Greece! Long live the Greek people!

Athens, 21 April 1967

The threat is getting more acute. There is every chance that the house in which I am taking shelter will be searched. I must find another place. Late in the evening the radio announces that the king has appointed Kollias head of the government. Kollias says over the radio:

11

The government is determined to carry its work through to the very end. It will not tolerate the slightest disturbance of order. All who are tempted to provoke disorder will be punished in accordance with the law...Greece will remain faithful to her Western allies...The country is on the edge of the abyss and the elections which were to have taken place before long would have changed nothing...

Nobody comes (nor will come) to Constitution Square. Our appeal has fallen on deaf ears. More than the tanks, it is the deception of our rulers, following so many mistakes, that has destroyed our people. The first battle has been lost. The resistance must now be organised. I move house and go to Viron's.

Saturday, 22 April 1967

Midnight The police are after me. I draft the first instructions for the formation of resistance groups. Viron's wife suffers from a heart complaint as a result of her husband continually being arrested by the police.

I realise I must leave the house as quickly as possible. But how? And where can I go? I carry on writing. Viron promises to give my manuscript to a printer friend who lives nearby.

I decide to return to Yannis's before dawn. I know the area like the back of my hand—ever since the Occupation. The large gardens in front of all the houses make it easy for someone who knows these parts well to move about. I know them by heart! It was here that I fought the Nazis in 1943–4. It was also here that I fought the British in December 1944, and later the Greek fascists.

As soon as I am back at Yannis's I must find a way of breaking through the ring which is surrounding me and of getting out of the Nea Smyrni district.

I disguise myself: I make a false moustache out of cotton wool dipped in black varnish. I kiss all the members of Viron's family and leave. It is pitch dark outside. I hug the low garden fences. At the slightest sound I hop over them. At Yannis's everyone is expecting me. Viron's children had warned them. In the afternoon I shall try to leave Nea Smyrni. The atmosphere is heavy all day. The police might knock on the door at any moment. Through the half-closed windows we watch the army and police vehicles coming and going in the streets. Time passes. It begins to get dark. Will the car come right to the door? The driver will need real courage. We are all convinced that if we are arrested we shall be executed on the spot.

9 p.m. A car draws up in front of the house. Friends? Enemies? I slip down into my hiding-place. The door bell rings. They're there! The driver brings two friends with him to cover up the transfer. New hands to shake. A quick glance down the street...I dash to the car. Bent double and covered over, I crouch between the seats. The two passengers in the back rest their legs on me. I try to guess the direction we are taking by the noise outside and the turns in the road. The driver is nervous. With good reason. Suddenly he jams on the brakes.

I whisper:

'What's the matter?'

'We've hit on a military patrol.'

I hear voices coming towards us. The car reverses so as to get round the army lorry which is barring the road. We get away. The driver lets out a sigh of relief.

The car climbs Filopappos hill. Stops suddenly. We have just avoided an 'ordinary' traffic accident. Finally we arrive at the refuge...a refuge which is to be followed by so many others.

Our two companions get out to see if the way is clear.

Leftheris is waiting behind the door. I get out of the car, though not without some difficulty, and dash into the house, and up the stairs...

From the window I can see the port of Piraeus and Falirou Square. Somewhere over to the left is my house. My wife, my children, my parents. How are they? The first things I see in the room are two tape recorders. I'll use them!

My joy at being in this comfortable place of refuge does not last long. Leftheris is afraid. His wife takes me on to the terrace, where there is a wash-house without a door, and at the back of it a wooden bench without a mattress. Just above my head, on Filopappos hill, I can see guardposts and sentries. If prying looks came from over there and the authorities sensed that I was in the area, I should be in a very sorry plight. I decide to lie still, and flat out. I cover myself with a bear skin. I keep a shot-gun at my side and this gives me an illusion of safety.

Sunday, 23 April

Leftheris's wife comes out on to the terrace. She is carrying a basket of linen which is to be hung out to dry; at the bottom of it she has hidden my food. She brings me the latest news, which is alarming. All the well-known politicians have been arrested. There is talk of mass executions, brutality and tortures. World public opinion must be informed. Further, the world must be shown its responsibility for the new crime which has been committed in our country. I ask for a pencil and some paper. I draft an appeal:

> The king, disloyal officers and perjured magistrates have, in collaboration with the American imperialists, abolished democracy in Greece. This act of treason is the result of their panic and it will lead inevitably and rapidly to the final denouement of the domestic political crisis in our country, with the monarchy being torn down by its protectors and protégés. By this action the pitiable fanatics who are in the service of the foreigners have banished themselves from the Hellenic nation. The Greek people has condemned them. Their end, which will not be long in coming, will be the end which free peoples always reserve for their tyrants.
>
> Our country finds itself today under martial law. Tens of thousands of arrests have been made. Hundreds of thousands of citizens are being hunted. Nobody knows the exact number of victims. Those who have been detained, among them leading elements of the Left, the Centre and even the Right, are being tortured inhumanely. [This alludes to the threats of death made against Manolis Glezos, threats which were later denied.] The executioners of the liberties of our people are preparing new death camps and emergency tribunals.
>
> Thirty years on and fascism is striking Europe again; it has struck the cradle of civilisation, the heart of democracy, the proud and shining Acropolis of humanism.
>
> We appeal to all the democrats of the world, and particularly those in Europe, to express their solidarity with the Greek people's struggle. At the same time, we Greek patriots are organising national and democratic resistance with both

14

optimism and confidence in the unconquerable strength of our people.

The history of our country is great and glorious. Dozens of times we have tested our strength against armed enemies and have vanquished them. The harder and more bitter the new historic battle is, the more decisive and beautiful it will be, for it will lead us to glorious victory, to liberty, to real democracy without kings, to national independence, to the patriotic unity of our people, to a national renaissance.

Greeks, workers, peasants, employees, scholars, intellectuals, artisans, officers, soldiers, sailors, airmen, patriotic gendarmes and policemen, proud Greek youth, men and women, young and old, all Greek patriots are rising as one man against those who are destroying our country. They set aside their political differences and unite under a common banner: 'Liberty, Democracy, Greece.' They unite in a national patriotic front to fight against the dictatorship. For us there is one single ideal, one common aim: to tear Greece from the shame of tyranny whatever sacrifices have to be made.

Our hearts burn with a terrible hatred for the tyrants.

Those who have abolished the Constitution, who have violated democracy, the enemies of freedom, the traitors of the nation who believed that by force they would bring our people, who are lovers of democracy, to their knees—they can be sure that soon they will be trembling before the anger of the great Greek people and that there will not be a single corner of Greece where they can seek refuge.

In the country where democracy was born, the tyrants are destined to die.

Down with the monarcho-fascist dictatorship!
Out with the foreign oppressor!
Down with the hangman Kollias!
Long live the Greek people!
Long live Greece!

Athens, 23 April 1967
Mikis Theodorakis

In the margin I add a few practical instructions:

Please make sure this appeal reaches its destination. Copy

it out by hand, on typewriters, duplicate it, print it and deliver it from door to door, from one town to the next. Send it abroad by all possible means. Get it—either in Greek or in translation—to foreign journalists, foreign press agencies, representatives of foreign firms, foreign diplomats and foreign embassies.

I spend the day and most of the night copying the text out by hand. Then I go down to the flat and record it. We make dozens of copies of the tape. On the cassettes I write imaginary song titles...

I arrange for this material to be sent all over Athens. From there it will get abroad. In fact, the messages reached Paris and Rome five days later. I thought that this statement would be just one among dozens of appeals which would be taken up by the political parties and national personalities. To my great surprise this was in fact the only voice to be heard beyond our borders and to tell the world at large of Greece's desire to resist tyranny.

24–25 April

I stay alone in my hiding place on the terrace, cut off from the rest of the world. I have paper and a pencil. I try to analyse the situation with what little, rather confused information I have. My aim is draw up a text which might serve as the basis for working out a plan of action for the first groups of the NEW RESISTANCE that we must get under way. The result of this was a text in the form of a letter addressed primarily to members of the Lambrakis Democratic Youth (DNL); the following is an extract:

ANALYSIS OF THE SITUATION
(for the members of the NEW RESISTANCE)
Athens, 25 April 1967

...Our people have been taken by surprise by the enemies of democracy and this has been turned to good account. They had made careful preparation to lull the democratic masses with the help of the policy of division, confusion and illusion carried out by George Papandreou.

In this way we have been surprised, literally in our sleep. It is now clear that the dictators had taken their decision a

16

long time before and that they had been implementing their plan systematically, step by step, right up to 21 April.

Who is hiding behind the dictatorship?

First of all, the Americans, who are very experienced in this kind of operation. The 'protector' Talbott[1] played an active part, letting it be believed that he was simply making his good offices available, that he was concerned about the country keeping calm, that President Johnson had sent a message to the king assuring him of his faith in democracy, etc.

What is certain is that the militarists of the junta never have been and never will be able to take a step without approval and formal orders from the Americans, who, beyond their political prerogatives, keep control of all the machinery of society, including the distribution of petrol and munitions for tanks and aircraft. Certainly the imperialists would have preferred a régime with a parliamentary façade but they understood that the relations between the political forces in our country would clearly not favour a régime of national resignation, that there had been profound changes, especially in recent years, and that the democratic camp embraced 70 per cent of the Greek people. They knew, moreover, that within this camp forces were arising in response to the invigorating influence of the ideals of the Left, that the Centre Union could no longer play the full role of European social democracy, that the people were attracted by the Left and were advancing resolutely in that direction.

They then decided to resort to stronger measures to secure their military and economic presence in Greece. In face of the censure which their Vietnam policy is encountering all over the world, they are feeling the need to secure strong positions for themselves by disregarding the wishes of the peoples. They see our country simply as a gigantic war base from which to counter the forward positions of the socialist camp and the insurgent peoples of the Middle East. Their next objective will be Cyprus and we must warn the world of it, by all possible means. The people's power in Syria irks them. At present, with a firm base in Greece, they are trying to fix the Arab liberation movements once and for all.

But it is not just the American militarists who are pushing the country to dictatorship, there are also the representatives of foreign monopolies, like Tom Pappas. Let us not forget that in our country there are powerful economic interests which are seeking, first of all, to protect their own privileges and then to step up the exploitation of our people in order to reap exorbitant profits.

These foreigners are backed up by a domestic oligarchy which is at their service—men like Onassis, Niarchos and Bodosakis, whose interests are linked with those of the foreigners because they too consider our country to be a colony: they want to keep wages and salaries down, and block any move by the workers for higher wages, so as to secure the most profitable degree of exploitation. They dream of making our country into an enormous camp in which each worker gets no more than a subsistence wage.

The Palace is compromised too. It is in league with the American imperialists and the domestic and foreign oligarchy. All the tales which are told about Constantine having been forced to sign the decree to abolish the Constitution, etc., are lies.

Having said this, we must give serious consideration to the role of the Greek Right. If the news of the arrest of Papaligouras, Kanellopoulos, Mitsotakis and other politicians is confirmed it would mean that they too have to some extent, without being aware of it, become tools in the hands of the dictators. They have been used and now that they are no longer needed they are discarded. But even if this is so their reputations are not spotless for they played a decisive part in bringing the dictatorship to power. Without the political assistance of the Right the dictators could not have seized power. Kollias had to make use of Kanellopoulos and the Radical National Union (ERE) in order to succeed. Without this decisive stage the route would have been barred to the dictators.

It follows that among all the Greek political parties it is the ERE which bears the heaviest historical responsibility for having accepted the role of hangman of democracy by bringing Kollias to power. If in the end they became victims themselves, quite apart from that being a harsh historical lesson, it reveals the deep contradictions and antagonisms which are troubling the Right and shows that behind the dictatorship there is the toughest kernel of the oligarchy, the darkest of interests: the fascist Right.

Then there is the responsiblity of the leadership of the Centre Union. George Papandreou's anti-communism and his refusal to collaborate, even unofficially, with the Left did not allow the democratic masses to unite at that critical moment. On the contrary, it created confusion, diverted the powerful popular current, spread illusions, lulled the people, the guardians of democracy, to sleep with slogans like 'The hour of democracy's triumph is come' and 'On 29 May we will be the government', etc., etc. In this way the one weapon the enemy fears—unity of action in the democratic camp—was lost by the obstinacy of the Centre Union leadership. One could say that the enemy sunk his knife into democracy at the very moment when the illusions which had been spread by the Centre Union leadership had not yet fully removed the people's readiness to fight. Hence the surprise and also the numbness of the popular masses, who were convinced that peaceful elections would disarm the forces which were enslaving the country and who suddenly found themselves attacked from behind by those same forces.

The warnings repeated time and time again by the Left had tragically been shown to be correct. It was not the first time that the Left had seen its policy confirmed by the facts. However, nobody could have expected such cruel and painful proof of its fears and predictions, both for the Nation and for the people.

Also, the EDA leadership had shown itself to be too conciliatory to Papandreou's contradictory policy. With a different attitude, by opposing every retrograde step by the Papandreou government, the Left could have helped the Centre Union to give up its fateful practice of dodging the difficulties and to finally take the path of democratisation by satisfying the political and economic demands of the masses.

Such a policy would have strengthened democratic government; it would also have made the Palace's *coup de force* of July 1965, the prelude to the dictatorship, impossible.

Unity of the democratic forces was the solution. We lost

the game because we did not understand it. It was obvious that when one of the adversaries holds the levers of power and the other has the popular masses with him, the decisive element which settles the issue is the dynamism, the degree of preparation, the resolution and readiness to fight of the masses. He who succeeds in dividing them or in uniting them to his advantage will be victorious.

On 21 April reaction prevailed because it had succeeded in dividing the democratic movement; it was we who were defeated because we had not succeeded in welding the democratic front together and presenting a clear and coherent policy.

But at least the lesson we have learned will serve us in the future. The Centrists, in particular, must understand that the catastrophe was caused by 'fighting on two fronts'. Those who urged George Papandreou to refuse any collaboration with us are now sharing the fate of the Left. All democrats now find themselves side by side in prison camps and deportation camps. Their jailers know full well that if the parties of the Left and Centre ever came to join forces it would be they themselves, the conspirators, who would take their places in the prisons and the camps.

History often creates terrible symbols. It is our job to hold them up for all to see. But what is done is done. Moaning is no way to criticise the past; one must be positive and constructive in order to correct the mistakes and light up the path which is to be followed.

There is no doubt that the wave of indignation will swell up at one and the same time against the tyrants and against the policy of the Papandreous.

We must be frank and straight: we must seek historical truth without compromising and by pursuing a positive aim, a political crystallisation. In other words, we must concentrate our efforts on achieving this unity so as to avoid making the same mistakes again. It is not too late. It is still possible to overthrow the dictatorship. And quickly!

What is this assertion based on? On the relative strengths of the two sides. It is clear that if, as we have said, the reactionaries had been preparing their *coup* for a long time, it is also true that the choice of the exact moment and the final moves were dictated by panic. This is proof that the

20

dictatorship has no popular base. Mussolini, Hitler, Franco, Peron and even Metaxas relied on the Army but they also had the support of a section of the people; Kollias, on the other hand, is almost alone. Apart from the Americans he can count on the support of only a few Army units. He does not enjoy the support of the people, not even one in ten of them. Equally, he does not enjoy the support of the whole of the Army, nor of the entire security forces, nor of all civil servants, and he is not supported by any political force. In fact, one can say that the greater part of the Army and the organs of state are opposed to Kollias.

Then again, as far as the people are concerned the conditions are ripe not only for them to free themselves from the present régime but also to strike out for profound political and economic changes.

One must not judge the democratic forces by how they appeared at the time of April *coup*; at that time they were very powerful not only from an electoral but also from a political and ideological point of view. As we have already explained, the people had been anaesthetised and were then struck in their sleep. It follows that as the people regain their senses they will regain their immense strength, too.

It is a fact that the Army's behaviour reflects that of the people. As the people rise up again, so the officers and troops will take courage and strength. And finally the people and the Army will join together and chase out the dictators.

What tactics must we adopt in the short term?

The dictatorship régime will accentuate—to the very extreme—all the basic contradictions between the oligarchy on the one hand and the working class on the other, because the exploitation will get worse. Discord will also grow between the oligarchy and the peasantry, and between those who promote a state of national resignation and the artists, intellectuals and scholars (because a medieval régime of interdicts and thought control will be set up). Finally a gulf will appear between the dictatorship and the young people, for one of the dictatorship's aims is to break the dynamic spirit of Greece's proud young people, to make teaching, thinking and convictions fascist, to create fascist organisations like EON,[2] and to condemn young

21

people to ignorance, unemployment, emigration and moral decline.

Finally, the dictatorship will accentuate the main contradiction within Greek society, which is expressed in the antagonism which exists between the Greek patriots and the American imperialists.

The Greek people's struggle, then, having as its main aim the overthrow of the Kollias government, must of necessity be patriotic, democratic, anti-dictatorship and anti-imperialist. In fact, the struggle for the release of detainees, for the economic demands of the workers, against the stifling of thought, against the enemies of youth, against the violent and repressive measures, etc., etc., converges on the struggle to chase out the dictators so that democracy can be re-established and the Constitution can come back into force, and so that the unwarranted foreign interference in our affairs ceases. It is under this banner that all Greeks will gather.

Our first duty is to set up a Patriotic Front against the dictatorship. All our militants, all members of democratic movements in our country, must convince themselves of this vital need and must assume this responsibility with full knowledge of what is involved.

Set up a Patriotic Front everywhere!

Actively organise democratic resistance! Our strategy and tactics are summed up in this call.

26 April

Leftheris brings Odysseas to the house; he is a militant of the DNL (Lambrakis Democratic Youth) and tells me that he is in contact with the majority of the DNL leaders who have so far escaped arrest. They all know that I am in hiding and are trying to communicate with me. I suggest that we hold a meeting on the spot. I am well aware of the dangers we shall be exposing ourselves to, but I am sure that the entire Greek people, and in particular our progressive movement, are at a decisive turning point, and that is why we must act upon the course of history. Who but a group of people conscious of their responsibilities could do it?

What is the latest news of the Party leaders? The majority

22

were arrested within hours of the *coup*. Five, or ten at the very most, have managed to escape arrest. For the moment they are in hiding. This is understandable because the entire police force must be on their heels. In all probability the leaders of the other parties are in the same predicament.

In fact, not a single voice has yet been heard to denounce the *coup d'état* and call for struggle. Are we left on our own then? What are the comrades thinking? I know they are burning to act! They have already formed the first cells at the University and in parts of the city. But what are their views? That we have been cheated. That everything must be changed...This is what Odysseas thinks.

We have regular meetings with the leaders of the Centre and Right Youth. We are all agreed on one point: that we must fight together without waiting for the leadership. There is a strong 'anti-leadership' current among the young people.

How far will we be able to come together? When? Where? How? Odysseas undertakes to speak to the others about it, and promises to get an answer as soon as possible. I give him copies of my appeal and of my analysis of the situation.

27 April

I am informed that the meeting hɛ ; been fixed for Easter Sunday and that I must get ready to move.

28 April—Good Friday

I am ready. False moustache, floppy hat, dark glasses—the classic get-up of the illegal militant! What else can I do? Unfortunately I am too easily recognised; I have no alternative but to disguise myself.

At nine in the evening two Resistance militants arrive in a car at the arranged meeting place. I get in the back seat. It is a dangerous stretch: all the streets in Athens are full of people going to celebrate Good Friday Mass. At any moment one could come upon a police block. The driver turns left and right, and in the Kypseli area we get stuck in the crowd. There are many policemen in uniform...looking at us unconcernedly!

We arrive at the house. It is only a couple of yards to the door but it seems an enormous distance: the street is brightly lit. A few yards farther on there is the entrance to a military camp, with guards and a constant coming and going of soldiers and vehicles. My companions shield me. I go through the door. In the lift—nobody. On the seventh floor—still nobody! At last as the door closes behind us I breathe a deep sigh of relief.

The room is small. It seems to be lived in by a bachelor. Nothing to eat. Odysseas and I stretch out. An empty stomach but a head full of dreams!

Saturday, 29 April

10 a.m. The first comrade arrives. It is Khristos, a member of the Presidium of the DNL. He is literally dying of hunger. He has been in an empty room, completely isolated, ever since the night of the *coup*.

11 a.m. Another member of the Presidium of DNL arrives— Aris. He is also here on behalf of two other Presidium members, Mikhalis and Thanasis, who have not managed to 'break through' the net to get to the meeting.

Midday Nikos, a journalist and member of EDA, joins us.

Everyone is absolutely worn out, but fired with an inexplicable, childlike optimism and joy. We are all burning to join the new resistance as soon as possible.

First decision : must eat! Odysseas enters triumphantly, loaded with tins; we open them and eat like gluttons. We tell our adventures and swap news and ideas.

Late into the night we decide to go to sleep. The next day, Easter Day, is to be the beginning of the resurrection of the Greek people. We all firmly believe it and that is why we feel the burden of responsibility which we are assuming.

We lie down where we can; some on the couch, others on the floor. The last few strands of conversation die away and we fall asleep. Before dropping off I go over the outlines of the report I am to present in the morning. The feeling of being surrounded by comrades gives me a deep sense of happiness and strength.

Sunday, 30 April. Easter

Through the half-open window we see typical Greek Easter

scenes. Only the heart is not there. Everything is paralysed. The people are going about like shadows. The sky is grey and tearful. It is suffering with us. In our room the tension is rising. We take our places around a small table. I want to say: 'Christ is risen!', but for us it is still the Crucifixion. I start to read my report, in a serious voice.

First, I explain the reasons for my Statement. Then I reveal the broad outlines of my analysis of the situation and go on to speak of our responsibilities.

'The first and most serious responsibility: How have we arrived at dictatorship? The second: How and why did we not foresee it? How and why did we not react to the military *coup d'état*? We fell without defending ourselves. We let ourselves be surrounded and taken—the movement, the Party and the people—while we were fast asleep!

'When an army suffers such a reverse, the soldiers and the officers remove the generals. I propose that we do the same: that we dismiss our strategists and assume the responsibility of reorganising our forces and of leading the New Resistance!

'In practical terms, it is we who are taking this initiative today. Those leaders who have not been arrested have had it. There has been no sign of life from them. You are members of the Youth leadership. I am your President, a deputy and a member of the Executive Committee of EDA—it is my job to replace them. But I suggest that we do take account of those leaders who are now in hiding and who will tomorrow no doubt want to take part in the fight.

'Because it is the Resistance which binds our hearts and because we need able organisers and leaders, we must judge each man not by the posts he has held up to now but by his abilities and, above all, by his willingness and ardour as a combatant. Later, when we are free, we shall all of us, without exception, give an account of our actions both before the movement and before the people.

'As regards the Politburo of the Greek Communist Party, which is abroad—in my opinion, they bear the greatest responsibility of all...However, we must count them, along with all our comrades who are living abroad, as a force to be reckoned with in our new fight. We must maintain the best fraternal relations with the Politburo and demand its constant collaboration, while at the same time making it quite clear that here it is we who are responsible! But let there be no split! At the present time that would be a catastrophe for our people. On the other hand, we must give proof that we are vigilant for the future.

'However, we must not forget that the struggle will be long and hard. Where is our support? The Central Committee and the Politburo of the Greek Communist Party, which are abroad, could provide precious reserves in material and perhaps in men, too. They could appeal for international solidarity and assistance; they could inform world opinion of our action and of the aims of our struggle; above all, they could organise concrete aid from the socialist countries and the world communist movement.

'How can we solve the problem of the Party? As I have already said, for us the leadership has not been up to scratch. There is a profound crisis. And this explains how we were surprised in the dead of night. What must communists do to save the honour of the Party and of the people? What is the immediate duty? To organise the struggle. To be once again at the heart of the battle which the people are going to join to combat the tyranny. That is what we are doing at the moment! And that is why we are in point of fact the active force of the communists, and of all people on the Left. It follows that we must think and act as responsible men, as leaders, in the certainty that our decisions could have a historic significance. I come now to the proposals:

'I propose the foundation of a Patriotic Front on the basis of the broadest possible participation, from communists to those on the Right who are against the dictatorship. The communists and the members of EDA and DNL will form the backbone of the Front. But we will not confine ourselves to it; I reckon that a new historic opportunity is presenting itself for us to create a new national and popular movement against the junta, in which the unity of the people and the democratic, and then radical and socialist, education of the masses will be realised.

'I conceive of the Front not only as a shock force to defeat the dictatorship but also as the political movement of the Greek people, a movement which will consolidate democratic liberties and will lead the country to a national renaissance.

'So, while fighting in the ranks of the Resistance we must, at the same time, once and for all settle our ideological and political problems, build up the Party so that it meets the demands of the people and the times, work out our short- and long-term programmes, form research and study committees from among the resistance workers to study the situation of Greece as it is and to work out projects in all fields of national life! This will be our most valuable contribution to the Resistance.

'It is essential that we make a rigorous examination of our differences and reduce them so as to organise the struggle effectively.

'At the present moment it is clear that we have alongside us the forces of the Centre and those of the Right which are opposed to the dictatorship. I propose that we enter into immediate contact with the representatives of the other parties with a view to creating a united Front. But first we must ourselves accept an equality of rights and duties, so that the Front belongs to everyone and our only privilege is to be in the thick of the fight and of the sacrifices. I judge that the struggle will be hard and difficult. Thus it is necessary to assemble the greatest possible number of forces in a common Resistance Front. Our slogans must be: Unity—Organisation—Struggle. Particular attention must be paid to the young people. It is significant that the first resistance organisations were formed in the University.'

These are some of the essential points from my report, which brought together the thoughts of those present and of those who are in contact with them. Each comrade spoke in turn. The long preliminary debates had already brought out the general lines upon which we were all prepared to build the New Resistance and to revive our movement. We now pass on to examine the measures to be taken and the delegation of tasks. We work in an atmosphere of exaltation and optimism.

We finish late at night. Each of us now has his own sphere of work. The comrades charge me with coordinating all this activity. The next contacts are fixed.

A new joy warms us to the core. Our only desire is to throw ourselves into the struggle as quickly as possible.

But practical problems arise immediately: where am I to stay?

The comrades say goodbye. We embrace one another. They can move about provided they take precautions. As far as I am concerned, I cannot take two steps in the darkest side street in the best known districts of the city.[3]

27

9 p.m. Two friends who are responsible for accommodating 'illegal' militants come up to see me. They propose three solutions, which are rejected *en bloc*. Finally, Nikos offers me his place and he will go elsewhere. I accept. He leaves to arrange the move. He returns shortly afterwards. I go down by lift, seven floors. Nobody outside. I get into the car. It is raining. Dimitris is driving. He tells me with real emotion: 'Your message has been taken up by foreign radio stations. You can always count on me for any service and any message carrying.'

We are going down Syngrou Avenue. As we pass my house and then my parents' I involuntarily turn my head. They could not imagine that I was passing only a few yards from them. We get into an area where there are a lot of gardens. The streets are deserted. We go into a house.

'Here's your room!' the owner tells me. He is surrounded by his family.

'Please give me some paper and a pencil,' I ask them. I get down to work.

Two days later I have my first working meeting with Nikos, who is responsible for the press. We decide to call our paper *Nea Ellada* (New Greece). Nikos has prepared a detailed report on its editing, printing and distribution. We also envisage publishing a satirical review and distributing other manifestos and printed matter.

Then I get to work with Aris, who is responsible for the political section of the organisation. It seems that everywhere there is a strong urge for joint action. We must prepare a Manifesto to serve as a basis for the contacts. Where are our comrades? Brillakis has had stomach trouble and is in hospital under a false name. Drakopoulos, Karas, Benas, Filinis, Efremidis, Iliopoulos, Abatielos, Vettas, Katharosporis and others are in hiding. We must bring them together at all costs.

1 May and the days following

Two more days pass. The master of the house buys boards and nails...to wall me up. I am still locked in the underground room. Most of the time I spend writing. When I get tired I read.

Aris walks past the front of the house. I see him through the slits in the shutters. But he moves on without knocking. A bad sign. Is he being shadowed? In fact, the area seems to be in the control of the police. I decide to move out. I warn Dimitris and move for the time being into a little lean-to in the back yard. I cannot understand why the police are around.[4]

It is almost pitch dark. I slip down the garden and into the car. I pull my hat down over my eyes. Dimitris takes me to his place.

We arrive there just as the police are turning the corner. (They had just raided Dimitris's block.)

The room is plunged in semi-darkness; it is covered with carpets, piled high with books, records and oriental curios. I find Babis—he too has found temporary refuge there.

We swap news. I must move on. Dimitris and his friend Roula come back after two hours of looking for somewhere. 'We've found a safe place. Let's go!' Dimitris reckons it is better to take the main roads through the centre. I disagree. He insists. He says the police and the Army do the rounds of the small streets.

We cross Kolonaki Square. (I later learned that several friends had spotted me.) A rendezvous with another car in a street. I leap quickly from one to the other.

'Hi! I'm Koula.'

'I'm Orestis.'

We arrive behind a building. I bend double and squeeze out of the mini-car. I walk the twenty yards or so as naturally as possible...A lorry comes past. Its headlights pick me out. First door. Nobody. Second door...The drawing-room. Lights. Comfort. Face to face with Petros.

'I've just come myself—less than half an hour ago,' he says, as if to excuse himself.

'I'm Antonis,' the fourth man says.

So I enter upon a new and decisive phase in my life. How many thousands of houses are there in Athens? And here I am with Petros in the same house and we arrived at almost the same time. And we are looking for one another!

We eat together. A kind of celebration. 'Everyone wants to fight,' our new friends tell us. 'Our circles are rather conservative ones and so we are all burning to do something.'

After dinner Petros and I retire to our room to talk. He is fired with enthusiasm when told of what has already been undertaken. But when I come to speak of the position we have adopted towards the Politburo and, in general, towards the leadership of the Greek Communist Party, he frowns. I know he has dedicated his whole life to the Party. He is a friend whom I value and whom I love enormously. We must fight together. 'We'll proceed with great care,' I tell him. 'We'll try if possible to avoid discussing questions of strategy. But as far as the leadership of the struggle is concerned we must be firm and resolute. It's we who are involved in this and nobody else. Certainly we'll get in contact with other cadres. We need well-informed advice. That's why we must form a powerful leadership committee, taking in former militants as well as the Lambrakis youth. For the moment it is the Lambrakides who are assuming the leadership. Come with us.' I leave him until tomorrow to think about it...

His answer is brief and to the point.

'OK! I suggest that you take the job in hand. We'll discuss the problems and then I'll talk to the comrades about them. Nobody must come here any more. And you will not leave. There will just be me to keep you in touch with those outside.'

We study all the current problems concerning the organisation and finally arrive at a series of suggestions for immediate action, starting with the Manifesto. I pass all the contacts to Petros...

He goes out. I watch him through the slit in the shutter. He strides confidently across the street.

He returns two days later as agreed. The draft of the Manifesto is ready. The other members of the new leadership must see it, and so must our allies. Petros has contacted them. The majority of them fervently want to join the Patriotic Front. On his second sortie Petros takes with him the *Little Guide of the Good Resistance Worker*, which we have both written and which contains practical instructions for everyone.

Comrade Koula is making some little coloured stamps to collect money. We gather material for our roneoed first edition. The text of the Manifesto has been corrected, completed and approved by everyone. Bouli types it on an antiquated typewriter. Andonis translates it into French and English. Petros adjusts the roneo machine: a rectangular frame, a piece of jaconet, a cylinder and copying paper. We apply the stencil and watch anxiously as the Resistance's first publication rolls off the presses:

30

NEA ELLADA, organ of the Patriotic Front, No. 1
Athens, May 1967
MANIFESTO

Greeks—

In the night of 21 April 1967 fascism struck our country. The assassins of democracy abolished the constitutional liberties and democratic rights which the Greek people had won by blood and sacrifice.

Directed and supported by the CIA, the Palace and the most fascist and reactionary political and economic circles in the country, the plotting officers and perjured magistrates betrayed the Nation and used the armed forces to reduce the Greek people to slavery.

They unleashed a wave of terror and violence which is without precedent, arresting thousands of people and setting up new Hitlerite concentration camps and tribunals. They are threatening to assassinate the leaders of democracy. They have imposed the law of the jungle (the law of tanks) and have transformed Greece into an immense camp in which tyranny reigns supreme.

Patriots, democrats—

The dictatorship struck a few days before the elections of 28 May, because the forces which installed it in power did not want the country to emerge from the political crisis and be led towards a normal democratic régime. They did not want there to be harmony, brotherhood, democracy and creative development in Greece.

The main responsibility for organising the dictatorship is borne by the CIA, which represents the most reactionary war-mongering forces in the USA—those who assassinated Kennedy, those who sow death in Vietnam, those who have provoked unanimous criticism even from the conservative leaders of Western Europe and from NATO members like France, Denmark, Sweden, Italy, the Netherlands, Belgium, etc. The dictators, Papadopoulos, Pattakos, Makarezos, Kollias and company, are the blind tools of the CIA. The Palace circles who, with Constantine, took part in establishing the military dictatorship are, equally, the organs and accomplices of the CIA.

The aim of the CIA and the Pentagon is to make Greece a military base, a centre of operations to be directed against

31

those West European democracies which are beginning to oppose the Americans' fascist and war-mongering plans, and a base for aggression against the neutral countries of the Middle East and the socialist countries.

It is for this reason that the American-inspired fascist dictatorship constitutes a mortal threat to the independence of the Republic of Cyprus. It wishes, with the help of partition, to transform Cyprus into a protectorate and into a NATO base.

On the home front, the fascist dictatorship's orders are to facilitate the looting of national riches with the co-operation of the local economic oligarchy. It must hinder all economic development, keep wages low, exploit the peasants, break up any movement for wage demands among the workers, crush the middle classes economically (the small factory owners, businessmen and entrepreneurs), and guarantee the colonialist exploitation of the Greek people.

The tyrants of Greece are leading the country to an economic abyss and all the signs are that they will go even farther and print paper money on a massive scale. In spite of their fascist demagogy they want to make our country into a monstrous camp founded on the system of 'order and work', and to make the Greek people into slaves who, deprived of freedom and rights and without preoccupations and personal thoughts, would work harder and harder to earn less and less and who, when necessary, would be called on to fight the peoples who are struggling for their freedom, as in Vietnam today.

Nobody is taken in by the efforts which have been made to get people to believe that Constantine and the Americans knew nothing of the fascist plot and only accepted it at the last moment. Clearly it is they who organised and led the fascist *coup d'état*. If there was any difference between them and the colonels, it is because the colonels outstripped their superiors in the junta and seized the leadership of it themselves. As for the promises about a Constitution, they were made in reply to the unanimous criticism of the Greek people and world opinion; it is a fascist parody of a 'parliamentarianism' controlled by the junta.

We must all draw lessons from the recent events. The people were 95 per cent against the fascist *coup d'état*.

32

There was a powerful upward surge by the democratic forces. So how was the fascist plot able to take effect? First, because the patriots, democrats and anti-dictatorship forces were not all gathered together to face the threat. Second, because a large part of the political leadership underestimated the danger of fascist dictatorship and allowed a climate of optimism to be created which held that everything was developing normally; so the people were surprised and unable to offer any resistance.

Greeks: The dictatorship will be crushed, the Greek people will be victorious and will go forward again. We are in 1967, not 1936. Since then much has taken place in Greece and in the world; there has been a radical change everywhere in the balance of forces, and to the detriment of fascism. The Greek people, which has been forged in the heat of great national, democratic and social struggles over the last thirty years, harbours within itself such strength that it will create the conditions not only to rid us of the dictatorship but to bring us on to more profound and more democratic changes.

The dictatorship régime is condemned to fall because it is hated by the people. Because the political world, the Left, the Centre and an important section of the Right, is against it. Because an important part of the armed forces—and not just ordinary soldiers, kids who have been enrolled—are either opposed to the fascist dictatorship or little disposed to assist it; the same applies to part of the security forces and even more in the civilian sectors of the state machine. And because the régime is censured by world, and especially European, public opinion and because world solidarity will become stronger and more decisive as the patriotic resistance of the Greek people within the country becomes stronger.

The decisive factor which will bring down the tyranny is the patriotic struggle and democratic resistance of the people. But in order to succeed the country's patriotic forces must unite in a PATRIOTIC FRONT and coordinate their struggle. The Greek people's Patriotic Front against the dictatorship must become the great hope for today and for tomorrow; it must become the Liberator, the Creator and the Regenerator of our country.

The PATRIOTIC FRONT will fight against Cyprus being delivered into the hands of the American military circles. It will fight against our country's participation in the Vietnam war. It will oppose the plundering of the national riches by foreign and local monopolies. It will struggle against the erosion of the standard of living of the workers and peasants, of all working people and of the middle classes. It will react with all means at its disposal against the fascist enlistment of young people and it will not sit back and see Greek schools transformed into Hitlerite propaganda centres.

The PATRIOTIC FRONT will struggle to save the lives of the democratic leaders and other fighters who are imprisoned and whose lives are in immediate danger; it will help political prisoners, those who have been condemned and their families.

The PATRIOTIC FRONT calls on all patriots: no collaboration, no dealings of any sort with the usurpers of power. No Greek must yield. Stubborn resistance to the fascist Constitution which the junta is preparing.

The PATRIOTIC FRONT will fight for a truly independent and peaceful Greece, having friendly relations with all countries, and will not permit any foreign power to determine our country's political course. It will fight for the overthrow of the dictatorship and for a government of national union to be formed by all political parties, a government whose task will be immediately to re-establish constitutional legality and real democratic liberties, to render the fascist movements harmless and to appeal to the suffrage of the sovereign people.

Greeks, the Present and Future of Greece are in our hands.

Forward! Let us crush the tyranny. Forward! Let us make the sun rise over Greece.

Long live Democracy! Long live Greece! Long live the Greek people!

National Council of the PATRIOTIC FRONT
Athens, May 1967

Petros is going through a bad patch. He is nervous; I understand how he is feeling.

'Don't be afraid of anything! The moment we have a correct strategy they'll have to follow us.[5] If they don't, they'll be left behind. Then they'll be cut off from the movement and from the people.'

But Petros listens with distress to all the broadcasts from Radio 'Foni Tis Alithias'.[6] And finally, a few days later, the Greek Communist Party Politburo's station solemnly announces the creation of the Patriotic Front[7] and reads from our Statement. Petros's face lights up. I cannot contain myself.

'Most of you are men: you've got common sense, experience, judgement and character. It's a pity you still can't think and act independently. You've got a blockage. You wait for all your orders from the radio. Let's take your case: you're enormously cultured, you've got experience and common sense. But, what are you doing with it all? At your age Lenin was making the October Revolution! And the rest of you, what are you waiting for? Are you going to wait until you're Comrade Grozos's age before you get responsibility?[8]

We stayed for hours, for whole days, locked up in our little room. Petros doesn't stop talking. I learn details of the activities of Gousias, Zakhariadis and Vlantas, three members of the former Politburo.[9]

When I was exiled in Ikaria in 1947, in the village of Vrakades, I wrote a song whose last verse praised our faith in and admiration for the Democratic Army, and of course its political leadership, the Greek Communist Party:

> Dawn breaks over the mountains
> The enemy is silent, freedom comes.
> Beat them, brothers, beat them hard!
> When Markos strikes the earth trembles!

Our faith was made of granite. We were one people, one party, one international movement, with one leader: Stalin! And his elected disciple in our country, Nikos Zakhariadis!

In 1945 Zakhariadis disavowed Aris Veloukhiotis, the capetanio of ELAS. We of course followed Zakhariadis!

In 1948 Zakhariadis disavowed Markos Vafiadis, the head of the Democratic Army. We of course followed Zakhariadis!

In 1948 Stalin disavowed Tito. We of course followed Stalin!

In our thinking we idealised our leaders. We wanted them

and believed them to be wise, pure, spotless and without any weaknesses. That is why, on a sign from them we could throw ourselves enthusiastically into the fire and to our death.

There were twenty thousand of us exiled in Ikaria. Tens of thousands were on Makronisos. Thousands passed through the hell of the Security Police or the Army's intelligence service, and then some were sent to prison while others went before the firing squad. But wherever we were we did not stop singing—during the transfers, in exile, in prison, at the moment of execution! Our faith was like a mountain and our will was pure steel!

Now I learn that the moment that a party, a movement, a whole people, was offering its life to its leaders, those same leaders were intriguing among themselves and one half were devouring the other half. I also learn that they had even gone as far as to torture entire companies of partisans in order to elicit the confession that there were agents among them who were responsible for this or that defeat. I later learned that in a partisan hospital in a socialist country one of the leaders had beaten seriously-wounded men on their open wounds.

When Petros had seen these leaders the first time he did not yet know all these details. That is why he was proud to meet them. But he soon had to change his tune.

Did we have leaders like that, he thought, leaders who commanded a movement and led people in this way.

We soon came to agreement with Petros that the movement itself was stronger than any leadership, that it was a great movement and that it needed a great leadership! Yet, how is this movement expressing itself? How is it that it still inspires and guides people? It is because we are all leaders, because thousands of militants, each in their own fields, became leaders. Because they implement, directly and creatively, the great principles of Marxism-Leninism which they had assimilated in life, in the struggle, in *action*! The socialist movement in Greece is a movement which rests upon a broad popular base and which expresses itself through an equally broad leadership made up of all the militants of the Left. And there are thousands of them. But the question is why this 'mass leadership' has not been able to be expressed in the leadership of the Greek Communist Party

Petros is quite categorical on this: 'Because this leadership did not emerge from the bowels of the Party; it was put in position by others.' (By whom? By our big brothers.)

And when there was a new wind of change after the Twentieth Congress of the Soviet Communist Party, and Zakhariadis and his group had to go, it was still from our big brothers that the change came. At the Sixth Plenum of our Central Committee who effected the change? Who was the rapporteur? The Romanian Dej![10]

So the progressive change took place in a reactionary way and this affected all subsequent developments, since it once again sanctioned the fraternal parties' 'interventionist' role towards the Greek Communist Party. The split which occurred in the Party in 1968 existed, in embryo, at the time when Zakhariadis was dismissed and replaced by Koliyannis. The point is that one can never strike at an irregular régime with irregular methods without oneself getting caught up in irregularity. One ends up by becoming an irregular régime oneself...

So the Greek progressive movement is growing in power, and it is doing so in spite of its enemies and also in spite of its 'leaders'.

It was my turn to speak:

'I have lived through the phenomenon of the "cult of personality". In December 1944, when we occupied the eastern sectors of Athens, all the responsibility fell on our shoulders. The secretary of the Party organisation was Achilleas, a superb, modest and skilful comrade. We lived together, ate off the same plate—we were inseparable. Suddenly, Achilleas became responsible for the lives of thousands of people. On a sign from him dozens could be arrested. Shops could be requisitioned. A prisoner or a suspect could be shot. The secretary of the People's Militia and the administrative chief became his principal assistants. And then suddenly Achilleas changed. Some of his group started flattering him. He now ate alone. He slept alone. He thought alone, he made decisions alone, he gave orders alone. And that is why the two companies of the local ELAS revolted. Then one day Triantafyllos, the captain of the second company, and I found ourselves condemned to death by Achilleas. Of course, I never associated the Achilleas of this last period with the Party; I always thought that his attitude was a deviation and a deformation of the way the Party operated.

'However, in the period immediately following the events of December (the regrouping of our forces in 1945–6, the abstention from the 1946 elections, my first exile in 1947, the Athens underground in the winter of 1947–8, the second exile in 1948, and

37

finally Makronisos in 1949), I was able to say that the "Achilleas phenomenon" was not the exception but, to all intents and purposes, the rule for the way the Party operated. So I concluded that there was a deeper reason for all this. But what? Logically, I could not find it because everything was confused. Don't forget that at that time all our attention was concentrated on the struggle against the enemy. We had neither the time nor the inclination, nor the opportunity, to undertake an analysis of this sort. And after all we still had an all-powerful movement. We had thousands of organisations throughout the country. We had our own army whose courage was admired throughout the world. And we had transformed the prisons, deportation areas and military tribunals into real strongholds!

'Then came defeat. I found myself back in my village in Crete. All the EPON fighters, who had been deluded, had rejoined the TEA![11]

'I felt like a waif. On the rare occasions when I left the house I met with two looks: hate or sympathy. I preferred the first. Out of spite I was doubly confident of the direction we had taken. The defeat was temporary. I told myself over and over again that it was due entirely to "Tito's treason", which had closed our frontiers. The wildest rumours were going round the villages and the town of Canea. A soldier in the National Army had said: "The Yugoslavs let us through the frontier. So we were able to surround the partisans..." Another soldier said the same: "When the Yugoslavs arrested someone they asked him who he was. They arrested me: when I told them I was in the National Army they let me go...Goodness knows what would have happened to me if I'd been in the Democratic Army." A third said: "I was in Yugoslavia and the Yugoslavs were friendly to me. There we learned that the partisans were being tortured *en masse*..."

'Zakhariadis cried over the Party's radio: "We remain with arms at the ready." I was a regular listener to the clandestine broadcast, "School of the Combatant", which gave news of sabotage and other illegal activities. Meanwhile everyone and everything was collapsing around me. But the longer I remained alone the prouder I felt. In the end I was completely isolated. I was also ill. Since Makronisos I had had several little attacks which laid me low each week. I no longer knew what to cling on to. I had only two rocks left to grasp: music and our people's fight. I went to Athens. I had hardly got back into the life of the capital when I realised that something was not going well with the Party's line. There were tens of thousands of comrades living around me: they were thinking, acting and developing freely, all fully engaged in the struggle. It was there that our strength must lie. It was a question of controlling this life of ours in a creative way. That was where the Front had to be: the Front of Life! It was on this battleground that victory would be won! At that time Party comrades came and told me of an "illegal apparatus". What was it intended to do? To supply the military tribunals? It was then that I took the great decision of my life. Without speaking to anyone about it, I declared myself the *franc-tireur* of the movement and assigned myself my own tasks.

'My personal relationship with life was that of a composer of music. So I had to arm myself solidly and prepare myself for a long struggle. Above all, I had to learn my art from the bottom. To arm myself scientifically, constantly to broaden my horizons. An artist must have a vast area of knowledge. Not only artistic knowledge. Every day I had to follow and analyse the events which were taking place in our country and the world outside. And when I finished work and had sufficient creative reserves left I had to put them at the service of the Greek people's struggle. I admit that by taking this completely formalistic attitude, and in subjecting myself to this iron discipline, I was taking as my guide the Marxist analyses we had made on Ikaria, and especially a series of articles which had appeared in the review *Morfosi* (Culture) under the title, "Stalinist Strategy"...

'From 1954 to 1960 I lived in Paris. I reworked all my old musical material: the First Symphony, the ballet "Carnival", "Oedipus Rex", and so on. I also wrote new music: the First Suite for orchestra and piano, the Second Suite for orchestra, the Third Suite for soprano, choir and orchestra, the Piano Concerto, the ballets "The Lovers of Teruel" and "Antigone", and other works.

'In 1958 I had just dedicated a first cycle of popular music to the elections which had taken place in Greece (and in which EDA came second): the music was "Epitafios", written to verses by Yannis Ritsos. When friends and EDA militants came to talk to me about the Party, I told them of my decision. The "Achilleas phenomenon" had wounded me deeply and the wound was still bleeding all those years later. I was distrustful. I would go to Greece and see for myself. In any case I was a part of the movement. The movement itself belonged to no one. As Ritsos says in his poem, "Greekness". "This land is theirs and ours". In the same way the movement belongs to its dead as well as to all of us.

'I returned to Athens in 1959–60 with "Epitafios", and threw myself enthusiastically into the Front of Life. I entered it, as I had decided I would, with my works and also with my presence, with this "attitude to life" which is the essential complement of any work and any renewal movement. The rest you know.'

The first rays of sunlight are filtering through the shutters. The cocks are getting ready to say good morning to the sun.

'Talk to me a bit about the Lambrakides,' Petros insists.

Clearly he knows nothing of the Lambrakis Youth. How could he? From the civil war until 1958 he was living as an outlaw. Then he was arrested and tried, and was imprisoned until 1966. He has probably not lived a full year in freedom. And here he is again underground...The following evening I talk to him about the Lambrakides:

'All those young people who overwhelmed Greece from 1963 to 1967 were ready to come forward and say: Here we are! And they did, as soon as we spoke to them in their own language.'

'The secret each time is to find the right language to meet the needs of the moment.'

'Exactly! The cultural movement, for example, produced a great and immediate response among the young people because in it they saw, as clearly as in a mirror, their own faces, their own anxieties, their own dreams, their own hopes.'

'Militant culture, as I have called it, that is living culture, that which directly and personally concerns the people and which is in a phase of great creative dynamism, touches on the very foundations of existence. In a single flash it illuminates our inner world and for the first time we are revealed to ourselves! For the first time, too, our common arteries and our common roots are thrown into relief. In other words, culture brings us together with those who are like us. With our brothers. With the community, with the nation. In a general way, with man. By helping us to discover ourselves culture suddenly enables us to say that the 'other person' is ourselves and that we are the 'other person'.

A new joy fills our hearts, a joy which becomes a strength. By taking part in some demonstration of militant culture, you suddenly perceive the other person and see flashes in his eyes. This poetry, this music, this colour that the popular singer's voice has, joins together with the sounds of popular instruments to make a kind of aerial chain which links you with your past, with your entire heritage. Suddenly Rigas, Kalvos and the poets of the 1821 revolution become your friends. Karaiskakis becomes your brother. You then begin to understand that the march is a unique one. The river bed is the same. You realise that you have already come a long way, covered great distances. Your duty now is to go farther, as the living part of a great body. You are the vanguard; you must open up the way. Thus aesthetic joy is transformed drop by drop into moral strength, and then into ideological weight and political action. This is the ineluctable march of militant culture.

'How in fact was this cultural movement able to give birth to the Lambrakides movement?'

'Beyond this march of militant culture, which leads of itself to politicisation (because in the final analysis what ideal can militant culture give birth to in us? An ideal of liberty and humanity! Conflict with the obscurantist and oppressive régime which prevails in our country becomes inevitable), beyond this process, then, there were real political events. In 1961 the Radical National Union (right-wing), which wanted to win the elections at any cost, organised an electoral *coup* with the help of the Army and the police.

'The elections took place as if in the jungle and, of course, the Radical National Union won. However, it was a Pyrrhic victory, because the reaction of the Greek people now started to become menacing. A vast democratic political movement began to take shape and in the midst of it the militant culture movement made its presence felt and developed.

'At the same time another big movement was emerging : the Peace Movement, with its impressive marches from Marathon to Athens. In 1963 between five and ten thousand demonstrators, and fifteen hundred arrests. In 1964 three hundred thousand. In 1965 five hundred thousand! The vice-president of the movement was none other than Grigoris Lambrakis, the deputy from Piraeus. At the time of the first Marathon march he was the only man to be able to set foot on Marathon Hill. From that day

41

on he became a popular symbol. Some weeks later, in May 1963, he was struck down in Salonika. As soon as this became known, the first committee was set up in EDA's premises and entrusted with attending his bedside. The committee consisted of Professor Imvriotis, the deputy Sakellaris, Manolis Glezos, Yannis Ritsos and myself. The whole town of Salonika was hanging on every beat from the heart of the dying hero. A whole town was suffering. There was not a single unmoved face. Some were dumbfounded, some were grief-stricken, some were full of shame. We hurried to the Ahepans hospital, on University Hill. Lambrakis was breathing with an artificial aid. We went in. There he was, his whole body quivering. His enormous chest, his great, strong arms, his powerful bulging muscles—how could a giant of a man like this be killed? His wife and brothers were waiting in the next room. The hospital director took us into his office. He explained the situation to us. Then the others left, and Yannis and I stayed behind. Night fell. In the darkness we heard the low strains of "Epitafios" coming from somewhere. I trembled. My mind had always had a craving for symbols, and finally I discovered where the singing was coming from. In the next room—like Digenis[12] on the marble floor—Lambrakis the hero of the democratic resistance, was fighting a great battle with death. Glezos, the hero of the national resistance, was at his side. The poet and the composer of "Epitafios", the first work, the foundation stone, of the militant culture, were there too. And at the hospital gate, sitting on the grass, young boys and girls were softly singing "Epitafios"...Yannis and I went to the door. They recognised us, but no one moved. They carried on singing, soft and with deep feeling. We walked across, cautiously, and sat down among them. The singing stopped. Silence...You'd have had to be deaf not to hear the roar of the rivers as they met! One river, the cultural movement. The other river, the Resistance movement...Then the poet spoke. The dialogue began...Then it was the composer's turn...Then a young man...then another young man...then a young girl...The two rivers had now joined to form one : the Lambrakis Youth...

'Later, whenever I went into a village and the young people gathered round, I would say to them :

"Who is really responsible for what happens in your village? The policeman? Or perhaps the mayor? No, it's you, the young boys and girls. You are responsible for everything that happens!

If a poor devil is ill; if the children don't have enough space to play in; if there's no public square; if there's no bridge; if the church is ruined; if the cemetery is overgrown with weeds; if there is no entertainment, if nothing is done for education. If there's injustice somewhere, terror and exploitation, then it's you who are responsible for it. We have given the word for the establishment of a thousand Houses of Culture for the young people." The Reaction was literally seized with rage. It forced the owners to throw us out. So the Lambrakides built their Houses of Culture themselves. When the Reaction blew them up with dynamite, the Lambrakides immediately rebuilt them.

'In the same way, we organised a national campaign called the Book of Youth. For three months the whole of Greece was inundated with books. We collected over fifty thousand volumes. We filled our Houses of Culture with them. The Lambrakides took those that were left over to far-off villages and they were put on show in the squares, and the young people danced round, singing.

'One day I went to Perama, in the heart of the shanty town area. "What's your main problem?" I asked. We were on top of the mountain. The gulf of Salamis opened up at our feet. Over twenty-four centuries earlier the King of Persia had been sitting just a few metres below where we were standing, contemplating his powerful fleet and preparing to win victory over the Greeks. Victory? The King had been lured to these straits by Themistocles's ruse, which had persuaded him he was to witness the massacre of the Greek navy. And then in the event, it was a question for the Persians of every man for himself...

'Now the descendants of those who fought the Persians at Salamis are living in wooden huts with neither water nor electricity. They have a half-hour or even an hour's walk to get the bus.

"That's our main problem: the road."

"So this is what I suggest: you provide us with shovels and cement. We'll bring the hands to do the work. OK?"

"OK."

'I went to the House of Culture in Piraeus and spoke to the Lambrakides about it. Some would work, others would sing. We would present artistic programmes all day. We'd play some sport and build the road! And that's what we did. One sunny Sunday five thousand Lambrakides set off to climb Perama. In the evening the road to the top of the mountain was ready. The people gave it the name: "Lambrakis Avenue".

'That's what the Labrakides did. In that way, then, we're linked to our milieu, to life, to the problems of youth. With a solid base in theory, we organised the struggle of youth with a view to achieving a real solution to its problems. And as these problems were only one aspect of the problems of the people and of the country as a whole, youth was thus also playing a part, directly or indirectly, in the people's struggle to solve all their problems.'

From all parts of the world come messages of enthusiasm for what we are doing and of confidence in us; ideas, thoughts and original suggestions. In this way we are able to build up propaganda groups, to organise the clandestine press, to expand our organisation, continually to broaden our alliances at the base as well as at the top of the pyramid, and to provide the international press with news, commentaries and statements. We plan the first resistance order to the entire nation for 28 May 1967;[13] we prepare the first spectacular demonstrations in the centre of Athens; we set up the first resistance committees for the clandestine taped transmissions 'Athens is speaking to you'; we lead the first resistance demonstration, a lightning demonstration in Ermou Street on 19 August 1967; our first bomb explodes on Constitution Square in July 1967; we set up groups of Resistance reporters and study groups; we set up a National Solidarity Fund, the Patriotic Front of intellectuals, the Patriotic Fund of young people, the Patriotic Front of workers, the Patriotic Front of women, etc.

Petros's comings and goings are regular and without any snags. Up to the present we have not had to suffer any hard blows, any losses. Day and night I stay locked in my little room. There are thousands of rumours going round about me: that I am in Greece, in Albania, that I have been seen at such and such an embassy, that I have been killed, etc. I manage to send a brief message to my family: 'I'm well.' I concern myself mainly with the problems of the Resistance. At the same time, I compose the first songs of the Resistance and begin writing a historical-political essay entitled 'We the Greeks' (which I eventually sent abroad in July 1967, with a thousand risks and sacrifices, so that it should find its way into the drawers of certain 'friends').

Petros leans over my shoulder and reads what I am writing. He says:

'At last someone dares to tell them the truth!' (He is thinking of the Politburo of the Greek Communist Party.)

One day, halfway through May, Petros comes in smiling enigmatically. We quickly lock ourselves in the little room.

'They've got to hear of it...' he says.

'Who has got to hear of what?'

'That you have...dismissed them! Now they want you to leave for abroad immediately. Just you, alone...For all the others, the order is that no one is to leave Greece.'

The clash came sooner than I expected. I have to gain time, and to convince the cadres, as I have done with Petros. But I have to proceed with care. I tell Petros:

'No, I cannot leave. I am needed here. My plan is first to create a strong Resistance which is capable of shaking the junta. Then I shall go and try to win Europe over to our cause. When I've done that, I'll come back...As for the leaders, no, we haven't dismissed them. We've simply taken over the leadership of the struggle in Greece. Let them send us a member of the Politburo to take charge here. In any event, we will not take orders from a distance. As for the strategy which is to be adopted, we await their analysis and their directives so we can discuss the matter and take decisions jointly. We are not refusing the very closest collaboration; we even want concrete help, and that hasn't arrived yet. Why didn't they send a little money along with the emissary who brought the "directives"? Don't they know we're living in complete illegality? Equally, we're waiting for them to provide us with various information media by which to disseminate the appeal to Resistance (for our part, we have sent them two complete broadcasts on tape—news, commentaries, music, presentation—under the title "The Patriotic Front Calling! Free Athens Calling!", which they rebroadcast as soon as they were received). Finally, there is the enormous problem of responsibilities. Leaders and members here have formally declared that they are not going along with the Central Committee until it pronounces openly, honestly and with courage on its responsibilities; until it gives proof that it has taken note of past errors. Has it made a self-analysis? If so, where is it? We

45

know nothing of it yet. Tell those comrades that our people here are now mature. That they are demanding responsible autonomous leadership. And that above all they are demanding the final and radical liquidation of the past...'

'I can't say things like that,' Petros says. 'You still don't know those comrades well enough.'

'In that case I'll give you all this in writing to send to them.'

The message is sent to the Communist Party's envoy.

Some days later Petros brings Alekos, a member of the Secretariat of EDA. We learn from him that another resistance group is being set up by EDA militants, who have already got contacts with Crete; that the other members of the EDA leadership are all hiding in a safe place, although certainly in bad conditions...that EDA has published a Statement (which was not very widely publicised).

We in turn give him the rundown on our activities. Alekos's face lights up. He is a loyal and crafty old comrade.

'Now,' Petros tells him, 'Mikis is going to explain to you *a*, or rather *the*, crucial point.'

He smiles mischievously. Alekos seems to have got the point. Anyway, I explain our position to him.

'In principle, I have no objection. I know there is an analogous historical precedent with the communists cut off in Sebastopol. In any case, our position here is a delicate one. As you know, we have been appointed by the Politburo. But I think that your view of the problem does make collaboration possible. But I must talk with the others about it.'

I repeat that at the moment the leadership is us and the young 'Lambrakides' and that nobody, in my view, would oppose our sharing the responsibilities of leadership—on one condition: that we lead effectively. We intend to use our brains in a sensible and balanced way and to take upon ourselves the responsibility of deciding on everything that happens here...

Alekos leaves the following morning. Petros meets him several times outside. Later he was also to meet two or three other EDA leaders. We agree to give them responsibilities. The 'Lambrakides' have no objection: there is enough work for everyone. The battle has put us in a state of frenzied joy. The Resistance is a purifying flame. Let's be confident!

46

July

I stay behind locked doors day and night. The heat is suffocating; the shutters are closed all the time. The only air I can breathe is what little gets through the cracks in the shutters.

The two tape recorders we bought to record our messages stand in front of me as challenges to the oppressive nature of the régime. When I start composing again it is songs of rebellion that I write. I shut the windows before recording them. By using two tape recorders at the same time I can add other voices, all on my own. At nightfall, when the comrades come round to listen to them, it is a moment of great emotion. We send the first recordings out straight away. Later, in prison and in the hospital, however exhausted I was, I would sing them to my comrades. They had to learn them in order to be able to teach them to the comrades in the prisons and camps.

The Front

The mountains speak in secret
So do the towns
Hymettus speaks to Parnis
Kokkinia to Tavros

Peoples speak in secret
So do brave young men
By day they grow wild
But they sing in the night.

Athens within my heart
Gave birth to my voice
I am the Front
I summon all patriots

I summon the youth of May
I summon the workers
To turn into an ocean
To drown the Pattakoses

Profound the sea
So great my sorrow
So vast the waves
So deep my agony

Open Sea

On Friday I was free
The next day a slave
At dawn on Sunday
Death called me.
Burn the wings of the mind
Burn the eyes of thy thoughts
Think not of suffering
Look not at pain.

Speak to me sweet death
Speak to me once more
I want to scale the heights
To greet the sun
I want to see the waters
Play with the shadows
To see again my mother
My sweet sad mother.

Ocean, O deep ocean
Bring me back my child.

Freedom or Death

When the sun is weary
Just before it sets
The brave young men emerge
From their secret hides

Once again the Front
Calls the Greeks to battle
Freedom or death
Is writ upon our banner

Their hands hold paint
To daub the walls of Athens
Freedom flashing in their eyes
Illuminates the Homeland.

48

Softly comes the dawn
Sweetly smiles the dawn
The front calls us
And points the way.

Dictatorship, fascism
Americans from Texas
The people will sweep aside—
A day of joy.

Filothei, July

I am in hiding now in Filothei, in the suburbs of Athens. The
house is spacious. It looks on to a garden in which there are
many flowers and apricot trees. At noon I listen to 'Voice of
Truth', the Greek broadcast which comes from Eastern Europe;
there should be a message for me. An international youth organisation is begging me, wherever I may be, to compose a 'hymn to
freedom' and send it to them. I am very moved. I write the
music straight away and sing it to my friends. I add a free text,
a general idea. This hymn will leave for abroad with the first
mission.

The Sun

A great crime has taken place in a small country
For this every young man and every young girl
Throughout the world must shed bitter tears.
For when a flower is trampled upon
So is the youth of the world
For when a song is killed
So is the youth of the world
For when a people is crucified
So is the youth of the world
Young men and girls
Help the sun to rise again in Greece
Our sun is your sun
The sun of all the world.

We decide to hold a meeting, this time with more people. There
are four of us: Petros, Alekos, Kostas (from the EDA leader-

ship) and myself. From the beginning I sense that something is wrong. Alekos and Kostas take up the same position: they suggest the leadership be reorganised with Alekos as Secretary and myself as his assistant. I accept on condition that we are both under the one roof so we can work out the programme together. They discuss it. Everything seems strange. 'They are following the Politburo's directive,' I tell myself. 'Yesterday they were different. Now their attitude is changing.' The Resistance is a flame which purifies everything, except...(In the end I was right: they and many others were later to be purified, or purged, themselves!)

Alekos and Kostas have a discussion in the drawing room which goes on until dawn. We had been celebrating Comrade Athina's birthday. I stay with Petros.

'So you didn't see them?' I ask him.

'Yes. You must explain your position to them clearly. Unfortunately, I'm leaving tomorrow morning.'

The next day there are three of us.

'I don't understand you. Before, you were looking for a personality of great standing to be at the head of the movement. Now, right now, you have in front of you someone who is known throughout Greece and is no stranger—in fact he is a leader of the Left; he has also taken the initiative, along with the "Lambrakides" and Petros, in setting up the New Resistance; and finally he is prepared to sacrifice his family, his career, his life, everything. *And yet you don't want him!* Why?'

'You haven't convinced us yet that you're a leader.'

They leave...

The next day my host, Takis, comes to the house in a mad panic. 'A black car has been past. It slowed down. They were all looking at the house. I'm certain they suspect something.'

I suggest that it's better not to react too hastily. We must wait and see if there are other signs.

The next day the same black car passes the house. Inside, it seems, Security men. They are indeed looking very closely at the house. We watch them through the shutters. In the small garden in front of the house little Andreas is sleeping in his pram. That's a good blind. But the car comes back. It's quite clear they've located us. They must have shadowed the French car which brought R...There's not a moment to lose. 'Warn Athina.' I lock myself up in my room and rush to finish my book: three or four pages. I record my message on tape. (I distribute a lot of little tapes in various parts of Athens.) My coolness annoys the owners of the house. They look at me as if to say: 'It doesn't matter to you, sure it doesn't. You're resigned to your fate. But what about us? What's going to become of our child when we're arrested?' I watch them out of the corner of my eye and decide I mustn't wait any longer—I've got to clear out. Athina tells us that her house is also being watched but that she'll do all she can. It is dark. I try to sleep. At the slightest sound I jump. I go to the foot of the bed and peep through the shutters into the garden. In my imagination it's full of fleeting shadows. Day breaks. Footsteps. It's the gardener. The real owners are at their house in the country, at Vouliagmeni. They would never believe that their house could ever be the focus of attention for the Security! We go down to the cellar, where there are two or three narrow rooms, hastily and sparsely furnished. We discover a second cellar beneath the first. We strike a match and go down the steps. It is immense, and as dark as a tomb. I shudder. If I'm to be executed I'd prefer it to be in daylight. Never in this cellar! 'You must hide down here,' Takis tells me peremptorily, 'and we'll cover up the access to the steps with the wardrobe.'

To gain time I say: 'Let's wait a bit.' Around midday Athina turns up: 'They're shadowing me. I stopped the car on the other side and crossed at my natural pace. Isn't it my brother's house?'

'But why opposite? On the other side? You should have parked right in front of the door.'

'It's too sunny. It's more normal to park in the shade.'

We agree.

'Where are they now?'

'I think they've gone.'

Takis's wife comes to warn us, under her breath—'The black car.' The car slows down and turns at the footbridge. It pulls up right behind Athina's.

I tell Athina: 'Get out of here, if you can...'

Midday, and we've not got much appetite. I return to the cellar. At first I hesitate to get back to my manuscript. But as soon as the owner has turned his back, I dive for my notebooks. At three o'clock one of our 'contacts' arrives. We examine the situation in the minutest detail: The fact that they haven't come back yet proves they suspected something but that they aren't yet certain. At nightfall I'll be able to get out the back way, through the gardens. That is the situation. It is for him to inform his comrades, who will then decide what can be done.

I'm ready. I start putting on my disguise. Helen cuts my hair with a razor. I stick on the moustache of a seducer and the uniform of a colonel. Then I go back to my manuscript. Suddenly Helen comes down the stairs, yelling: 'They're in the garden!' I collect my things together. Takis and Helen push the old wardrobe across the hole behind me to block access to my tomb. I strike a match on the wall, and just manage to pick out a bench, which I crawl across to on all fours. I lay my bag on it, with my fortune inside—the manuscript. I remain standing up. My eyes get used to the darkness. A tiny hole is letting in some light. I try to move towards it. I press my eye to it in order to try and make out which part of the house it gives on to. I spot a man's shoe: there's someone—or several people—on the other side of the wall, just a few centimetres from me. Here they are—they're moving the wardrobe. I expect shouts and shots. It's Takis. I grope my way towards him.

'They came into the garden, and then left again. What are we to do? Athina has just arrived.'

'Get me out of this hole.'

'Are you mad?'

'I want to get out of here. I must speak to Athina.'

She is full of emotion—her hand is trembling slightly. I smile to reassure her.

'Why did you come? You know perfectly well we're done for.'

'I've come to get you out of here. We'll leave like a pair of lovers and walk past them.'

'A colonel six feet tall! I've never seen that...They'll recognise me straight away.'

'In that case, we'll escape by the back way.'

'A colonel who jumps over a wall! An astonishing sight! We'd do better to try next door—it's the Yugoslav military attaché's house.'

'They've blocked the rear passage with box bedsprings and old mattresses. It's impossible to get through.'

'Let's take a ladder.'

'We haven't got one.'

'Well, go and ring at the door.'

Athina is composing a message in English, which she gets me to copy out: 'I am Theodorakis. I am trapped and surrounded. I am asking you to grant me sanctuary in your house.'

Athina and Helen step over the little wall into the Yugoslav's front garden. He is on the doorstep. I watch them from the window of my room. They speak to him and give him my message. They make signs in my direction. I move my head forward a little. The Yugoslav stares at me boggle-eyed. He's just arrived in Greece and doesn't know me. And, I completely forget, I'm wearing a magnificent colonel's uniform and a military moustache!

'No, I don't know Mr Theodorakis…In any case my government has diplomatic relations with the Greek government…'

The attaché suspects a trap. The two women come back in despair.

'Leave quickly,' I tell Athina. 'Nothing more can be done. Just make sure and send me somebody who can perhaps help get me out of here.'

Athina lets herself be persuaded. Her eyes are full of tears. I fear lest it's too late for her as well. The house is being watched. They'll follow her and arrest her whenever they want to.

My hosts again insist that I go down into the cellar. I tell them it's useless but in the end agree to. Pointing to the hole, I say: 'Stay near this hole so I can get my bearings.'

Back in my tomb. I go over to the hole. Takis comes to speak to me. He is calmer. The hours pass. I persuade him to let me out so we can have a chat. We go up into the large drawing room. The house is surrounded by trees and beneath them one can clearly make out shadows. There are a lot of cars. The Yugoslav's house is all lit up. Great excitement. Could it be Security spies? The idea crosses my mind. But I decide to reassure the others.

'It's certainly not for us. They'd be here already if it were.'

'You're mad,' Takis shouts, beside himself. 'You've fucking landed us in the arms of the Security with all your carelessness. What's going to become of little Andreas? I'm going to open the window. I'm going to shout : "Here we are!" and be done with this agony.'

He is holding a bottle of wine. He doesn't stop drinking. He has lost all self-control. Helen gives me a wild look. I try to keep my cool. I speak softly and calmly.

'I'll tell the police I took advantage of you, that I forced you...'

'We know you too well, clear off,' shouts Takis. 'Is it an accident that the Security comes back when all the others have gone?'

'What others?'

'The militants! The leaders!'

My eyes must have been flashing with anger. But luckily it was too dark for them to notice. I want to calm them down at all costs. At that moment a silhouette emerges from the shadows and is visible against the surface of the road. The figure is coming towards the house.

'They're coming...'

'But it's...It's a leader who's come to be arrested with me...'

Petros comes in. He looks at me stupefied. I must be pale with fright.

'What's happening?'

I explain briefly. The sound of a car stopping. We slip down into the cellar. But even before they have finished pushing the wardrobe over the hole, they are moving it again. It's Yannis. He has come in the red MG...I greet him warmly. This is real courage.

We put the light on in the porch and go out completely normally. At the top of the steps I wave for Petros and Orestis to bring my cases, just as servants do for colonels. They open the door for me. I salute and get into the car. The police watch our movements from between the trees. I look Petros straight in the eye.

'You know that I've always considered our chance meeting to have been a miracle and for the good of our people. Now, frankly, I can't say if it's been for good or ill.'

'I understand what you mean,' he says. 'What do you reckon on doing?'

'We're going ahead. I want you to put me in contact with the Lambrakides, whether you're in agreement or not—it's your duty. I don't know what *you're* going to do...but you must decide—this side or the other side. I believe the illusions have vanished—a new organisation is needed.'

4 August

When I was back in Leftheris's house (whence I made my statement of 23 April 1967) I had met Nora, to whom I had given the job of finding money and places where one could take refuge. She immediately went into action in earnest and succeeded in finding an American Jewish professor who was returning from Tel Aviv to New York and was stopping over in Athens. She gave him my statement and accompanied him to the airport. They had agreed that if everything went well at the customs he would raise his handkerchief as he entered the plane. The same evening I was informed that the professor had indeed raised his handkerchief at the top of the gangway. This wasn't, however, the only route taken by my statement. We dropped it into the letter boxes of many Greek and foreign journalists. Nora told us she had slipped it under the door of a family she knew well. She went back half an hour later and rang their door bell. No answer. She rang again. Someone came to the door and opened it just a fraction; they were taking exceptional precautions, for the family was hiding a well known writer, K.K., whom Nora met. Immediately everyone set to work…copying out my statement and they asked Nora if she would make as many copies of them as she could!

Nora got in contact with a small group led by Gl. (the same Gl. who had some days before called on Andreas Papandreou on my behalf to suggest that we cooperate). The members of this network wanted to get in contact with me personally. But I considered it was still too soon to expose myself to danger in that way, and a little later I was to find out just how wise I had been. In fact the Security had planted one of their agents right in the heart of Gl.'s network, and this explained the insistence on making personal contact with me. When the Security saw that this manoeuvre had failed it struck: the majority of the members were arrested—the others managed to get abroad.

When I met up with Petros, our first decision was to break off all relations with Nora, for we believed, and rightly, that the Security must be keeping a close watch on her. We got a message to her that she was 'to go into the country' for a while.

The last mission I entrusted her with was to get a note to my family, written in my hand and saying: 'I'm well.' Nothing else. It was enough to give my wife and my parents reassurance. The message finally managed to reach them after passing through a number of hands in the relay. Nora was sensible for a while but then fairly quickly resumed her activity. She stubbornly sought to contact us, organised her own network, and sent militants to get training abroad. So I suggested to Petros that we go back on the decision we had taken: 'By refusing to see her we are running the risk of disappointing a recent recruit.' But Petros was still adamant: 'Any contact with Nora would lead to our arrest. The Security is allowing her freedom to move so she'll put them on to us.'

Here we are, then, in the first few days of August 1967, after the coolness which had set in in my relations with my friends in the Interior Bureau. I tell Petros that I am going to organise the Patriotic Front on the basis of new elements. It is quite natural, then, that my thoughts turn towards Nora, who, moreover, had come a few days before to get a taped message from me for an operation which had been christened 'Constitution Square'.

This operation was to develop in two phases. The first was to get the crowd to hear the message on a tape recorder, while at the same time making it clear that the latter was a snare. The second phase was to blow it up. The police succeeded in discovering the tape recorder, which had been placed on the square one evening towards the end of July. The tape bearing my message went into the Security archives. Lambrou had learned it by heart, and after my arrest he would often come into my cell reciting it in his imitation of my voice. It was his way of being funny...

With the three comrades who were hiding me in their house I spent a long time trying to decide whether we should collaborate with Nora. We decided the principles on which we would collaborate, knowing at the outset that we were playing with fire. I couldn't sleep for nights and kept hearing the voice of the worker, Kimon, who had told me: 'You must not at any cost be arrested...' Then I would see Petros sleeping as he had been a short time before in the same room as me and on the floor. We had spent many nights discussing things under our breath! We would go off to sleep at dawn after being locked in the

56

room. As I tend to snore, Petros would wake me with a start to remind me that there was a maid in the house. She had been told that our room was kept locked because it was full of very valuable pictures. One day the owner's brother turned up from Europe and I had to hide in the cupboard with a thermos full of iced water to save me from the heat. Petros would tell me time after time: 'We mustn't get caught. That's our first duty.'

However, Andonis was given the job of making contact again with Nora. In the evening he returned looking very anxious.

'We were given the Loumidis café in Stadiou Street as a rendezvous. And all of a sudden a bomb went off in the passage next door. We cleared off quick.'

'Did you have time to talk at all?'

'Sure. I told her of our fears that she was being shadowed by the Security. She assured me she hadn't noticed anything.'

I remembered how scrupulous Nora was in preparing everything she did. She went into the finest detail—for example, she would want to know if the person she had to make contact with held his brief case in his left hand or his right.

'If she gave an assurance on that, then it's true,' I said.

'Anyway,' Andonis went on, 'I repeated the conditions of our agreement and she accepted them.'

We had decided, in the event of our collaborating with her, that we would suggest exceptional precautions.

'She also told me that L, the Centre deputy, is prepared to join the Front on condition that he can meet you.'

'Another condition!'

'Yes. And Nora, too, places a condition on her collaboration and on the meeting with the deputy—that she can meet you herself.'

The danger was as great as the attraction was tempting: a well-known Centre leader joining the Patriotic Front could serve the cause of the Resistance in a big way.

Ever since the early days of the underground struggle, Petros and our leading cadres had been in touch with Centre elements. Almost all of them hesitated to follow us...Most of them told us they were waiting for the word from the Papandreous (father and son). There was just one exception, though: a leader of the Centre Union who had been a candidate at the legislative elections and was one of the founders of the Front. Through him I sent two personal messages to Andreas Papandreou. One said:

'I beg you to address an immediate appeal to members of the Centre Union inviting them to join the Front. We are struggling for the same ideals. As far as you are concerned, you have and will always have the place which is yours by right—in the bosom of the new Resistance.'

I still don't know how much of this appeal reached Andreas Papandreou, but I do know that George Mylonas, the former Centre deputy, did receive a message in this vein. Still, I must admit, at the top of the Centre party there was still great hesitation about whether to join us. Only lower down did one encounter an enthusiastic desire to join forces. That's why winning a leading cadre of the Centre seemed so important to us.

We decide on the principles to be adopted in these two meetings—with Nora and the deputy—and make a careful study of the measures to be taken.

7 August

During the day, when everyone is out—including the maid—I can sit in the drawing room. I am always overjoyed to escape for a moment from my room. The drawing room is spacious. It has a library, a record collection and record-player. I am 'allowed' to put records on provided the music doesn't carry more than two metres!

Today, 7 August, I shave and go into the drawing room. It is eleven o'clock. The sun is shining brightly. That penetrating cool freshness which is characteristic of Athenian houses in midsummer dominates the house. My meeting with Nora is in a few minutes. The die is cast!

Nora falls into my arms. We hadn't seen each other since the first days of the dictatorship. She wipes her tears and gets to the heart of the matter. We are agreed on the conditions and the practical aspects of our collaboration. As far as the deputy is concerned, she confirms that he is prepared to join us. All we have to do is to see to all the material questions—shelter, protection, money. She adds that the deputy has already prepared a statement for the Greek people. I decide to examine the problems raised by this meeting with my comrades and to keep her posted. Nora came and went 'cleanly', as we say in our underground jargon: she had not been shadowed.

Andonis and Orestis have a rendezvous this evening with Nora. They have chosen Constitution Square so as not to arouse the interest of possible 'shadowers'. They tell her what is to happen: the deputy is to leave the house alone, take a taxi, get out of it, take a second one, then a third. Then he will go and meet up with Nora, who will drive him to Andonis—who will bring them both to our hiding place.

Past midnight. I'm playing patience. Footsteps. Orestis and Andonis enter the room, looking uneasy. What's happened.

'The rendezvous on Constitution Square went off without incident, nothing abnormal. Only after we'd got back into the car did we notice we were being followed. We took the road around Mount Lycabettus to make absolutely sure: the car was still following us. Finally I decided to accelerate. They gave us up at the first bend. I can't understand it,' Orestis says. 'Why did they give up? If it had been a Security car it would have followed us right to the end.'

'But now they've got the details of the MG: they know the number, the owner, his friends and his parents.'

'OK…What are we going to do?'

'When's the meeting with the deputy?'

'In four days' time.'

'We'll chance it. We must dump the MG in some yard.[14] And on the evening of the meeting, or at the latest the day after, I'll disappear.'

'Where'll you go?'

'I've just got to get out of this habitual cycle of different homes, one after the other, just that…'

'Just what?'

'There's the underground printing press in Odysseas's house. My place is down there.'

'The press has been moved to a house in Khaïdari, or had you forgotten?'

'Well, I'll go to Khaïdari. You know that the publication of *Nea Ellada* is closest of all to my heart.'

Up to now our underground publications had been roneoed. At first we did it with the comrades who were hiding with us in the same house. One copy at a time. Then Petros arranged for them to be printed in different places, further out of Athens, in the country. There are a thousand printing presses in Athens. All of them have been seized by the police and registered. All printing work was controlled by daily visits which were so thorough that not a single piece of type could be set aside for clandestine work. The day Orestis went to get some printing paper, the supplier immediately rang the Security and Orestis escaped arrest by only a few seconds. We then decided to buy the materials we needed for *Nea Ellada* at different places and a little at a time. Then we found blocks of a religious work which were going to be melted down and Petros bought them up. To move them from one place to another an extremely careful plan was worked out which made it quite impossible for us to be shadowed. At the last stage but one the journalist Nikos was to hand them over to Odysseas's wife. Petros thought it would be better to use a taxi to move the blocks. So at the last stage Nikos and another comrade had loaded a taxi with a bag crammed full of plates; Katie, Odysseas's wife, gave the driver the address and got in. At her destination she got out and went to take the bag. It was so heavy she couldn't lift it. She went to ring the doorbell. Nobody came. She went back to the taxi and tried again. The taxi driver asked if he could help. She hardly had time to think of an excuse when he seized the bag. As they walked up to the house the driver turned to Katie and said:

'Well, my little lady, what is it you're transporting here? One might almost think you're moving a printing works?'

I only learned of this incident from the lady concerned when we were sorting out the plates at her mother-in-law's—where I was to be caught.

13 August

At nine o'clock in the evening we had to get the Centrist deputy to the house. This was a new and serious twist to the regulations we had made for the underground : according to them, no rendez-vous—however important—must take place in the house I was using as a hideout.

Andreas had left alone at about six, to be at the right stage in the deputy's itinerary on time.

For the past several days Orestis had been alarmed to discover that he was being shadowed. He told us how, when he was in his MG on Constitution Square, a black car behind him had moved off just as he did. To make sure he was not seeing things, he had set off on a slalom through the centre of Athens. In the end the car disappeared, but he found it again a few moments later as he got back to his house, parked in the road.

All these signs were very disturbing. However, our organisation had hit on a warning device to enable us to spot the moment of real danger. It wasn't possible to move each time we were in danger for in fact we knew only too well that the police were everywhere and that we were never safe from them. And, to make a move without informing the others, without taking precautions and making necessary preparations, and without a concerted plan, was to risk losing contact with the network (and therefore to condemn ourselves to being completely ineffective and to become vulnerable in another way...by virtue, quite simply, of being isolated).

Our warning device was as follows: I was in a house rented under a false name by Andonis and his wife. They lived in another house not far away and kept in contact with Orestis, the owner of the MG and Andonis's brother-in-law. If the MG became marked and was being watched, the investigators would logically go first to Orestis's house, then to Andonis's, and then to me. So we kept a constant check by telephone (in code, of course) to find out if everything was normal. Moreover, Petros, who was outside this circuit, kept an eye on each house with daily telephone calls (also in code).

Andonis and the deputy turned up at nine o'clock on the dot. Andonis asked me if I needed anything and then left. After the introductions I asked the deputy:

'How did it go?'

'Your precautions were excessive.'

'What did you do?'

'I left my place quietly. Nobody was following me. I stopped suddenly in front of some shop windows to make sure. I then walked on a little way to get to Nora's car.'

His rashness appalled me. He had neglected all our recommendations! Now, I was certain that I was about to be shadowed. But I didn't show my concern. I just said:

'You shouldn't have underestimated our precautions. I fear that it won't be long now before we find ourselves together again in the Security jail. However, be that as it may, let's talk about what brings you here.'

L then stated his position with regard to the dictatorship, the colonels, the Americans and the Greek people. He told me he was getting ready to go to Crete to organise maquis activity. Friends were expecting him. He also told me of a journey he had just made to the islands. He had met all the cadres of the Centre Union there, and they were determined to fight.

He had been talking for a good hour when I decided to interrupt:

'We haven't spoken yet of the object of this meeting.'

'What object?'

'Your joining the Patriotic Front.'

'Well, you see, I've changed my mind. I'd rather confine myself to just cooperating with the Front. Besides, I can't contemplate living the underground life...'

'If that's the only problem, we're prepared to take care of all the material questions.'

'Yes, but I can't stand being kept shut up...'

'You said you wanted to meet me so you could join our organisation.'

'It was only a possibility.'

'You have no idea of the risks we're running by meeting like this. I'm even running the risk of being disclaimed by my own people. I did it in full awareness of the dangers, because I thought it would serve the cause of the Resistance. And here you are here announcing that you've changed your mind! I'm sorry, but in conditions like these that's the sort of casualness that could be fatal.'

L frowned.

I had already accepted the inevitable. All I now had to do was to save what could still be saved!

'Anyway, let's see what can be done,' I said.

In spite of my objections, he stubbornly insists that he wants to get to Crete. Anyway, we are able to agree on one point: he will work with Petros.

'Perhaps we'll end up together, after all...' he said, trying to make amends for our disagreement.

We say goodbye and he leaves. Exactly eight days later we were to be using the same toilets on the fourth floor of the Security headquarters in Bouboulinas Street. We both had to pay the price of disobeying the most elementary rules of underground activity.

When the door closes behind the deputy, Andonis comes back into the room:

'Teddy,[15] I must say, some alarming things are happening.'

'Yes, yes, I know,' I said icily.

'I left about six. About eight thirty I was walking down Pindarou Street. I was planning to make a big detour before going back to the rendezvous. Then what do I see? Nora's Volkswagen parked on the right-hand side of the street. I quicken my step. At the first crossroads I see the deputy turning the corner. He gets into the Volkswagen and it drives off immediately. Suddenly I see two guys setting off in hot pursuit. Nora's car turns and disappears from sight. I carry on along the road, but the two guys, who have stopped, are watching me. I slip into the dark of a building. It's a private clinic. I stay there until ten to nine. Nobody around. I get to the agreed place and run into a patrol of plain-clothes police. "Police. Your papers!" I show my passport. They are examining it just as Nora's Volkswagen comes into sight. The cop hands me back my passport and moves away. I get into the car.'

Andonis has finished. After a short silence I say:

'I'm still staggered at the number of mistakes we've made. I feel hundreds of cops are watching us behind these walls.'

The Security Police are at our doors. What more is there to say? No comment is necessary. We discuss it all night. We decide that the first thing is for me to move out immediately. Athina has been warned. I'll go to Khaïdari, Elias Hill. That's where the printing press is. But I must first tell Petros (one can get him on the telephone) so he can give the green light.

The comrades are going to close this house and rent a bungalow in the Varkiza region under a false name in the hope that the Security will lose track of them. The MG will be hidden somewhere. On the last Sunday in August I am to go to the bungalow and when it is dark I shall swim to a foreign yacht which will be moored some distance from the coast. I shall cover my body with a black substance so I can't be seen when I'm swimming. I shall also blacken my face.

15 August

The day passes feverishly and with some anguish. Andonis goes out to make a telephone call. We expect to see him arrested at the corner of the road. But instead we see him coming back triumphant. 'Petros says that Odysseas *is a good doctor* (the code phrase). Athina will come here at ten o'clock tonight. Her brother is looking after the transfer; he has a big car. Odysseas will follow in his car: his wife will drive. So you'll be covered.'

In the evening an unexpected suggestion was made to me. An actress told me of another very safe house. If I could get there, I would slip out of the Security's vice. But the first difficulty was what would happen to the publication of *Nea Ellada*? The suggestion was turned down. Once again, the usual preparations for a move. The uniform. The moustache. I try to acquire the character of a colonel. We laugh heartily. Final instructions: the passwords. The rendezvous. Dates, timetable. At ten o'clock precisely Athina arrives with her daughter. It is dark outside. Two cars are just visible. Now and again a car's headlights tear through the night. We leave the house. The pine wood which covers the slopes of Mount Lycabettus is in front of us. What if there are gunmen there? On the look-out? Or on the terraces of neighbouring buildings? Absolute calm. I get into the first car and stretch out, as I have been told to, between the front and back seats, hiding under a cover. The mother and daughter get in and sit over this cover. We drive for some time and then the car stops. Change of driver. We are starting to climb Elias Hill. They tell me to get out. For the first time I see the friend who is to guide me. The route we are to take is scarcely visible. We walk very warily. A couple pass quite close. I turn round and clear my throat. My comrade gets the key out and opens the door.

I recall that the scene had been exactly the same two months before. Just the comrade was different. We had gone inside the same house and had sat down in the same drawing room. The mistress of the house had made her entrance, with her daughter.

'May I introduce my friend, Theodoros?' the other companion had said.

'Very pleased to meet you.'

'You look very like a composer I'm very fond of,' the girl had said, in an ironic tone of voice.

'Which composer?' I had asked stupidly.

'Theodorakis. Have you heard of him?'

'Of course. But his music leaves me cold.'

'Quite the opposite with me.'

She had got up to get a pile of records bearing photographs of myself.

'You're really very like him. Unless you are Theodorakis?'

'Well, yes, I am.'

The two women had chuckled with joy. (There was an unexpected result. They were so attentive that I put on fifteen kilos, although it must be said that my enforced immobility accounted for some of this. Anyway, that was what finally put me into the heavyweight class!)

This time the first thing I ask Maria is:

'Where is it?'

'Upstairs, in the attic.'

I am unable to resist: I go up just to lay eyes on the piles of plates and all the gear. It was very late before I got off to sleep that night: I could not get the typographical dreams out of my head!

16 August

'Happy birthday, Maria! My present is that I'm back here.'

We go and sit out on the veranda. Myself at the back in the shade. Although I am letting my beard grow, I still add to it my false archbishop's moustache.

Below us, out of sight, twinkle the lights of Athens, the holy city. Over to the right, Piraeus. To the left, in the far distance, Alexandras Avenue. Straight in front, Ellinikon airport.

'It won't be long before Mount Hymettus is illuminated,' I tell Maria. In fact a group of Lambrakides was to carve a huge luminous D (for Democracy) into the side of this ancient mountain which dominates the capital. But nothing happened. (I later found out why: they had been arrested, and some were hideously tortured.)

I spend the whole day with the printing press, sorting the letters one by one into little heaps. All this time the Security is getting closer. The worm is in the fruit and is burrowing on all the time. Nora and her network find themselves—as it later transpired—surrounded on all sides by the police net. A young intellectual got involved with Nora's daughter, who was unwise enough to introduce him to the network. The result is that the KYP and the Security are following, through the young man, all the activities of Nora and her friends. They are noting all the addresses so they can easily reach us. Our sudden disappearance seems to have caught them off their guard. So they decide to move into action. But this would be of no use to them if I were to observe two strict principles: (1) Not, for any reason or in any way, to establish a link between my previous residence and the new one; (2) to make sure that Petros comes to take me away so I can get into a completely different circuit of lodgings.

Friday, 18 August

We work at the printing press from dawn. A young Lambrakides came out of the blue to join us. He lives in the suburbs of Athens. We think we can get the newspaper out in a week. I compose the type. In order to finish the job successfully there are two or three things we need and which we must get next week. Especially paper. Maria, who had gone out, comes back about two in the afternoon. With Andonis.

'You really *must* give an interview to a Swedish newspaper in French.'

While she is getting the meal ready, we record the interview. I talk with Andonis.

I ask him if the others have left the old house.

'Not yet. We're still looking for the bungalow.'

'And you're not being shadowed?'

'Not that we can see. We're beginning to wonder if we were seeing things.'

The operation which is due to get me out of Greece seems to be seriously endangered. We must meet tomorrow to discuss it. After Andonis's visit I become very pensive. How can he talk of seeing things when we were able to state the facts very precisely? I must get in contact with Petros. He's the only one who can get me out of this trap. Just one big leap, and the Security Police would lose track of me for ever. I decide to send Maria out at once to make contact, as had been agreed. She is to ask Petros to come and get me, and also to warn him that the danger is getting nearer all the time. In the evening Odysseas's wife comes with Nikos, who is a journalist and a member of the Easter Committee. Two days before, I had been asked to do this interview and I had agreed to him coming round. He had given me to understand that he had a very serious reason and had to see me as soon as possible.

We chat for a long time. Since Nikos is circulating, talking and living in the normal world—far removed from ours—what he has to say is very valuable. What he has to say about the Front, the Party and the movement in general moves me greatly. I had been thinking that my doubts, my bitterness, were just a purely subjective phenomenon, but here is Nikos telling me that these feelings, these fears and these thoughts are shared by almost all the militants with whom we are currently fighting hand-in-hand.

'The burning ardour of the first days is gradually cooling down,' he says.

It is perhaps because at the beginning we thought we could build a new world and now we see the same faces popping up again just as if nothing had happened. For my part, I maintain that we must make use of all the goodwill that is going.

'But why don't they work with you? We have the feeling they're seeking to isolate you.'

'The links are kept by Petros.'

'But, you see, we prefer to meet you in person. We're afraid something's not running quite right. Once again one can feel that numbness that prevailed before the *coup*. The Politburo—will it intervene? Have you seen the people of the Interior Party?'

It interests me to find out what the other members of the Easter Committee are thinking. I am not certain that they're prepared to make the great leap. But Nikos assures me that all the comrades he has seen recently are determined not to go back and to accept no compromise with a leadership which is responsible for the Party's defeat. In his view, they remain faithful to the spirit of Easter.

'If we decide that we have to break all our ties with the former Party, do you think we could rebuild the forces of the Left on a new basis?'

'I'm convinced of it.'

'You think our friends will follow us?'

'Absolutely!'

I tell him of my last, rather depressing, experiences in this field and of my determination to start everything again from scratch—even if I have to do it alone.

'Naturally, only one thing counts today—the Resistance. But how can one speak of resistance if there is no revolutionary party to lead the way. The Greek Communist Party has been no help to us so far. After four months of clandestine struggle what have we received in the way of funds, material or any other form of assistance? Practically nothing. Sure, the Greek Communist Party is only interested in us to the extent that we inspire confidence. But one has to see what others have managed to do through the Patriotic Front, and it's only a beginning.'

'What others?'

I quote some names, and continue:

'And may they do a lot more! As far as I'm concerned, I have no wish to go back to the old set-up. I'm fighting for something completely new, for the rebirth of a rejuvenated Left. And we're achieving our aim quite nicely: by working flat out to lay the foundations of a new Greek progressive party. We're making a check on our friends, the comrades in the Easter Committee, and other leaders of the Lambrakis Youth. Will Petros agree?'

'I think so.'

(A little later Kostas, a member of the Bureau of the Interior Party, was to tell me that after my arrest Petros and certain other Lambrakides had shown absolutely no desire to stand up for an enterprise which they considered was...divisive!)

We agree that I should write a small pamphlet which will set out the problem and prepare the ground for a meeting to set up a Greek New Left. On the basis of this pamphlet, Nikos is to speak to seven or eight members, assuming they are in agreement with us, and they will then come to see me in Khaïdari, for it is our view that we must share the responsibility and the honour of an act of such great historical importance. We fix a day for this meeting: the following Friday, 25 August.

Saturday, 19 August

The decisive day for the Resistance. We have decided to move on to a new form of action: demonstration! To begin with (to use our own terms) 'fleeting', or 'lightning', demonstrations. Up to now the shock brigades have had a series of spectacular successes in the centre of Athens. One form of demonstration is to unroll banners carrying Resistance slogans across the fronts of buildings. First you have to find a building which is prominently situated. The banners are made of pieces of tissue or

68

paper joined together and fixed in place with glue or staples. Hundreds of leaflets are rolled up inside them. One end of the roll is fixed to the edge of a terrace and the roll is held by a piece of cotton. A lighted cigarette is placed under the cotton, and then you retire. In a few minutes the cigarette has burnt through the cotton and the whole thing unrolls automatically and covers the top of the building. The leaflets which flutter down also attract the attention of passers-by.

Another form of demonstration is the tape recorder. You have to have an empty, well-situated office. You get in and set up the tape recorder, making sure that the loudspeaker is facing the street. Within a quarter of an hour all the traffic stops and the crowd is listening to the appeal of the Resistance! We are lagging a bit in the field of explosives and this is because explosives require extra care and greater organisation.

But the demonstration is still an advanced form of struggle, for it elicits an immediate response from the enemy. There is less chance of escape. One goes straight to the confrontation and runs the risk of being seized on the spot. Twelve Lambrakides are chosen for the first demonstration. They are to go down Ermou Street in two lines, at midday on a Saturday, in other words at the height of the rush hour. Everything goes according to plan. On the stroke of twelve, the twelve volunteers go out into Ermou Street and begin chanting 'Down with the junta!' 'Long live democracy!' They hand out leaflets. The demonstration lasts just as long as was planned—two minutes. Each demonstrator vanishes into the crowd. But just at the last moment an informer who happens to be there hurls himself at one of the Lambrakides. The young man calls for help. The crowd gathers round and tears the young militant away.

Sunday, 20 August

Andonis and Orestis did not turn up yesterday evening as arranged. I am convinced that danger is approaching. Petros didn't show up either. But I have changed my mind. I am going to stay on here until the New Left is on a good footing.

However, I can feel the vice tightening: to start with, why didn't the other two come? What happened to them? Have they been arrested? Maybe they are being tortured at this very moment? But then, why didn't Petros come? He has got my message; he knows I'm in danger.

(I later learned that Andonis and Orestis had noticed, just as they got to my house, that they were being followed. It was too late and their car was already in my district. As for Petros, he later told me in prison that he had found out I was surrounded and he could neither come nor warn me.)

During the evening Maria's daughter asked me to hide behind the piano. I must say something about that hiding place; it did turn out to be fatal for me but there were good moments (the life of a member of the underground is full of anguish but there are comic moments, too, which one cherishes all the more because one knows at what price one is enjoying each minute of fragile freedom). So, in Maria's house, where my presence of course had to be concealed from any strangers who visited the family, I had chosen as my hiding place—every time I had to disappear—an upright piano which stood across a corner of the drawing room. There was enough room behind it for me to sit on a cushion reading a book, while the conversation was going on in the room. In this way I heard visitors making remarks about me, calling me everything from a hero to a pederast (to the great embarrassment of my hosts who knew I was listening to everything). But the funniest thing was the way these ladies gossiped. So as not to arouse any suspicions, neighbours were still welcome to drop in for tea or to use the telephone. I had never realised that between themselves women have very special topics of conversation.

That evening when Maria told me to get behind the piano, I sensed an unusual nerviness:

'Why, so suddenly?'

'Lakis, my fiancé, is coming in a minute.'

I grab my cushion and squeeze behind the piano. I sit down with my legs crossed. I start writing. Lakis arrives. He is talking a lot of nonsense out on the veranda. He is a journalist. His family is very well off and has a magnificent house. Lakis sits down at the piano; he likes classical music. Maria's daughter and he want to live together. As for getting married, maybe later. They have found a little flat near Koliatsou Square. They are now painting it. When will they be able to move in? Lakis insists that they should move straightaway. *Tomorrow at the latest*! It is strange but this Lakis really disturbs me.

(At the very moment that I was squeezing behind that piano, the police were knocking at other houses: Leftheris's, Takis's, Athina's and Nora's. They arrested every member of Nora's network and she was the first to be tortured.)

Monday, 21 August

I am working at the press. In between I am trying to write articles for the first issue of *Nea Ellada*. I am also dictating into the tape recorder the last chapter of my book, *We the Greeks*.

The atmosphere is very heavy. What if Petros were to come? What would I do? Would I leave with him? Or should we postpone the meeting arranged for Friday? There is one solution: to leave immediately and postpone the meeting. I send Odysseas's wife out with an SOS for Petros. Just that: he'll understand.

At this moment the Security men are knocking at Andonis's house. They take him away but lock his wife in the house under guard. The poor woman has to stay like this for several hours while they are torturing her husband at the other end of Athens. Koula is lying on a divan, and underneath it is the typewriter we used for the statement on setting up the Patriotic Front. It is an old machine, with a very characteristic type face, so that it would be easily identified and would unquestionably compromise Andonis and Koula. So, patiently and without undue movement, she slips her hand under the bed while the guard's back is turned and twists the hammers off one by one; then each time she goes to the toilet she jettisons her little handful of scrap iron. She does not have to feign illness for these visits to the toilet, for in fact she is ill because she chewed and swallowed, one by one, the pages of a notebook which I had left there and in which there were many compromising addresses in my own handwriting.

Odysseas's wife returns empty-handed. She is not sure if Petros has received my SOS. Maria is clearly very tired. She can do no more. A minute later her daughter and Lakis come to get their things. They are going to spend the night in their new flat. I return to the piano. The atmosphere is highly charged. Lakis's car drives off.

71

'You can come out now.'

I am not hungry. I carefully hide the tapes, take the type up into the attic and tear up all compromising papers.

'No news of Andonis or Orestis?'

'Nothing. It's as if they'd been shipwrecked.'

I hide my manuscript and the pamphlet I wrote on the New Left behind the piano (all this is now in the Security archives).

'Do you think Petros will come?' I ask Maria.

'He doesn't usually come as late as this.'

'Maria, if they ever come here without warning to search the place, don't forget—let them think you're using *my* bed. They mustn't find out there are two beds, or we're buggered.' In fact Maria sleeps on a couch on the veranda, without any covers, so my bed is the only one not made up; with this little trick one can pretend that Maria is the only person in the house, and that she has moved out on to the veranda because of the heat.

It is after midnight. There are knocks at the door. I leap out of bed. There are sinister shadows cast across the window, I open the door on to the veranda. I whisper: 'Get up, Maria.' She went to bed dog-tired and she is sleeping soundly. Hurried steps hammering up the veranda steps. I hardly have time to get behind the piano...They find Maria asleep on the divan and then look across at my unmade bed. I hear her explanations: 'I was hot and got out.' They turn round and round again like hungry animals. They search everywhere. My heart is ready to burst open. 'The printing press, where is it?' 'Whose is this uniform?' They search, search...Then silence. Have they gone, or is it a ruse? Bent double, I try to stifle my heart beats by pressing my chest with my hands. The door opens. More steps. Someone is coming over to the piano. 'There he is!' He is leaning over me, staring. He shouts: 'Over here, boys, here's Mikis.' 'Get up! Hands up!' He points his revolver at me and with his free hand tears my pyjama trousers off. I am now naked. 'On your knees!' I refuse. 'Hit him! Tie him up quickly! No, no! Hands in the air! No, in front, on his chest! Or, rather...No! Hands behind his back! Yes, that's it! And very tight! So it hurts. Like that...Down!'

The soldiers came to arrest me while I was asleep. They made me undress and ordered me to kneel down. Then they tied my elbows behind my back as the Americans do with

72

Vietcong prisoners. When Maria came in I felt ashamed and asked them to put my pants on. They put on my pants and my trousers. I was barefoot and I told Maria to put my shoes on. She bent down in front of me and as she was tying the laces I whispered: 'Courage, Maria'.[16]

'We're off.' 'Go on ahead...' 'No behind...' 'At the side!' 'Be careful he doesn't escape!' 'What?' They cackle and fool about like street kids.

I am bent double. It hurts because they have tied my hands very high behind my back and by the wrists. One of them is kicking me. The other one is digging his baton in my sides and stomach: 'You'll see, it'll be fun.'

Outside there is not a living soul to be seen...No! In a moment a car is spotted coming up the street. A few steps away, a group of people. Over by the hill, various movements. Headlights. Lorries on the Sacred Way.[17] The grocer has his shutters half-open. Is he going to see me? Has anyone seen me? The houses are silent, frightened, compassionate...

The road slopes down and at the bottom there is a car waiting. 'Not this way; over there towards the trees!' To the right— Athens, the holy city. High above it—Hymettus. Higher still— the dark sky, the stars, the moon. They tell me bluntly: 'Mikis, you're going to die!' 'Mikis, you're enjoying your last minutes of life!' 'Mikis, what are you feeling?' I am taking in the morning air. I am thinking of nothing but the beauty of the starry sky, of the silvery light of the moon. I am smiling. I am proud. The end is just as I would have wished it. I look down on Athens from the heights. The others are asleep: I am going to die for them. A mad kind of music suddenly swirls into my thoughts like a flurry of snow—it is the song of Federico Garcia Lorca: 'Down there, beside the river, where three tongues of land stand out in silhouette, his blood was drained away.' Just like him! It was also night. The others were sleeping. He counted the stars. And he is dead!

'This is where you're going to die! Right here...No! Take him away from here...Somewhere else!'

We go down the slope. The sinister red car...the same one that used to take me from house to house. Now it is driving me to my death! Has Orestis been arrested too?

'Put a hood over his head!' They stick their batons into my

73

stomach, belly and testicles. They twist my hands behind my back. The bones crack and about to break. I tell myself : What a pity! The end won't be as romantic and as simple as I thought. They're going to hit you, flay you alive, burn you. And when you give up your soul, your face will already have disappeared, thanks to your torturers. Maybe they'll gouge your eyes out: maybe you'll die in darkness. Maybe they'll drown you in a pit of dung, like a rat. Maybe they'll pull your nails out. That hurts, horribly! The pain is unending. Pitiless. You'll pray for death to come and deliver you.

We stop. Move off. Stop again. Whispering. Stifled laughs. Move off. Stop again. Orders: 'We're off.' 'Halt.' 'Get out!' They make me get out. I cannot see anything. I am in terrible pain. I climb some steps. Now I know: they are going to throw me off the terrace. The void. Here I am before the void. No, not yet. They push me. Into the void? No. I am going up. Still going up. Out of breath. They want to throw me from the very top. To reduce me to pulp. To remove all trace of me. For ever.

Faces. Dear faces. The faces of Margarita, of Yorgos, of Myrto flash into my mind. My mother will never see me again. The void...? No, still going up. My people will not be able to wash my dead body, caress it, kiss it...Steps...The void? No, a landing...Just the memory will remain...Farewell, mother! Farewell, father! Farewell, wife! children...

They push me. They stop. They guess what I am thinking and laugh. 'Sit down.' They lift the hood. I breathe again. Enter Lambrou.[18] 'Hi Mikis! We had some trouble getting you, but anyway here you are. You're in General Security head-quarters. Now you're going to have a rest. It's the Koukoue, your Party, who gave you away...'

And once again I encounter the traditional methods of the Police.

References

1 The US Ambassador in Athens, Phillips Talbott.
2 Ethniki Organosis Neolaias (National Youth Organisation) closely modelled on Mussolini's fascist organisation. It was set up by the dictator Metaxas (1936–40).

74

3 Mikis Theodorakis cannot ignore his immense popularity. 'At forty-three Theodorakis is the most popular musician in Greece. A legendary man. A god from Olympus. His music has the aroma of thyme and jasmine, of retzina and grilled mutton. It can speak of the sky and the sea, the air and light, sunsets and the colours of the anemone. Above all it is the cry of downtrodden Greece, a country which was murdered so many years ago that no living person can remember having known what the world means by a Greek word—democracy. His music has made the greatest poets sing out in the smallest villages. In this land of misery and exodus Theodorakis's music has given back to the Greeks their pride in being Greek.' (Extracts from Jacques Coubard's *Mikis Théodorakis. La Grèce entre le rêve et le cauchemar,* Julliard, Paris.)

Equally one cannot ignore the fact that Theodorakis's stature, both physical (he is 1 metre 90 cm tall) and as a hero, is known to everyone. (Translator's Note)

4 Three years later I was to meet a Dutch friend in London who gave me the explanation: he had been arrested at that very time, hauled in to the Security Police and told to say where I was hiding. He did not know. They hit him. A note was found on him bearing an address—'What's this?' He did not remember. He was hit again. The next day he remembered: 'It's the address of an inn. A friend gave it to me because it had good wine and excellent hors d'oeuvres.' The inn happened unfortunately to be near my hiding place. And that is what brought the police so near.

5 Between us 'they' means all the leaders of the Greek Communist Party who are outside the country.

6 'Voice of Truth', the Greek Communist Party's radio station which broadcasts from abroad and is currently in the hands of the Koliyannis group.

7 A year later it became the Patriotic Anti-Dictatorship Front, PAM (Patriotiko Antidiktatoriko Metopo).

8 Seventy-nine-year-old President of the Greek Communist Party. (Translator's Note)

9 His denunciations were later confirmed when I heard similar denunciations from other comrades.

10 Gheorghe Gheorghiu-Dej, First Secretary of the Romanian Communist Party, 1952–65. (Translator's Note)

11 National security battalions (extreme Right). (Translator's Note)

12 Digenis Akrites Basileios, a legendary hero of Byzantium, whose exploits gave rise to many folk ballads and a written epic in the tenth century; the figure of Digenis has captured the imagination of modern writers and poets in Greece, who see him as a symbol of modern and medieval Hellenism and its heroic spirit. (Translator's Note)

13 The day fixed for the general election, which could not take place because of the military *coup d'état* of 21 April.

14 Alas, the MG was too precious to be put out of service.

15 I had a nickname in each house so that when I was mentioned through carelessness in the presence of third parties it would pass unnoticed. At Maria's I was referred to as Mitsouko... It was the cat's name.

16 See 'Exodos', p. 231.

17 Iera Odos.

18 Deputy director of General Security.

AVEROF

Bouboulinas Street

So I was arrested in Khaïdari, a suburb of Athens, on 21 August 1967, five months to the day after the putsch. I was immediately taken to the Security headquarters in Bouboulinas Street, to await torture and death in Cell No. 4 on the fourth floor. I spend interminable days and nights in total isolation. Not until 4 September do they provide me with paper and a pencil. Then I write thirty-two poems in succession.

I had stayed awake every night, leaning against the wall, expecting someone to come in at any moment to take me away to torture me or execute me. My existence was in suspense, in this expectation of certain death. But as neither time nor my thoughts stood still in the midst of this anguish, I had constantly in my mind the very vivid vision of my last moments: the morning sky was deep blue, the atmosphere crystal clear. What would be my final cry? It had become an obsession.

At midday the heat became torrid. I was sleeping naked, on the cement floor. I used my shoes as a pillow. I had several weeks' growth of beard. I ate with some difficulty, as I had neither a fork nor a spoon. Sometimes I would sit down on the chair—the only piece of 'furniture' in the cell—and at other times I would start walking up and down like a madman. I counted. Five hundred paces up and down. Five hundred paces in a circle. I also kept counting the cell bars. I would look at my jailer's neck. Did he really hate me? Why?

No doubt he had hummed my songs. When was he going to lay his hands on me? When would my turn come?

On top of all this anguish, which bore down on me all day and every night, there came, inexplicably, a period of morbid euphoria. I was happy. In the last resort, death is not so terrible. 'Maybe it is even beautiful,' I said to the warder. As soon as a new day broke and the sun shone into my cell, life gained the upper hand again, and with some force. Once again I would see my children's faces. I did not want them to be thinking of me and crying. I was disappointed they had not executed me on the spot. What fate were they keeping in store for me? What sort of execution? I had dreadful headaches and my temples were thumping like mad. Two o'clock, three o'clock, four, five, six o'clock. The afternoon passed and nothing had happened. 'In the Paradise of my skull, a yellow sun journeys on the wings of time.' I cry. I shout. My heart is giving way. Someone must be thinking of me at this minute. But nobody knows I am here. Call, I beg you. Here is my telephone number: 934.303, 934.303. I shout it out. Maybe someone will hear and will lift his telephone and announce: 'Mikis is alive!' I am thinking of my comrades all the time. They arrested Maria at the same time as me. But the others—Iason? Leloudas? No doubt they have been caught. Sylva must be still at Vouliagmeni with Elena. They may still be tasting some of the joys of life, bathing on the beach. Sylva was in love with Pepito di Capri's voice. When I was in hiding at Filothei, we used to listen together to Markopoulos's last song. When evening came, we would walk into the garden. It was getting darker every minute and we would sit under the apricot trees. Elena had a harmonica. 'Wings, mouth-organs, echoes of waters, lizards, moons.' Kostas, Andonis and Babis were also hiding in that house. Yannis and Dora were smoking 'Xanthi' aromatic cigarettes. And here I am, today—I am going to die.

But when I am writing music, I become master of time and death. I am time. That is why the cycle of poems I was writing at the time—'The Sun and Time'—became one of life and death, and in the end, a cycle of victory. A bitter victory, certainly, for the poet suffers for all men, even for those who hate him and torture him.

The first things I scribble down are the notes of one of the popular tunes I am very fond of:

Night without moon
The darkness is deep
Alone a young man
Cannot find sleep

Then images and thoughts erupt in an impetuous rhythm. Sounds, chromatic sonorities seeking to express themselves in words:

'...Five intervals of augmented seconds with a minor third interposed lead to monochromatic bifurcations whose values depend on the amplitude and degree of vibration.

'We end up with hypersonority of sound leading to the stressing of meanders of sound with intervals of diminished fifths.

'The beginning of a series of opposing currents of chromatics which could well contain some hints of diatonicism.

'But at this juncture a rhythmic cross-cutting motif must come in otherwise there would be a confusion of aesthetic levels. In this way we progress in the investigation of the relationships between the chromatic quantities and the diatonic qualities. The determination of the golden number is the basis of the calculation. The relationship between qualities and quantities according to the sum of the rhythmic factors leads us to a hyperchromatic representation of the main theme. Then comes the more elaborate construction of the remaining elements. Which are they? Moments of consciousness sensitised with humour? These elements are enriched by the addition of new chromatic vibrations leading to new chromatic sonorities. To new transformations of consciousness. *Ad infinitum.*

'It is the sign to move on. Very important, to heed this sign. But manifold and complex problems immediately arise. Which problems? The relation of the whole to the part. A qualitative relation, naturally. How does one determine it? By the total of the speeds times the masses.

$$\frac{V^2 \times M^2}{\text{central idea}} = \text{internal rhythm}$$

'Essentially the internal rhythm must be the acceptance by the consciousness of the most general criticism which the work is making of tradition...'

And for the first time the title appears : SUN AND TIME. And the first verses :

>Times dissolves in a moment
>The lowly becomes the greatest of tyrants...

The following verses were not to be used in the final version of the work:

>The trees separating us have become rooms
>The flowers, men
>The fields and insects,
>Offices, files, padlocks
>Abyss upon abyss
>Love.
>
>Kappa Ypsilon Lambda full stop.
>Alpha colon Phi
>Semicolon Ita Sigma[1]
>Patras, Rion, Mesolonghi, Aitolikon
>Mules loaded with laurel wreaths
>Mules from Akarnania
>Light coloured scented tobacco
>A caique smelling of fuel oil
>Numb from hunger
>Vonitsa
>Numb from hunger
>A September night
>You look suspicious.
>
>Loquacious star
>Hanging
>Beyond the grille
>What is the sky?
>What is the earth?
>What are the waves?
>The sky is your mother
>The earth your dwelling
>And the waves your friends
>They lament for you.

Nine in the evening
A still ship
The caress of the weather
Myrto's sea remembers us
Memory claws at us
When the sky has shed its tears
I go to the window
When the bolt has fallen
And day has waned
All the drops of rain
I have collected for you
All the sufferings of life
I have collected for you
Your love is but a drop
When my heart is an ocean.

A sky of deep blue
Looks on us sadly
This sky had been
Propitious to us!
Such a deep blue light
Blinds man
Rattlesnakes, chameleons, jelly fish,
Engraved copper serpents
The hand of a seventeenth century hagiographer
Polykarpos, the theologian of Messinia
Shoe tassels from the Officers' School
Epidauros ancient theatre tunics
Lycurgan press agencies
An ancient civilisation
Ancient, very ancient,
Most ancient.

Eleni Vlakhou, press magnate, yacht, Rome, balcony,
The frightful facing the worse
Blue June sea
August festival
Staccato whistles and military marches
Blankets, sheets, mess-tins, bolts
Glory glory glory!

Hellenic August dedicated to music
The musical demon of the race
Byzantine hymns, canticles, psalms
Popular symphonic ensembles
The entire treasure of Stournara Theatre[2]
Seats reserved in advance
Concert starts nine o'clock sharp
Book seats because of heavy demand
Entrance free exit prohibited
By Police order.

I try to unravel the tangle of circumstances which led to my arrest: the mistakes and the negligence. How did the Security find me? Who has been seized? They arrested Maria at the same time as me. They took me in Orestis's car. So, he too has been seized. But what of his friends and collaborators?...

Four or five days later, Lambrou comes to see me. He sits down beside me and crosses his legs.

'Today we are all socialists,' he says. And then suddenly: 'Anyway, I must admit, you've given us some trouble, *Lambros*,' he says, pretending to have let this name slip out...and correcting himself immediately: 'Sorry! I meant Mikis.' Lambros was one of my underground pseudonyms. Which house did I have that name in? Ah, yes! So they've arrested them, too. But how? I pretended not to have understood. But my eyes were flashing: he must have noticed.

He came again another day, this time with his secretary. 'I've come about the regulation statement, so we can file your dossier,' he said. 'What do you know about the Patriotic Front?' I replied that I was one of its leaders, and that its aim was to overthrow the tyranny and re-establish constitutional order. And I outlined the main aims of our struggle.

'With whom do you collaborate and who told you of the house where we arrested you?' I said: 'I knew that house already—a friend in EDA had told me about it. I visited it a long time ago. On the morning of the *coup d'état* I took a taxi and went straight there. The women were frightened. I threatened them and paid them handsomely. After that I got in contact with my friends.'

'Which friends?'

'That's no concern of yours.'

84

That roughly was my first statement. Then Lambrou suddenly spoke to me of Comrade Irini, of one of my refuges with which I had severed all contact. So the knife had gone in deep, it had struck the bone.

After about three weeks they open the window. And through the glass I can make out the shadows of the women in the next cell. I hear their voices. Sometimes they sing. From the cells below I hear men's voices which seem familiar. One day, as I am leaving my cell, I spot Sylva at the end of the corridor... So, I am now convinced that there is no-one still free. During the month, another interrogation. This time a military justice captain conducts it. The indictment concerns my Statement of 23 April 1967. I am brought to justice under Emergency Law 509. I dictate my statement to his secretary, who trembles while writing it down.

'You're going straight to the firing squad,' the captain tells me, adding: 'It's a pity—you're a great composer...' Always the same line.

First, a visit from Savvas Konstantopoulos (director of the pro-dictatorship paper, *Eleftheros Kosmos*); he is accompanied by Papaspyropoulos, the director of Security.

'You must be very pleased that Greece has become a prison,' I tell him.

He breathes deeply, and replies:

'Nobody is satisfied. We must, however, see how we are going to get out of it without a national catastrophe.'

'Well said! I'm thankful for just one thing: that there's not been a bloodbath yet.'

'We must avoid *that* at all costs, and that's where you come in—your contribution could be important.'

'Things are on the move. The colonels would do well to go quietly back to their barracks before it's too late.'

'I'll come back and talk to you again.'

We go down together to the director's office. There are many people in the corridors. A crowd of reporters and journalists in the room. They want to see if I am still alive. If I am fighting in the terrible Security building. I am struggling. I am confident, even optimistic and joyful. It is your love, you people of Greece, which more than anything else puts me in your debt, and I want to repay this debt. These are the thoughts which are passing through my mind as I go down the stairs and along the corridors. These are my thoughts as I stand smiling before the cameras. But I did not know then how many people were going to reproach me for that smile! Oh, how everything becomes suspect and distorted in this world which is deformed by the monstrous pressure of the dictatorship!

One day, after an interminable period of time, I am taken from my cell to Lambrou's office. He is sitting at his desk. Sitting opposite him, my father and Myrto. I had not seen her since the morning of 21 April. She is in tears. Her hair is done up in a chignon. Her eyes are open wide. She is burning with despair. She throws herself into my arms. I am happy. Momentarily I leave this hell and want to laugh! 'Don't worry. All will be well!' She looks at me, terrified: 'How can everything be going well?' 'I'm very strong,' I tell her, glancing at Lambrou out of the corner of my eye. 'They won't dare send me before a tribunal. That wouldn't serve their purpose...' But Lambrou has just told her that the trial is to take place and that my neck is at risk. He wants to break down her resistance, as well as mine. Myrto must have understood, for she says, hastily for fear that she may be thrown out: 'Do your duty and don't worry about us. We're used to the idea of seeing you condemned to isolation, of even seeing you facing execution. Don't think of us! Do your duty! Because if you give way, all four us will drown.' Lambrou gets up. He wasn't expecting that.

'Are you a Communist Party militant, madam?'

'No, sir, but I have dignity.'

'Take him away.'

I had to wait four weeks before I saw her again.

I have already spent forty days in solitary. I am woken up one night. 'Don't worry,' Lambrou's assistant says, 'get dressed.'

We go down to the second floor. The corridors are deserted. Lambrou is hidden behind a pile of papers. 'Sit down!' We are alone. The clock strikes two.

'This letter you have sent to Bithikotsis[3] is very serious.'

He shows me it.

'How did you get hold of it?'

'The waiter at the Taverna is one of our men. This letter could send you to the firing squad.'

'Just that...? But you've got enough "proof" to have me condemned to death a hundred times over...'

'So, what are you going to do? Sacrifice yourself?'

'Do I have an alternative?' I look him straight in the eye.

'Listen! I think there's a way out.'

'The declaration of repentance?'⁴

'No, not that! We don't want things like that. What we want is for you to write down on paper your reasons for disagreeing with the others.'

'I still don't get it.'

'We know everything. For example, we know that you are critical of the Politburo and of those in this country who follow it...'

'They're family affairs. You can be sure that in front of a military tribunal and public opinion I shall be a firm defender of the Politburo.'

'And you, in your turn, can be sure that you will be executed.'

'Listen, Vasilios, you know only too well that I drive a Citroën at two hundred.⁵ I've lived at close quarters with death, and an absurd death, too...And you come and offer me a noble and heroic death! You're bluffing! You can't kill me. Just think: for years to come millions of people would hear my music and they'd say, "That man was killed by the colonels...by the Security...by Lambrou..." No! I'm aware of my strength. Don't you worry...'

He bursts out laughing, in a rather sickly way:

'I wanted to test you,' he says.

The following morning Papaspyropoulos comes up to my cell.

'It's absurd to ask you anything. I hold the view that it's not yet time for this trial. First, because apart from you no cadre has been arrested [Filinis had not yet been caught]. Second, because those who are with you are members of important Athens families. And third, because you're the only communist: all the others are nationalists.'

'So, what are you going to do?'

'I know that you're suffering from the knowledge that you're responsible for the misfortune of so many innocent people. But we'll find a way—perhaps by shelving the case—of setting them all free. All of them without exception. Except you. Your case is a tricky one. If you're on trial, we'd have to condemn you to death. And you know as well as we do that that would do us more harm than good.'

Two more days pass. I am woken at daybreak. I see Babalis and Malios kneeling at my side.[6] They are unshaven. Their eyes are red. I get it!

'Get up!' They take me to Lambrou's office.

'The case is closed,' he says. 'Once the interrogation is over, you will all leave here. All we need is your statement.'

'But you have it in your hand.'

'The service considers it's absurd—a tissue of lies. Now you know that we know everything: people, addresses, discussions, etc. Look at this statement, for example. It's forty pages long. Do you want me to read out the details? There are just three elements missing: (a) where did you go on the first day? (b) who took you to Filopappos? and (c) who took you to Khaïdari? We know everything else. We know the time you take your bath and the kind of soap you use.'

'And so, what then?'

'Well, so that everything is in order, we must cancel the first statement. You only have to tell us the houses where you stayed —the owners are all arrested.'

It's a trap. But what's the object?

'And if I refuse?'

'If you refuse, then you'll stay here two, three, five, ten months, until you're completely exhausted.'

'But when you know everything and you have arrested everybody, why do you ask me to go over it again? What do you want to get out of it, exactly?'

'Come on now, it's just a formality,' Malios says. 'We have to wind up the case. And all that's missing is your statement.'

My thoughts are running so fast that I can feel my head spinning. I feel bad. What do they want now? To all intents and purposes the investigation was over long ago...Maybe they want one day to be able to defame me. But what would I have to fear? I can understand why they don't want to start a trial. There are so many awkward names: Leloudas, Akrita, Loulis, Skarpalezou, Yavassoglou...Formidable propaganda for the Resistance and especially for the Front...

Meanwhile the resistance is being stepped up all around us. One evening we hear bombs exploding. A sudden silence descends on the Security. But it is from that night that the cries, the blows and the yelling begin. And in my ears they merge with the cries and wailing of women, for they have moved me to the other end of the corridor, to Cell No. 1, where the deputy, L, had been. My window has iron bars of course but it does face on to Tositsa Street and there is a new maternity hospital across the road. So every night from then on the cries of mothers giving birth mingled with the cries of men being tortured on the terrace.

When I go to the window during the day I am recognised by the women opposite. And I can see by their faces how deep their affection is for me. A young woman sits up in bed and gives me a big wave. A young father lifts his baby up and indicates that I am to be the godfather. A family, one of whose members is a colonel in uniform, throw me kisses and make signs that I am to hold their newborn at the font. Nine out of ten of those who spot me indicate their sympathy and their indignation at my fate in various ways.

After fifty days of being on my own I get company. Dimitris, one of the comrades who arranged my moves when I was underground, comes to share my cell. He enters, deathly pale, and collapses on the ground, gasping.

'What's the matter?'

'I thought they were taking me to the terrace.'

'What terrace?'

'Eh? You don't know yet? It's hell. You'll hear this evening. I've been living in that cell for a month and I know...'

'They torture people?'

'Of our people they've already tortured Andonis...and Comrade Nora...You've not heard the cries yet?'

'Yes, every day at noon. I protested to the warders. They called Lambrou, and as he came in you could hear the flogging clearly. I asked what was happening. He started talking in his rapid, "persuasive" way: "Oh! That's nothing. The cries are coming from the Narcotics Section. You know, we have to beat the drug addicts otherwise they don't tell where they're hiding the heroin and what not. And that's death. What are we to do? We've got to protect society." I insisted on knowing if they were beating *politicals*, too. "You're joking!" he said. "You've only to think of your own case. Do you have any reason to complain of any pressure on our part? We haven't even asked you any questions. Why? Because we have perfect archives and we do our work scientifically! Flogging is archaic! Everything nowadays is a question of archives and statistics! Oh! I know, I know...We're accused of putting the prisoners in solitary, of depriving them of water, of binding them hand and foot, of hanging them by their wrists, of giving them the 'falanga'! That's all lies! On my word of honour as a soldier, we haven't even given a clout round the head!" '

'Listen!' Dimitris interrupts suddenly.

We hear footsteps on the terrace.

'He's getting the apparatus ready...' Dimitris says. 'Here come the others...They're tying him to the bench...Now they're interrogating him...They're gagging him with a rag soaked in urine.'

Suddenly the walls shake. My God, what a terrible blow that must have been!

'What are they beating him with?'

'They take his shoes off and beat the soles of his feet with a club. But usually they leave his shoes on and use an iron bar on the soles. The feet swell and the pain lasts several days and sometimes even weeks.'

We count the blows.

'Write it down!' I tell Dimitris. 'The day, the month. Eleven o'clock—120 blows; twelve o'clock—70 blows; 2.15—180 blows...'

Dimitris lies down in his corner. He feels sick. I talk to him so as to give him courage. Perhaps to give myself some, too.

'It seems terrible to us because our imaginations are at work. But for him there's only the physical suffering...' (I lie: I remember that on Makronisos, when I lay on the hospital bed in the evening after the tortures, I used to say bitterly: 'What lies we stuff our heads with—and those of other people! The suffering of the soul! The moral suffering! The intellectual suffering! Those are words...In fact, there is nothing harder, nothing more painful, more *real* than ordinary physical pain, the pain of the flesh.')

The blows fall thick and fast. And all of a sudden a horrible cry, like that of a wounded beast, rends the darkness. Then— silence...Dimitris says:

'Now they're untying him...dragging him away...wrapping him up in a blanket. If they've finished, they'll take him back into solitary. If they're carrying on, they must first make him have a pee...'

'Is there a doctor with them?'

'Yes. Kioupis. They say someone succumbed to the blows. They took him down to Number Four, next to the women.'

'My old cell!'

'Didn't they make you go out one morning, at dawn?'

'Yes. Now I can understand why. When I got back the floor had been washed.'

'They had washed the blood away.'

'Did anyone see him, poor fellow?'

'They said he was a thin man of medium height.'

'Aristide?'

'Could have been...'

'We must warn those outside...I know what I'm going to do...'

'What?'

'I'm going to talk to Lambrou about it...I'm going to protest violently in front of him...'

'Are you mad? He's capable of pulling your finger nails out. With me the policeman who conducted the investigation got a pair of pincers out of his office drawer and said: "No funny business...You're going to talk!" Don't you know where we are?...'

It is in this new cell—just below the terrace where the tortures which were to be denounced by the Council of Europe took place—that I complete on 17 October the music for 16 of the 32 poems which make up 'Sun and Time'. Then I teach them to Dimitris. Sitting at the window, behind the bars, we sing before going to sleep:

Sun and Time

1

Greetings, Acropolis,
Tourkolimano, Bucharest Street!
The Pole Star
Casts its light
On the steadfast part of the world

91

Athens First
From the timeless depths
Through their masks
The fish hunters see you
Galleys, private cars, secret brothels
The dead centre of the world.
The Pole Star turns steadily
The chimney of the cookhouse
Marks in smoke
The centre of the Firmament
The Pleiades, Aphrodite,
Dina, Soula, Evi, Rinio.
Five million light years
Draw a straight line
Five billion Galaxies
Pole Star, Acropolis, chimney
Five metres
Five metres
Only five metres
From my cell.

2

Time dissolves
Within a moment
The slightest trifle becomes
The greatest tyrant
Tortures flourishing
Wounds
Smiles and promises
For something else—that something else
For we live every moment
Thinking we are living another
But the other does not exist
We are our Fate
The Sphinx that looks at us sideways
That has lost its enigma
We have nothing to solve
There is no enigma
There is no way out of the circle
The fiery circle
Of the sun and of death.

Sun, I shall look you in the eye
Until my sight dries up
My sight will fill with craters of ash
Let it become a weightless immobile rhythmless moon
A shooting star lost and extinct for ages
Condemned to hear the cries of men
To breathe the poison of flowers.
Man is dead! Long live man!

On the dry soil of my heart
A cactus has grown
More than twenty centuries have passed
I have dreamt of jasmine
My hair smelt of jasmine
My clothes smelt of jasmine
My voice had taken something
Of its fine aroma
But the cactus is not evil
It does not understand and takes fright
Sadly I look at the cactus
How have such ages gone by!
I shall live an equal number
Hearing the roots grow
In the dry soil of my heart.

Between the sun and I
There is but
The variation of time
I rise and I set
I am and am not
They see me
But I can not see myself.

When time stands still
My cell is full of months

Months, days, hours, moments,
Tenths of seconds
Tenths of seconds
Tenths of seconds
A step before chaos
Chaos exists
A step after chaos
Chaos exists
I exist a little before and a little after
I exist in chaos
I exist not.

7

The cells breathe
The cells high up
The cells low down
The rain unites us
Nikos, the sun was ashamed to appear
Yorgos, I have only a flower to contain myself.

8

The sun bites me
It has no teeth
Deceitful
Deceitful promises on the wall
On the white colour, the white colour
Shaded, shadeless
I am alone motionless
Immobile in the light and the white
I hover aloft unmoved
On the floating mosaic
My thoughts plummet to earth
The parachute has not opened
The earth comes towards my thought at a gallop
The sun contracts, revealing the void
Three voids clash
My thoughts, the earth, and the sun.

9

Down on earth all is dispersed
Law of Laws, O Law!

The Law does not argue with nothing
When it wears a helmet it smokes
Filter-tipped cigarettes
When it wears pyjamas, when it wears pyjamas
Of silk
It smokes not, it smokes not.
Villages, woods and ricefields smoke
Mothers do not
Soldiers smoke before they go to sleep
They sleep deeply up to two centuries
I always smoke before I die
Strong tobacco from Lamia and aromatic from Xanthi
Sweet perfumes just before the end
The end has sweet perfumes
Aromatic from Xanthi and strong from Lamia.

10

I am the teeth of the sun
I am the one biting me
I am the one I desire
I am the one who desires not
I am the one when you remember
I am the one when you forget
I am the one when I am not
I am you when I shall be no more
For I am you.

11

The Aegean has risen up and looks at me
'Is it you?' it says.
'Yes,' I reply, 'Is it I and another whom you know not?'
'No,' it says, 'Don't you know that the other one is you?'
The Aegean has fallen back
The sun has coughed
I am alone
Quite alone.

12

Not quite alone
I don't want you
I want you so much

That's why I don't want you
Plane trees, cool waters
Myrtle, myrtle, myrtle
A symbol, an ideal, a belief
I want you so much
Earth covered with weeds
Myrtle, myrtle, myrtle
That's why I don't want you
Because without you
I cannot be alone
Quite alone
Alone.

13

Shoot at time, kill time!
Time is an outlaw
I want to hang its body in Aiolou Street
Time is for sale at a bargain price
In Monastiraki Square
Buy it at the bargain price
It is quite fresh
We shot and killed it yesterday
Yesterday, yesterday, yesterday
Between yesterday and today
Which means that we did a fine thing!

14

No way out of the circle
You won't get out of the circle
You'll stay there
You, the sun and the time.
Your movement is run by clockwork
You wind it up by night
It runs down by day
Bow, smile, cry, curse
Everything is ordained
By the Maker.

15

Whatever you may be
Sea, mountain, woman, bull

If you are a man
Tree, song, toll, death
If you are a man
If you are a man
Gently release the handbrake
Set off down the hill in second gear
Whatever you may be
Bus, lorry, Citroën, DKW
Margarita Myrtia Rodostomi Theodorakis
If you are a man
It will cost you less
Old memories
As old as today
As tomorrow
As never
If you are a man
Whatever you may be.

16

The First Sun, the First Athens
Mikis the millionth
One hundred thousand follow
And as many again
Yet another hundred thousand innocent
And so on
To the end of the world

17

Never, never, never
Shall I be able to unfurl all the banners
Green, red, yellow, blue, mauve, sea green
Never, never, never
Shall I be able to smell all the perfumes
Green, red, yellow, blue, mauve, sea green
To touch all hearts
To cross all seas
Never, never, never
Shall I know the one banner
The unique one
You, Tania.

When I lay on the shore
The bathers ran into the sea
When I entered the sea
The bathers returned to the shore
When I drowned
The bathers went home
When I came to life
It was too late
The bathers had got into their cars.

You are my image
My hand is yours
When I press it, it is pressed
When I raise it, it is raised
But this grille is mine alone
What is being destroyed is yours
(Mark the feeling of private property)
Mine, yours
The grille
Ours
Eyes
Lips
And hands.

In the Paradise of my skull
A yellow sun journeys on the wings of time
Birds with wooden wings follow
Angels in jets lead the way
A grandiose march over the banana trees
Eucalyptus and pines which cover
The left side of my brain
Nymphs and celestial prostitutes on the right
Red lizards covered with jasmine
Listen to the flowing waterfalls
In the caverns of the marrow of my spine
The earth has begun, the universe is ending
Suddenly the grandiose procession comes to a halt
Six in the evening

Exactly six o'clock
Procession, time and sun all stop
Only the birds go on
The wooden wings flap
And the jets
Whine in angelic fashion.

21

I have the labyrinth of a private car
A 12 horse-power minotaur
I want a cheap second-hand Theseus
I would exchange a Japanese radio
For Ariadne, a widow if possible
Under 40, income over 5,000
Time limit
One tenth of a second
In a tenth of a second
I shall be dead.

22

Elytis, Gatsos, great Seferis,
Tsaroukhis, Minotis, Hadjidakis,
Vera, Dora, Jenny,
Cinema, theatre, music
So many others
Poets, poets
So many others
You, you and you
Friend, enemy, opponent, rival
Sleep secure
The account is paid
The friend paying
Has money.

23

Celestial rivers
Underground torrents
Flow down rippling
Street of dreams, Omonoia Square
Silva, Sigma, Yiota, Lambda
Vita, Alfa

Filothei and Haidari
Their bright waters
Two bright streams
Two green streams
I, a red locust, in their midst
Wings, mouth-organs
Echoes of waters
Lizards, moons
Plunge in, immerse, drown
Grilles
Grilles
Grilles.

24

When you call out
I am asleep
When you are in pain
I yawn
When you shudder
I scratch
September
The sixteenth day
Of the Creation
Dionysis.

25

On the fourth floor
Your mother is asleep
Elena
Her dreams divine music
Her dream Pepino di Capri
Over the sea
Don't wake her.

26

The false teeth of the sun
Threaten me
The grille of time
Protects me
Yannis, Iason,
Viron, Petros, Alekos
Raise high on the masts

Raise the oranges and lemons
Sandals on the sand
Shrill voices, Crème Nivea
Horseplay, card patience, Nescafé
They hold
Expensive flags of cheap material.

27

Sixth September
Eleven in the morning
Birds bathing
In the rivers
The fir trees moved
By the North Wind
The Turk beat you
At Bizani
You drink coffee
You distil poison
Love, love
The sun roasts
The grapes
Eleven o'clock
In the morning.

28

Suleyman the Magnificent
Constantine Palaiologos
Stop shouting!
Smuggler, pickpocket, procurer,
Vocal chords
Andreas, Ilias, Anthi
Throat of animal, throat of man
Saint Sofia, hordes of barbarians
Heavy fire
The Old Man of the Morea, a maggot
I stumble at every step
To left and right of Borneo
To the right the flames of Nagasaki
Ahead the ovens of Buchenwald
Behind the cell of Makriyannis

Up, down, east, west
Knives, javelins, whips, hordes
Of saints
Of demons
Of generals
I am a weed sown in the crater
Farewell sun
Farewell light
Good night.

29

East of Sirius
The light rains fall
They hold yellow umbrellas
Green sunglasses
They wear miniskirts
The light rains of September pass by Mars
Next Wednesday they enter an Earthly course.
Hanoi, Washington, Moscow
The Desert of Sinai
Tositsa Street, Athens
West of Chios
East of Corinth
Inside, outside
A pine tree deeply etched
Miniskirts
Green sunglasses
They hold yellow umbrellas
The light morning rains
East of Sirius
West of my cell
In September.

30

When the Meteors shall dance the Syrtaki
I'll know you my country
When the Akheloos shall spend all night in taverns
The White Mountains swim the crawl
The Aegean play the pools
The Roumeliots dance the Tsamiko

The Sea of Crete violates Milos
And I write bad verse
Then I'll know you
I'll know you my country.

31

The Nine Muses dwell near me
The other side of the corridor
Two doors, four guards
Dora, Maria, Takis,
Anna, Tonia, Roussos
Perhaps they know better
Particulars, numbers, addresses,
Techniques, schools, museums
The Muses are close to the museums
Music is close to the museums
Music, Muses, museums.
However,
Thoughts, techniques
Can be tried
Rain, dust, sun, laughter,
A vast conservatoire
Pianos, musical scales, singing
The Nine Muses wash
Comb their hair, go to bed, knock on the door
To have it opened for them
Pindar, Aeschylos,
Mozart, Chopin,
The guards
Take them
One by one
To the loo.

32

City of violet
Give me your hand
Caress my hair
Grant me your voice
To lull my dreams
Show me your face
That I may see your might

103

My source of strength
My Mistress
From Oedipus
To Androutsos
No one
Has loved you
As much as I.

Petros has been arrested. They have also uncovered at Comrade
Nora's an entire network which had bombs and so on at its
disposal, and which had branches abroad...They will all be
brought before the military tribunal.

'They're new boys,' Dimitris says. 'They're asking us to tell
them what attitude to adopt in front of the tribunal.'

'You've got the chance to join them, for they'll certainly give
me a wide berth, as they always do with those who have been
their leaders. So I'm going to give you detailed instructions for
each of them. I believe this trial is a decisive stage in the struggle.
I still don't think our enemies are so stupid as to start it.
But if the "hardliners" end up getting their own way, we must
make this trial into a tribunal from which we will make known
our personal point of view and the role of the Resistance.
Nobody must be under any illusions: first, all of them will be
given heavy sentences; second, nobody apart from me runs the
risk of being shot; and third, even if they gave way they wouldn't
get a lighter sentence. Conclusion: we must choose attack. And
how are their spirits?'

'Not bad on the whole, apart from a few cases one can count
on the fingers of one hand. But they're all preoccupied with
your arrest. They are, or rather *we* are, consumed with remorse
because we have committed grave errors.'

'Tell them they mustn't attach too much importance to that.
It all belongs to the past. We've all committed grave errors. I
was the first. Now we're paying for them. One or more of them
is bound to have squealed. Luckily, nobody outside a very small
circle knew anything. That's why Lambrou gets so mad. Such
a storm, and to get what? Except for my arrest, the discovery
of the hiding-places and the brutality meted out on the people
who sheltered me, our enemies have not made the slightest progress
as far as destroying other networks, cadres and organisations is concerned...The question of my arrest doesn't preoccupy me. You

must tell everybody that. And tell them they must stop spending their time trying to find out who has spoken or who has denounced whom. The important thing is that they have all kept their faith in the struggle. No-one has crossed over to the other side. Let's look to the future! Let's prepare for the trial. Then we'll see...'

'Most of us, you know, are new to the movement. Before, I was with the Lambrakis Youth. We used to have some good discussions. The boys used to say that everything started to go wrong on the anniversary of the Gorgopotamos affair. Can you tell me exactly what happened?'

So we spent time talking about the past: 'In November 1964, as every year, Greek patriots came to Gorgopotamos from all corners of Greece to celebrate the anniversary of the first great military operation by the Greek Resistance against the Nazi occupiers.[7] That year the authorities took part : we had a centrist government. So the secret service and the CIA organised a diabolical provocation. First they surrounded the place with heavily armed military units. Then they placed an old reactivated mine near the officials' dais. An agent was holding the fuse. He lit it at the appointed time and ran. Then the first demonstrator to walk over it set it off and was blown to smithereens; the mine was powerful enough to kill fifty men. There were agents provocateurs in the crowd who shouted: "Revenge!" so as to turn the anger of the crowd on to the political and military personalities. And from the hills round about Army units would have to intervene to protect them. Among the dead would be ministers and generals : a good opportunity for the press to shout—"communist *coup d'état*" and to justify the Army's intervention for the safety of the country. But events decided things otherwise : when the mine went off the ministers and generals had left. If there were 13 dead and 60 wounded, they were all ours.'

'What role, then, did the Lambrakis Youth and you personally play?'

'I was a deputy in the Chamber and President of the Lambrakis Democratic Youth. We were preparing for our Congress at the time. Brillakis telephoned me at home to warn against any untimely reaction on our part to the provocation. My immediate reply was: "I'm going straight to Gorgopotamos: how many dead?" "Twelve or thirteen, it seems." "Well, we'll have a Lambrakis funeral twelve times over." It was obvious that the assassination had been planned in cold blood. I went to the spot where the bodies were and I aimed my headlights at them to chase away the wild animals and to prevent the secret agents searching them, and so on.

'In the evening I was still there with Kyrkos and Paraskevopoulos. The reporters were pressing us to give our views. We drew up a communique which spoke of assassination. Representatives of the Executive Committee of EDA[8] came the next day. They brushed me aside (I was not yet a member of the Executive) because they held me responsible for the "erroneous" interpretation. The following day EDA publicly adopted the official version of the "accident". At the funeral of one of the victims, at Perama, Papadimitrou[9] made the assassination sound like a picnic at which death had accidentally intruded...We Lambrakides were indignant and went back to our premises in Piraeus Street. For the first time ever we all approved a text which went against the Party line: we reckoned we had to arouse the people as we had done at Lambrakis's funeral. The masses could exert pressure on the Centre Government, which was wavering. In the end the Government decided to crush the fascists who had been plotting within the Army and in the para-state organisations. The best policy for us to pursue to achieve unity is not always to be content to avoid putting obstacles in the path of the Centre Union, particularly when it is weak, but on the contrary to put pressure on it to gather its forces against the main enemy—the fascist threat. I went to the Chamber in person to obtain the approval of the EDA leadership for publishing the text in *Avgi*,[10] but they replied sharply: our proposal was rejected. On the other hand, the Rightist Party, ERE, the very same evening went on to the counter offensive in the Chamber: Kanellopoulos called us assassins, and our dead were not yet buried. The Centre Union, now under pressure from the Right, was turning against us! It banned the funerals. Later it was to condemn the relatives and friends of the victims to heavy sentences! Four months later, in the spring of 1965, the Lambrakis Democratic Youth held its Congress. I was elected President and in this capacity I addressed my first message to the new members of the Central Bureau: "The Party's policy towards the Centre Union is timorous. In order to achieve the

106

necessary unity to defend our rights in the democratic camp, we must be courageous and denounce all the Centrist Government's equivocation and shifting of policy. If we don't we're heading, with mathematical precision, straight towards a tunnel —I can see its entrance clearly, but I don't see the exit..." '

'The boys speak about a good story you told them a week before the dictatorship was set up.'

'Which one?'

'A ship in mid-ocean. A storm. The boat is tossed about by huge waves like a cockleshell. You wake up. You go up on to the bridge. Nobody there. You go down into the engine-room. Nobody there either. You go into the captain's cabin. No one. You go to the helm. No one. The tiller is turning on its own, this way and that, at the mercy of the waves and the wind. So, you run to the wireless operator's cabin. And there you find them all, leaning over the table. What are they doing? Studying the map? *No, they're waiting for instructions from the radio*! Another question: When you met at Agrinion ten days before the advent of the dictatorship, why didn't you talk openly to the people and to the youth?'

'It was I who held the others back from doing that. I remember Khronis's words: "If you want to, President, we break with EDA from tomorrow. The young people will follow us. And all the active elements in the Party with them." "We're getting towards the elections," I told them. "What's more, we've got another opportunity: the Congress. Now we must reflect and analyse the problems and prepare ourselves..." '

'Why should you have seen things more clearly?'

'Because we hadn't abandoned our common sense to the voice of the radio giving us orders from two thousand kilometres away. We were perhaps the only people on the Left who thought and acted with initiative...freely. If the leaders of EDA had taken account of the reality they would have seen even more clearly because they had experience and competence which we didn't have. *The fault is not with individuals, but with the relations*...We had broken off these relations, but at the level of action. Not yet at the level of working out a political line. My field was limited to youth, culture and contacts with the masses.'

At last the dossier for the trial is ready. A visit from my father.

In the office next to Kolonias's. Several high Security officers are present.

'You are to be brought before the military tribunal, under Emergency Law 509,' one of them tells me.

'Please be so kind as to give me the Law to read: I have forgotten it,' my father says

...'*the Count...the death penalty*' is underlined in red.

'They've underlined it for fear we might miss it,' I say to my father with a laugh.

He drops his glasses and looks me in the eye. In a strong but calm and solemn voice he says: 'Death on the battlefield, my child, is a normal thing for a Theodorakis. Remember your great-great-grandfather, Khalis: he was at the head of the first insurrection agaist the Turks in Crete. Your other great-great-grandfather, Spyridakis, was impaled by the Turks. Your uncle, Manolis, was skinned alive. Your father faced the Turks at Bizanti fort when he was sixteen...Well, you'll only be following in the heroic family tradition. If they kill you, you will have my blessing. I'm at the end of my days...'

Saint Paul Prison Hospital
November 1967

I half open my eyes. Doctors and nurses are bent over me. Both my arms are bristling with enormous syringes. I am unable to move. I feel bad. They use a probe. A bearded prisoner doctor is taking my pulse all the time. Our eyes meet. 'I'm Kastro,' he whispers. 'I'm from your part, from Khania. We've saved you.' I sink back into a state of lethargy. I'm like this for I don't know how long...

Scraps of phrases float to my ears. Now I can make out words. An insult, an obscenity. The words smell of bad places and brigands' dens. My eye falls on the bars at the foot of the bed...A nurse is passing. Someone calls her. 'Margarita!' No! That's intolerable! I don't want to hear my daughter's name in this place.

I get out of one hell only to fall into another. If anyone dares utter my daughter's name again I shall do something desperate...

They give me an injection. I calm down. My thoughts pass to Themis.[11] 'Goodbye, comrade!' he had said, throwing himself on the stretcher to embrace me. He had helped carry me from our cell to the fourth floor of the Security. Themis wiped my brow, I remember. The warder, a fellow from Peristeri, had come in, terror-stricken. Themis had said to him sadly: 'My friend is going to die!' The warder looked at me: 'Why aren't you eating? Eat a little, I beg you...' Then my wife and my father arrived. Voices. Cries. Then silence! Then a crowd of people : officers running up...Then they lifted me up...

Then next day I find myself in the infirmary. a ray of sunshine falls across the middle of the ward. My fellow prisoners march past in front of me, each carrying a towel and a bar of soap. Some acknowledge me with a nod of the head, others with a glance. Terror reigns. In the middle of the adjoining ward someone is lying on his bed, his head buried in a book. Could it be Peponis?

The days pass. They transfer me to the other side. The ice is gradually breaking. General Koumanakos shakes me by the hand. Peponis is sitting on the bed. Colonel Srallis offers me some jam. There are still some political prisoners. Those who come from the prisons. The others are the 'common law' men. Soon we all become one family. The Lambrakides act as medical orderlies. In the evenings they sing songs. We play chess and read; above all, we have discussions. In the other wing of the infirmary there are the 'politicals' from the camps. We are forbidden to have any contact with them. We take walks in the same corridor but it is separated by a grill. We greet one another secretly: usually we run our hands though our hair. But Ilias Iliou is completely bald. Sometimes one hears someone shout 'Hi!', whereupon the warders rush and take him into the barrack room. Among the deportees who are in hospital are General Avgeropoulos, Kostas Loules, a member of the Central Committee of the Greek Communist Party, the deputy Khiotakis, Dr Manolis Siganos, and others. About thirty cadres of the Left. I devise a thousand little ruses for communicating with them. As I receive through the underground organisation a regular bulletin giving all the news, I pass it on to the others. The young nurses, who are also prisoners and come from prisons for minors, bring us presents, poems and flowers. They've now got rid of them and we're left with one solitary male nurse for sixty patients.

109

Every morning Spyros in the next bed raises his fist, makes the 'V' sign and shouts: 'We shall overcome!'

One morning the chief warder comes in. 'The director asks to see you.' The heavy iron door opens and then closes again. The warder leaves me with a colleague, who changes my uniform in the ground floor corridor. A lot of people. Most seem to be policemen. I have a nasty sense of foreboding... 'Director's Office': the door opens. I find myself face to face with Tournas, the prison inspector. There is a squat little fellow sitting at his desk. He has a fine moustache and is wearing dark glasses. He introduces himself: 'Ladas.'[12] He turns to Tournas and says: 'Leave us alone!' and to me: 'Take a seat, if you wish!'

I flop into a comfortable armchair. He says:

'I have called you so we can have a bit of a chat. I hope it doesn't put you to any inconvenience. Myself and my colleague here: we come from poor peasant families. We have lived in the villages. We have known hunger. We have suffered with the peasant, with the poor. My mother worked for foreigners so as to feed us and educate us. I had to walk to school for hours in the cold and barefoot. Well, my poor mother—the communists killed her...' He pauses; 'Basically, what divides us is the national question...'

'In other words?'

'We agree on the social level. But we don't allow one square metre of our territory to be given up to foreigners, especially to Slavs.'

'In fact, we are in disagreement on the national level,' I say, laughing. 'But the other way round. You belong to the Right. The Right bears the responsibility for the ills that have afflicted and continue to afflict our country. Think of the disastrous Asia Minor campaign. Or the collaboration with the Nazi occupiers. By the way, what were you doing during the occupation? That period sorted out the real patriots from the false patriots. Because I saw the communists defending the Nation's honour, independence, life and liberty, and to the last drop of blood. And what happened afterwards? You delivered the country first to the English and then to the Americans. What national integrity are you talking about? Your "revolution"—isn't it just a CIA *coup de main?*'

'I assure you that we acted alone. As for the Americans,

110

we've got the better of them! Certainly our position is difficult and that's why we must be vigilant.'

'But the Americans are in control of everything.'

'But not us.'

'And what's your aim?'

'To make Greece independent.'

'In other words, neutral?'

'We don't rule that out. We want to improve the lot of the Greek peasant.'

'Would you be prepared to enter into conflict with the Greek oligarchy?'

'We detest the Greek oligarchy as much as you do.'

'Being cut off, as you are, from the Greek people, even if you really wanted to oppose the Americans and the Greek oligarchy, you would be overthrown in a few minutes.'

He slams his fist down on the table, then gets up and almost shouts:

'No one is capable of overthrowing us!'

'Certainly they are. The Greek oligarchy can. Twice in the past three decades we have raised an army to fight them. We know only too well that they have strong support...'

'That's precisely why I've got you here. Papadopoulos said yesterday: "Gentlemen, Theodorakis is one of us." You must help us.'

'You know perfectly well that I am always prepared to enter into a dialogue, and where a hand is held out. When I said that you were not on good terms with the Palace, I asked myself if we were witnessing a positive nationalist movement like Nasser's. In fact I said to Filinis at the time: "What if it's a 'Nasserite' movement in disguise. And what if these unknown officers have seized power and don't know how to go on from there. Maybe we should make contact with them?" But it wasn't long before Papadopoulos's speech (the first one he made in public) and that decided us on the programme we should adopt...But, even now I'm quite prepared to discuss things frankly and honestly. But I fear there are too many things which divide us.'

'Such as?'

'Torture, to begin with.'

'What torture?'

'Don't pretend you don't know. Is it possible that such serious

111

things can happen without your approval? Huh! Without your express orders?'

'I swear to you this is the first time I've heard anything about torture. Personally, I've given orders that all prisoners are to be treated humanely...In your opinion, who's to blame?'

'For seventy days I've been right there—where the men are tortured! Who's responsible for it? You! Of course! You in person, as their chief. Everyone in the Security takes a part in it. So when they put me in a cell right beneath the terrace I asked to see Lambrou. They took me to the office where the preliminary interrogations take place. I said: "You assured me that torture no longer took place and you put me in a cell just under the terrace so that I could count the blows of the 'falanga' and could hear the cries of those being tortured. You bear a grave responsibility, you personally. I've already told you once before that that seat you now occupy—I'll have it..." '

'And what did Lambrou say?'

'He began by threatening me. But soon he regained his cool. Karapanayotis[13] came in and "explained" the reasons for their violence. Anyway they agreed to stop the beatings on the terrace, because...I was "sensitive". But, some days later they began again and with redoubled fury.'

'I promise you I shall start an enquiry immediately and inform you of the results.'

'You must understand that you can't build the new Greece on acts such as these. That's the first barrier which divides us. There are others...'

'Go on. I'm listening.'

'Let's start with what you called the "national question". We don't want to be dependent on anyone.'

'Not even on the Russians?'

'Right. Not on the Russians. Not on anybody! We want both independence and neutrality. Are you prepared to subscribe to that? Our foreign policy will be determined exclusively by the Greek people; it will respond to our national needs, objectives and interests.'

'And Macedonia?'

'For us there is no Macedonian problem. There is just a problem of minorities—Turks, Slavs, Macedonians, and so on

112

—to whom we must guarantee all the rights laid down in the United Nations Charter...'

'What about the statements of the Greek Communist Party, then?'

'Right, you must read them again, carefully. Our position is quite clear. As far as we're concerned, there is no Macedonian problem. Anyway, I tell you: *first*, we will not allow a single metre of Greek soil to be handed over to anyone, and *second*, we will not allow any control, patronage or division of our sovereignty, by anyone, no matter who he might be.'

'Go on!'

'Then, there's the big problem of the just distribution of national income. Of course you know that 80 per cent of the national wealth is in the hands of 5 per cent of the population. So what must be done? If you haven't forgotten your village and poverty, you'll agree that a programme has to be worked out to put the land to better use, so that the peasant's income is doubled and trebled, and in the shortest possible time.'

'We agree.'

'In that case, how do you reckon you're going to achieve it? With the Security, with Kyrou,[14] or with Ventiris[15]? You need people who are fired with a high ideal. Well, you have locked those people up in the prisons and the camps...You can't create the new Greece without us: without Filinis, Diamantopoulos, Kyrkos, Iliou. Without Stefanos...'

'Which one is he?'

'His bed is next to mine. He's been in prison since 1946. Always for a good reason!'

'They're communists. They're in the pay of foreigners.'

'We've seen who's in the pay of foreigners. But if we want to do something, we must have done with the past! Let's look to the future! As for me, I'll forget Makronisos. You must forget personal rancour. It's the only way of finding a way out.'

'Good! So you're coming with us?'

'But...I am a communist.' I laugh.

'But you're not like the others. You're different in our eyes. What's more, we all like your music.'

'Are you sure you're not setting a trap for me?'

'Why should we? There's no sense in doing that...I came here for a frank and honest chat.'

'In that case, here's my suggestion: you've told me you

113

seized power in order to help the Greek people. In other words, you seized power in the name of the Greek people...'

'Certainly.'

'It's a big thing for a people to take power itself. Have you read the article Konstantopoulos[16] wrote about me some months ago?'

'On your conversations in Zürich?'

'Yes. In fact, I had asked him if there were any patriotic officers, that is, officers who were not subject to the Americans. He said yes, there were some. My second question was : why, in that case, didn't the Army and the people make a pact to chase the foreigners out and put forward a joint programme of national recovery?'

'And what was his reply?'

'That's what the Nation has been waiting for since 1821. We agreed to speak about it to EDA and to Andreas Papandreou.'

'He's an agent!'

'If you want to have a discussion without making propaganda, you've got to admit that Andreas Papandreou is a true patriot, educated and able, who came to serve the country. You know that quite well. And that's exactly what I wanted to come to: if you genuinely intend to put power in the service of the people, then you must make an appeal to all their genuine representatives. Especially to those who stand for progress. And here, as I was saying, there's Iliou, over there there's Kyrkos, Filinis...and there's Papandreou. We must all agree on a joint programme. After that we'll call the people to Constitution Square and we'll tell them: "The power is in your hands. The Army is your servant. Here is the programme of national recovery which we propose." To the foreigners we'll say: "Your domination is over. Now we—the People and the Army—are united and we have decided that our country will be sovereign and independent. All we want is good relations, on the basis of mutual interests." Of course, in this general reconciliation we mustn't forget to condemn, once and for all, violence and torture...'

'Of course, of course! I believe we've both spoken frankly. Would you like to meet Papadopoulos? He's a genius! You'll see for yourself.'

'I've no objection, but it must be on 'the basis of what I've

114

just said. Why aren't you going to speak to Papadopoulos and the others yourselves?'

'That's what we are going to do! Now I'm going to start an on-the-spot enquiry into what you've told me and I'll keep you posted. 'Bye!'

"Bye!'

I am convinced that Ladas's visit is directly connected with the big Patriotic Front trial which is coming up. His main aim is to sound out my intentions and to see what he can get from me. An idealistic man who is also an artist—he must be a naïve, even simple-minded, person. Certainly Ladas knew that he had an interest in avoiding any threats with me. But, on the other hand, what a sensational piece of news: Theodorakis has joined the 'Revolution!' and how useful it would be at the trial.

It later turned out, of course, that Ladas's report was negative.

Just the very thought of seeing me up there being cross-examined at the military tribunal, under the arc lights of Greek and world public opinion—this was what scared the colonels.

In fact for nights on end I went over and over the main points of my defence in my head so that it should become an indictment defence, a defence call to the Resistance. Then they employ another method of getting me out of the way: lies. Early on the morning of the trial the chief warder comes to tell me to get ready. I get dressed and wait. The next moment they come to tell me I am not leaving. Colonel Pattakos has just told the press I am seriously ill. My fellow-prisoners' lawyers then demand that the tribunal be postponed. The tribunal dismisses their request.

The trial begins. The defence demands that my testimony be read out. It is clear that beneath the defence lawyer's gown is hidden an ally of the Security, which has put on this whole farce because in this way I appear to be abandoning the defence of my cause and my network. The next day the headlines of *Eleftheros Kosmos* read: 'Theodorakis has betrayed his fellow-prisoners.' Lambrou and the other policemen give evidence. When they speak of me they have honey on their lips.

My brother's wife comes to the prison and shouts out to me: 'Tell this English reporter who is standing beside me that you asked to go before the tribunal! Say it in English...' In reply I

115

utter a Greek swear word. That was all there was to say! Every man is free to believe what he wants, I tell myself. Or rather, every man is free to believe what he wants to believe!

However, I send a letter to the president of the military tribunal asking to be tried with my comrades. My jailers dare not let me appear before the tribunal. *Because my persecutors know, better than anyone else, that I might let out truths that would be better not heard.*

24 December

Eleven o'clock in the morning. The chief warder takes me to the director's office. Ladas is there again:

'A promise...You're going to spend Christmas with your children. I've come straight from Papadopoulos's office. "Tell him his music will be set free," he said. He wants to meet you. Because the officials of the Ministry of Justice put certain restrictions in the amnesty decree, he called for the director and told him: "I don't want to know anything about that. What I want is that Theodorakis be allowed to go home today." '

'Go for me,' I tell him. 'What are you doing about the others? How many are being freed?'

'About three hundred.'

'But it's absurd! Why, then, have you made so much of this amnesty? Here even the "common law" fellows believe they'll be amnestied.'

'Oh! That was in a moment of exultation after the failure of the royal *coup d'état*. But gradually everyone will be freed.'

'When?'

'During the next session, at the latest. We'll only keep a small number...And now, get ready to leave...Happy Christmas...'

I go up to my cell, humiliated. What am I going to say to my companions?

I tell them the truth. We are soon ready—myself and Peponis, who has also been freed. I embrace all seventy of my fellow-prisoners, the 'politicals' and the 'common law' men. The majority have tears in their eyes. I go past the grilled front of the 'deportees'' block. Handshakes. 'Good beginning!' 'Open the way for us!' they shout out warmly. They make every effort to smile, but bitterness lingers in their eyes. The heavy doors open. I think of my folk. I go out, but the chief warder takes me to another building, where the director of the Averof prison has his office; he holds the papers for the formalities of my release.

Outside the family and friends of Andreas Papandreou are waiting. He is also about to come out. Reporters. A large crowd. Joyful holiday faces. The heavy doors open and close again. Once again I am back inside the prison, in the director's office.

'The order isn't printed yet. We're expecting it at any moment. Please come over to this side. You'll be told...'

Peponis, who finds himself next to his old cell, starts telling of his past misfortunes.

'That's where my cell was. Next to the dustbins. That fellow over there used to sweep Papandreou's cell. He would carry notes between us...This chap here is the prison "torturer".'

The 'torturer' comes across to us.

'Go through that door...'

We are directed back inside the prison.

'But...we are free.'

'It's an order.'

Another heavy door closes behind us.

Peponis gets anxious:

'They're delaying. Do you think they've changed their minds?'

We are called back to the office:

'The order has arrived. You don't figure on it.'

Tournas, the prison inspector, gives the order:

'Put Peponis in his old cell! Theodorakis with the others!'

Averof prison

Searched again...Then, the first door, the second, third, fourth and fifth...and then the cell again.

'It's Mikis, boys,' shouts Khronis, who throws his arms round my neck.

Who am I to begin with: Paraskevopoulos, Tsakiris, Iason, Sofoulis, Notaras, Tsakarestos, Protopappas, Anastasiadis?... And the others come down from their cells. Filinis. Leloudas... Kyrkos takes a running dive on to my bed. Papayannakis stays on his bed: two months after the tortures he has still not recovered. The Lambrakides are wearing slippers. They are

117

walking with sticks. The 'falanga' has broken the bones in their feet.

I ask one of them:

'When were you beaten?'

'Twenty days ago.'

'And you?'

'Eighteen days ago...'

And the enquiry Ladas had ordered?

We are in the annex of the Averof prison, in fact. On the left, as you come in, is the hospital. On the right, two large cell-dormitories. There are about sixty of us in them. The other prisoners are in narrow cells. Alone or in pairs. My bed is under a large window which overlooks the courtyard. The window sill, which is fairly large, serves as a writing desk. Day and night I sing my latest songs to my comrades. They write down the words. Then, they come a group at a time to learn the tunes. They are avid and impatient: this music makes them free, as free as me. Art—this art which is ours—is our strength, our trump card. Our oppressors have chains. We have songs. We organise musical evenings. At the end of each afternoon two hours are set aside for folk dancing. Sofoulis is the best of the lot. Petros, Notaras and I—three huge men—dance the Khasapiko. The others watch, doubled up with laughter. Papayannakis, who is stretched out on the floor, makes one explosively witty remarks. Khronis has found no rival on the chessboard. Tsakiris does some drawings on the subject of my songs. Potis pinches my tobacco. Leonidas whistles Sibelius's 'Finlandia'. He also adores the tune of Seferis's 'Lullaby'. Filinis and Leloudas go round and round like madmen without stopping. Iason puts on a smile which says: 'Here I am in this famous prison, but, also, it has no tunnel...' Before our arrest we had planned to free our comrades by digging a tunnel under the Averof prison! Christmas is approaching. The chief warder, whom we have christened 'Eichmann', has confiscated our volleyball. No matter. We continue the games as if nothing had happened...using an imaginary ball. Eichmann becomes furious.

Petition from the prisoners: 'We demand our ball back. We need an oil stove. We want 60 watt electric light bulbs.'

Discussion with the prison director, Tournas. 'Once I hummed one of your songs, "Sto Periyali",' he tells me.[17]

118

I am granted permission to use music paper, but on condition that it is initialled by the director in person.

They have put us 'politicals' in with the 'common law' prisoners, an old trick of oppressive régimes. Among them there are two pederasts who prostitute themselves in exchange for a modest payment. At dawn they are to be seen sweeping the courtyard. Sometimes 'Julia' comes to knock at my window to entrust me with her secrets and to complain of her friend, whose prices are in her opinion too low. And as always in dismal prison life, there are uncontrollable rumours. Tanks have been seen on the streets. Is it a rebellion? Almost certainly they were units on the move.

A film show in the dining-hall in the evening. Drug addicts and communists excluded!

Visits! We are taken to a special building where our visitors deposit their parcels and they are searched. All round the room there is a double row of roped-off passages. We're allowed in for ten minutes. We barely have time to spot our visitors and as everyone is talking at the same time we have to yell to make ourselves heard.

In the middle of the courtyard there is a twisted tree surrounded by barbed wire netting. We walk round it during the exercise period.

Christmas has passed. It is New Year's Day. Leonidas Kyrkos comes up to me:

'You must find something new, something exceptional, for your music.'

'Too true. I want to break the bonds of the song, to free it.'

'As you did with Ritsos's poem "Greekness".'

'I want to go even farther, following a line of inner progression. And outside the classical framework.'

'Oh, you've got something simmering...'

'I've got this collection of Seferis's poetry here. You remember that poem I set to music called "I Have Kept Hold Of Life". Do you know how many verses I took from it? Four or five. Well, I'm going to take the whole poem and make a song, an immense song.'

'You're going to start on it?'

'This very evening. As soon as they've closed the gates.'

Thus the new musical form which I have called 'flow-song' was born.

119

AVEROF EPIPHANY

(Flow-song composed in the Averof prison in Athens on 3 and 4 January 1968. The work was continued at Zatouna and completed on 26 March 1969 in its final form as a 'Cantata for singer, six voices, mixed choir and orchestra'. Poem written by George Seferis in 1937 and published in the collection of his work under the title, *Epiphany*, 1937.)

The sea in flowers and the mountains at the wane of
    the moon,
The big stone near the Arabian fig trees and the
    asphodels,
The pitcher unwilling to dry up at the end of the day,
And the closed bed near the cypresses and your hair,
The golden stars of the Swan and that Aldebaran.
I have kept hold of life, kept hold of life by travel
Among the yellow trees and the rain-swept slopes,
The silent slopes heavy with beech leaves.
No fire on their peak at dusk.
I have kept hold of life. A line on your left hand,
A mark upon your knee, there may well be
In the sands of last summer
Remaining there where I heard the North Wind blow
Its strange voice around the frozen lake.
The faces I see ask nothing, nor does the woman
Walking hunched forward, giving her child suck.
I climb the mountains. The dark valley, the snowy
Plain, snow-covered all around, asks nothing,
Nor does the weather enclosed by hollow chapels,
Nor do the hands stretched out to beg, nor the roads.
I have kept hold of life, whispering in the endless silence.
I can no longer speak nor think. Whispers
Like the breath of the cypress that night,
Like the human voice of the sea at night on the pebbles,
Like the memory of your voice saying: 'Happiness'.
I close my eyes, seeking the secret meeting of the waters
Under the ice, the smiling sea, the blocked-up wells,
Feeling with my veins for those escaping me
Where the water-flowers end and that man
Walking blindly on the snow of silence.

I have kept hold of life, with him, seeking the water
    touching you
Heavy drops on green leaves, on your face
Within the empty garden, drops in the still basin,
Finding there a dead swan with pure white wings,
Living trees and your eyes absorbed.
The road is endless, unchanging as you seek
To remember your childhood years, gone by
Lost in the sleep of deep, deep tombs,
As you seek the bodies you loved,
Bending under the hard plane tree branches,
Where a ray of sunshine stopped directly.
A dog started and your heart missed a beat,
The road is unchanging : I have held on to life,
The snow and frozen water and the prints of horses.

Composing 'Epiphany' and reading the Seferis collection, I
had found new pleasure in his poetry. Some days later I took
the poem 'Mythology' as a subject, and I chose four extracts
from it. I wrote the music in a state of high tension and in spite
of the special, not to say exceptional, conditions of prison life;
but my comrades in the prison did all they could to create the
most favourable atmosphere for composition. The moment they
saw me turn my back and lean on the window-sill to write,
they fell absolutely silent. The cycle of these four poems from
'Mythology' was completed around 9 and 10 January 1968
and Tournas, the prison director, noted in the margin in red
ink: 'Authorised to be taken out, 18.1.68.'

MYTHOLOGY

(Composed upon four extracts from 'Mythology' written by
George Seferis in 1933 and published in Athens in March 1935.)

Now that you are leaving, take the child with you
Who saw the light under that plane tree
The day trumpets sounded, weapons flashed
And sweating horses bent to touch
The green surface of the water

With their damp nostrils in the basin.
The olive trees with the wrinkles of our forefathers,
The rocks with the wisdom of our forefathers
The living blood of our brother in the soil,
Was a great joy, a rich order
In the souls that knew their prayer.
Now that you are leaving, now that the day of reckoning
Is dawning, now that you are doing this,
As he does not know whom he will kill, how he will end,
Take the child with you who saw the light
Under the leaves of that plane tree
And teach him to study the trees.
I am sorry I let a broad river slip through my fingers
Without drinking a drop.
Now I am sinking into the stone.
A small pine tree in the red earth,
I have no other companion
What I loved has been lost with the houses
New last summer,
They have crumbled in the wind of autumn.

In my breast the wound reopens
When the stars come down and join my body,
When silence falls under man's foot
The stones rolling through the ages, where will they
      draw me?
The sea, the sea, who can consume it?
Each dawn I see hands beckon the vulture and hawk
Tied to the rock made mine by pain,
I see the trees breathe the dark serenity of the dead
Later the smiles of immobile statues.

Sleep has enfolded you like a tree with green leaves
You breathed like a tree in the quiet light
I looked on you in the clear spring
Closed eyelids engraved the water with their eyelashes.

A little more
And we shall see the almond trees blossom,

The marbles shine in the sun,
The sea, the waves unfold.
A little more
Let us raise ourselves a little higher.

We are walking round the old mulberry bush in the little yard; Khristos, a member of the Easter Committee, is putting me in the picture:

'We've started regrouping our forces. The Party has taken the thing in hand. Our entire effort is concentrated on the organisation. A critical analysis has been made of the policy of the previous leadership. Its line was fundamentally wrong. It exposed our forces to the blows of the enemy. Hence the terrible extent of our losses.'

'But I thought we worked that line out together.'

'Yes, but later we were cut off from the leadership. It was Petros who transmitted the line to us.'

'What? Don't you agree with the demonstrations we organised? But it was you who used to talk to us with such enthusiasm of the work that had been done. Can one do all that without any danger? Now what are you doing?'

'Work in depth.'

'What depth? Perhaps that's why you've forgotten the surface! For over two months nothing's been seen to move. Well, mark my words: you're too content with this "work in depth".'

'I thought you knew what was happening.'

'I take full responsibility for everything that was done up to my arrest. And I'm prepared to give an account of it.'

This whole story distressed me a great deal and chilled my feelings a little towards Khristos...Only the day before yesterday he was the one partisan who was most in favour of the radical change in our policy and methods. And here he is a 'wiser' man now that the 'Party' has shoved him up in the hierarchy...Was I being unfair to him? Was he seeking, groping for, the right path in the dark? We're all looking. That's the truth.

Our beds—mine and Potis's[18]—are very close. Every night we chat for hours under our breath.

'So we've been in agreement for a long time!' I say. 'Why have you never spoken to me about it?'

'Who dared speak?'

123

'Not even to me? Still, I gave my opinion frankly, with no fear of anyone. You could have had confidence in me.'

'But you saw how they got rid of me from the paper. Why did you say nothing?'

We burst out laughing. What chaos we've been living in!

'Well, good night! God preserve us from the worst...'

I talk to Kyrkos; I explain the facts, my views. He explodes.

'Never, never, against the Politburo. Everyone must stand by it! It's the most sacred thing we have...'

Poor Leonidas! Who knows what damp cell you're in now? How many times have they spoken of you—the radios of the socialist countries, our friends and the 'holy of holies'? You have lost your father. They didn't even let you kiss his brow. You have lost your mother. They didn't let you embrace her...And your wife struck down by cancer...Your children scattered around the world! You have given your whole life to the movement, to the Party, to your people...Your lucid intelligence could have given you a comfortable life, an enviable reputation, satisfaction and strength. You preferred to do your duty. You believed, along with the whole of your generation, the generation of EPON,[19] in the great illusion.

> Up and down, up and down
> From East to West
> Knives, whips, javelins, hordes
> Hordes of demons, hordes of saints
> Hordes of generals
> I am a weed sown in the crater
> Farewell sun, farewell light
> Good night.

We talk about my imminent release and about the probable lifting of the ban on my songs.

Most people think my songs must be authorised at all costs. At all costs—but also with great care, as the path is full of traps —I must return to my creative work. In the atmosphere of the dictatorship? Yes, in the atmosphere of the dictatorship. Our people will draw strength and courage from being in the active presence of all representatives of culture. I decide to take it upon myself to talk to the latter as soon as I am free.

The first 'public' performance of my new works is like a great festivity: Vlakhos recites and analyses the poems of Seferis, then I sing two or three of them. 'Sleep Has Enfolded You' and 'A Little More' had been great successes in prison. Tsakiris takes keenness as far as designing the sleeves of the records, which didn't exist yet, though none of us had any doubts that they would soon. As always, we are great optimists. Rumours begin to spread about a general amnesty. Echoed in the press and public opinion.

This famous amnesty does come: the mountain finally gives birth, but only to a mouse. There are just a few releases and on a purely individual basis. They notify me. 'You leave as soon as the gates are closed.' I have time to go and say goodbye to my comrades, who are going back to their cells and solitary confinement. 'We'll all be at the windows to wave,' they tell me, and as I leave there they all are, clutching at the bars and singing:

'A little more
And we shall see the almond trees blossom...'

I catch a last glimpse of the twisted tree in the yard. One gate, then another, and another. The big deserted yard. My comrades are already far away, behind their walls. A fifth, a sixth gate. The formalities of being released. The final search! 'Empty your pockets. Take your shoes off. Raise your arms. Open your bundle of things.'

References

1 KYLAFIS: The name of the Secretary of the Lambrakis Democratic Youth in western Greece. He was in a cell on the first floor and made the letters out of silver paper from cigarette packets and held them out of his window so I could see them.
2 The Security headquarters are on the corner of Bouboulinas and Stournara Streets.
3 One of the most popular interpreters of Theodorakis's songs.

4 Dilosis Metanoias (q.v.).
5 Two hundred kilometres per hour.
6 Two well-known torturers of the Security.
7 In November 1942 the Gorgopotamos bridge was destroyed; it was used by convoys carrying supplies to the Afrika Korps.
8 Kyrkos and Paraskevopoulos were leading cadres of EDA; Kyrkos was also a deputy in the Chamber.
9 Another EDA deputy.
10 The Party paper.
11 The comrade who replaced Dimitris in my cell at the Security.
12 Secretary to the Minister of Public Security; a colonel and Papadopoulos's right-hand man.
13 Lambrou's subaltern.
14 Director of the ultra-reactionary paper, *Estia*.
15 Retired general, former Chief of the General Staff of the Army; during the civil war (1946–9) he directed the 'cleaning-up operations' which are remembered with such horror.
16 Director of the pro-dictatorship newspaper, *Eleftheros Kosmos*.
17 'By the Shore.'
18 Potis Paraskevopoulos, director of *Avgi*.
19 Youth organisation during the occupation (q.v.).

126

VRAKHATI — Freedom under Surveillance

I leave the Averof prison on 27 January 1968. When the fever of the first few days finally dies down, my closest friends gather round and I begin giving them my views on the new tactics which the people's struggle must adopt. In particular, I stress my intention to carry out and pursue the work of an artist in spite of the undeniably unfavourable atmosphere of the dictatorship. I soon realise that these ideas (which were shared by all, or at any rate most, political prisoners, at least those I had left behind in the Averof prison), far from meeting with a favourable response, are provoking violent reactions among the leading cadres in the outside world. I try hard to demonstrate the absurdity of their reasoning and their attitude, but in vain. I point out that their words and deeds are wildly out of joint, but this too has no effect. In their words they are ultra-revolutionary; in their deeds they are ultra-conservative.[1]

I manage to make indirect contact with certain intellectual circles: the majority of them do share my views. But all are afraid of being accused of collaborating with the enemy if they carry on with their artistic activity.

I decide to leave Athens and go to my house at Vrakhati, near Corinth.

I start composing again...and I think of Marina. When I was in the Security, after my arrest, Marina was in the corridor, opposite Cell No. 1, with another girl who wore trousers. She was later to be transferred to the women's block. When I was on hunger strike, I used to hear her bawling out to the warder.

129

She was to write a poem, a poem which is incomparable in its beauty, its strength and its truth. From the moment I first saw it each word, each image, each meaning entered the pores of my skin. Wounded me. Gave me comfort. Delivered me. It was the voice of all of us. All those hopes which according to one image in the poem 'turned out to be a rotten grape'. It was our anger. Our bitterness. And our strength. I took the first part of the poem and wrote the music straight off in one go, from beginning to end.

Now, at Vrakhati, I get on to the second and third parts. From the point of view of musical form, I have the opportunity with this work of continuing along the path I had started out on with 'Averof Epiphany'. It was a new 'flow-song' in three parts. Originally the title was: 'Averof Women's Prison', since the poem had been written after Marina had been sentenced by the military tribunal. She tore this poem up immediately she had finished it. One of her fellow-prisoners, Athina, managed to save it and sat up at night copying it out:

STATE OF SIEGE

(Flow-song composed at Nea Smyrni in March 1968 and at Vrakhati in May 1969, on a poem by Marina.)

1

Like the child scarred by the first experience of solitude
Time and endurance will end by breaking my heart
I shall have lost my way for ever, if I am allowed to get
    out of here,
Shall I go searching for you everywhere, in flat places,
    in the pieces of the mirror, in wasted glances
Again to find your face, my heart searching?
Shall I alone speak the language that was once ours,
That was once the only thing left to us,
In the shades of the dead—the dead colours—images—
When our nights were simple incidents,

130

In the great night that began so long ago?
How shall I measure the time in here, its lunar intervals
    its starlike bounds,
How shall I measure my blind progress, the unforeseen
    span of your absence
Within this inexorable spaceship
In the heart of the city that was once ours
Now governed by tanks?
Sevenfold confusion, sealed, besieged within and without
    by fear of the thousand faces,
The cries of the incurable subside at half past five every
    evening,
The sirens shatter the silence
Those asleep inscrutable dead,
Again and again—where are your hands? Where is your
    voice?
Will the walls resist tonight? Will darkness prevail?
How shall I measure?
Just as the first experience of solitude scars the still
    young child,
Your absence has driven a knife up to the hilt into my
    place and time
Ugliness has everywhere released mad tongues ensnaring
    and devouring me,
Wounded time spread unnatural blows,
I am doomed to die
Round me, everywhere, in my breast, in confusion,
    in my wounds,
The bloodstained path from innocence to murder, from
    murder to remorse, lament and again to murder.
How shall I sing your praise?
My voice that loved has been stabbed.
In my wakefulness my hair that you loved is celestial
    seaweed.
My hands move in despair
Wherever I look I find you not
Square holes of darkness through the bars.
Hellenism betrayed, treachery, a knife to the heart,
Wounded light after ten, unexplained noises, breathing,
Vain sacrifice, siege, absence, the guard's cigarette.
I shall only speak in this language

131

The others will say: 'How that fellow has changed!'
Looking at me with the single eye of a Cyclops tourist,
Asking me to speak of heroes,
Others who sleep through these labyrinth nights when
    treachery shouts from the house tops,
Drowning the tanks and aircraft, the fear, the step of
    the guard,
The nights without you, when treachery shouts from the
    house tops
And my broken heart likewise shouts
Like the children of Zenobia, scattered to the ends of the
    earth in despair.
The nights without you, nowhere.
For I shall have lost you
In the moving darkness
Like the struggle
That was 'difficult yet fine'[2]
And turned out to be a rotten grape.
How, without you?
Just as the child is forever scarred by its first experience
    of solitude,
My body will break up, my cells dissolve one by one
On this Procrustes bed of time,
The sunspot of my body will explode
Will write your name throughout the heavens,
My cells will one by one graft on to people
With the age of suffering, in the mauve light of dusk
    behind the grille.
I shall send my dreams to disturb their sweet slumber,
Send hatred to nest in their unsuspecting glances,
When the warder comes to call the roll,
The others will say: 'Escaped',
Misunderstanding my death.
You alone will know,
I alone shall remember your hands,
The dull whine of the dog outside the prison,
The men's cries on the terrace,
The despair in the Chinese drawing,
Greek enigmas: 'What is it that comes up on its feet
    and goes down on a blanket?'
Will you alone know

How my body was lost,
My voice scattered, I was kept awake,
How fear has echoes, the face of despair?
You alone will know.
I shall go on speaking in that language.

2

Far, far away life is heard
High, high above the lights shine—maybe—
The lights stolen from us of the city stolen from us,
The memory of the last sunset, our mountains around.
Far, far away you exist. It must be so.
If only I could hear your bright laugh, behind the soiled
    walls.
One day when all becomes known
When the frozen memory has thawed.
Now everywhere—'My statement, I must remember
    what I said in my statement'
Colours will return—perhaps.
One day the doors of the tombs, the houses, the prisons,
    will be opened
We shall count our dead, share our new songs
One day
You will learn
The rest
You will remember
That life exists far, far, away.
You will be far away
And I
Shall be no more.

3

Time has made a change. The years have made a change.
You know where to find me.
I am fear, I am death,
I am unbridled memory,
I am the memory of your tender hands,
I am the sorrow for our spoilt life,
By my agony I shall besiege the 'mind your own
    business',

I shall break their sleep with noisy fearful fireworks,
Countless bullets will strike the indifferent passers-by
Till they start to tremble
Till they start to ask questions
They won't be able to kill me
But I think that the only ones who may understand will
    be the children
Rich in our heritage
For the first time
The children
Harsh in memory, harsh to us,
May read in time the clumsy message of the previous
    wrecks,
Correcting the mistakes, erasing the lies,
Naming correctly,
Dispassionately, the children, correctly by age,
Scarred by the lightning knowledge of the solitude of
    strength so late in reaching us.
If now I seek you in despair in the mighty waves of my
    wakefulness
If I call you with every breath
When I come to return to the dark roads of the world,
With only a handful of moonstones to lead me
Blinding the world with the peals of mad laughter from
    the nun holding the key,
Deafening the world with the echoes from the terrace
With the cries of the tortured and those torturing them,
Shaking the world with that language of death
You may have found the way in your labyrinth,
You may be a proud tree on the crossroads of the world,
With all the rivers secretly reaching your roots,
Your children and all the children
May rejoin time and life—one moment before chaos.
Nothing of me will be left

Neither the remorse I planned to be
Nor the touch of your hand
Nor my most important part, my tongue,
I shall have dissolved in all the rivers of the world
I shall have written your name in all the snows of the
    ravines

I shall have gone through the darkness I feared to the
   other bank
My body perhaps dead but once more intact will rest
With the memory of you and the sunlit life around it.

June

Stelios the gardener and I are sitting on the beach unravelling
fishing nets. We go out each evening in the boat and cast our
nets in semicircles around one part of the coast; then we beat
the side of the boat and the fish take fright and rush into the
net. We repeat this three or four times and get several kilos of
fish: ample for a fry-up. We moor the boat in front of the
tavernas, and with our catch we have a 'country' salad,
washed down with a little rough local wine. We eat like kings!
We sing and when we are alone we dance. Two kilometres from
the house there is a taverna where the owner's two beautiful
blonde daughters work as waitresses: it is a feast for the eyes to
watch them. This little taverna is buried beneath large trees
which are hundreds of years old and give off an intoxicating
aroma. Often we land our boat nearby and run to the kitchen
to give (so-called) culinary advice. But our eyes are elsewhere.
Then we sit out under the trees, listening to songs; when someone from another table gets up to dance the 'zeïbekiko' we clap
our hands in time with the rhythm.

Stelios is a man of few words. He only speaks to tell me a
fishing story: the day he caught a fish weighing over ten kilos,
and so on! Be that as it may, for the two months we have been
together his nets have caught nothing bigger than my finger.

'We're out of luck. It'll improve.'

'Mister Mikis, someone is asking for you.'

I can just see—at the bottom of the garden—Georgia
Anastasiadis. She is distressed: they have arrested her only
son, Sotiris.

'I've still not been able to see him...But yesterday a dreadful thing happened...They sent me his clothes...They were
stained with blood...'

'Have courage.'

Her son and Dariotis had had prices put on their heads as
criminals some months before. They accused them of murdering

135

a woman—after there had been a bomb attempt in Piraeus Street. A bomb had gone off on the terrace of the Ministry of Justice and a tile had fallen off and hit the woman on the head. The junta had immediately exploited this death and had put a price on the heads of these two young people.

Both belonged to the Lambrakis Youth. Dariotis was secretary of the Athens branch and Anastasiadis was a member of the bureau. That is why they and all the other Lambrakides were tracked down by the Security. I was convinced that they were going to be tortured. But, worse, there could be a trial and death sentences might be passed. Perhaps even a showpiece execution...

'How were they arrested?'

She told me.

'This goes back to when?'

'It's a month ago now.'

'We'll see what we can do. The thing is to get them out of their clutches. I'm going to try the impossible.'

'What can you do, my boy? Aren't you in their clutches, too?'

As soon as my friend Georgia had left I telephoned the Security.

'Mister Lambrou, please.'

'Who's speaking?'

'Theodorakis.'

'Malios here. What can I do for you?'

'It's personal.'

'I'll call him immediately.'

Lambrou and I fix a rendezvous in a tea shop near Exarkhia Square in Athens. He turns up in an American radio car.

'What's up?'

'It's a month since you arrested those kids.'

'Which kids?'

'You know perfectly well. You've tortured them, for sure.'

'Who told you that?'

'You sent bloodstained clothes back to Sotiris's mother. You must be very pleased with yourself.'

'They killed an innocent woman.'

'Who killed her—them or you?'

'What were they playing at? Distributing leaflets?'

136

'You know very well that's a lie. Why do you want to kill these kids?'

'We need to make an example of them!'

'That's exactly why I wanted to see you. I was their leader in the Lambrakis Youth. So I'm responsible for all their actions. They were carrying out our orders.'

'So?'

'So I'm going to assume my responsibilities in public. I'm not going to let you kill them. And for a start, you can consider me as being a witness for the defence. We'll see all this comes before the military tribunal.'

'Could you say all this to the director?'

'Which means we have to go to the Security?'

'If you like.'

'Let's go.'

As we get into the car, Lambrou cannot refrain from saying to the driver, just to see his face:

'To the Security! Mikis is arrested!'

I ask myself: 'what if that's true?'

The familiar gates of the Security. It was not so long ago that I passed through them the other way.

As we go up the stairs, he whispers in my ear, almost joyfully:

'Tell me how you feel to find yourself on these stairs again!'

I glance at him out of the corner of my eye and say, loudly: 'Nothing.'

And I add immediately: 'I have no intention of satisfying your sadism.'

I look to the left at the top of the stairs: my cell. A shadow. Who is there now? Lambrou guesses what I am thinking:

'They're your lads. Lambrakides. Think of the magnificent book we could write one day, you and I. You could say what you knew, and I could say what I knew. It would be a famous best-seller!'

We enter the office of the director of Security, Papaspyropoulos. It is where I met the foreign journalists and my father. He shows playful surprise. Karapanayotis, who is beside him, says:

'Director, if we had Mikis with us, all the young people of Greece would line up behind us! That's where his real role is: at the head of our national youth...'

137

Lambrou explains the purpose of my visit. The director says: 'I advise you to do no such thing.'

'You can count on my being a witness for the defence.'

'He's determined to appear before the military tribunal,' Lambrou says.

'You know perfectly well that those two kids have got absolutely nothing to do with the death of that woman.'

'The investigation is not complete,' Papaspyropoulos says. 'When it is, I shall ask you to come so I can give you the results.'

'Is it possible for Sotiris's mother to see him?'

'Tell Lambrou.'

The next day I see Georgia and tell her everything. She is very relieved.

'We'll fight together. As we always have.'

We embrace one another, and say goodbye with tears in our eyes. A week later she sent me two poems which I set to music:

With You

Amidst the wild waves
In the fire, in the fire
In the fire with you
With you, with you
In the evening stillness
In a tender serene dream
My light of dawn, my morning star.

In the fire with you
With you, with you
In the fearful starless night
Among the pitiless beasts
Roaring, roaring
In the fire with you
With you, with you
In loud joy
Invincible rivers
On the wings of the eagle
In the fire with you
With you, with you

Lament

Pain has no words
The abyss no bottom
Hell no measure
Chaos no order
More bitter than gall
The world exists not
All its vipers
Gnaw my entrails.

It was in my house at Vrakhati that I returned to the work of
my teacher friend, Yorgos Fotinos. During the civil war
Yorgos had been condemned to death; he was not shot and
we met again at the concentration camp on Makronisos in
1949. Sometimes we were on the same working party—one
of the 'national re-education projects' which meant transporting rolls of barbed wire. We were filthy dirty and had several
weeks' growth of beard. The north wind, which blew so strongly
on that desolate island, was beating everything down in its
path. We put our collars up and pulled our caps down: all
that was visible was our eyes. When we spotted each other, we
dropped our rolls and fell into each other's arms. On 26 March
1949 I was transferred to the first group, which was to suffer
the most terrible cruelty and which we called the group of
March. The notes of my First Symphony were going round in
my head continually: we had written a first draft in the tent
where the Resistance generals were cooped up.[3] Like all the
others I had my daily ration of blows on the head and far from
disappearing, the notes of my symphony drew enormous
strength from this brutality.

Six years later, in 1955, the First Symphony was played by
the National Orchestra of Athens. I was in Paris at the time,
at the Conservatoire, and Yorgos was teaching in a small village
in Greece. By chance he heard my symphony on his radio and
with great emotion he wrote 'Our Sister Athina', a poem which
is full of barbed wire fencing and orange trees.

OUR SISTER ATHINA

(Flow-song composed at Vrakhati in May 1968 upon a poem by Yorgos Fotinos.)

The sun will rise
On the groaning breasts.
The sun will rise
Over prisons and ravines.
Just as the ants come out
Of their underground cells
Four-sided sun.
The cannon mouths cannot
Kill it.
They aim at the curve of its eyebrow
They fly off its corner-stone.
Brave men will rise from the folds of my pain,
Brave men with strong hands.
They will engrave the bars and our heavy dreams
Inscribing the forehead of the day:
We want to live.
Violins will emerge from our tortured breasts,
The barbed wire will become violin strings
The broken bones will become flutes,
There will be a wild dance.
We are marrying truth,
We are marrying the earth
Disdained yet unique.
We are marrying its laughter,
Its milk, its veins,
To its children.
Dawn had broken
When they took our sister Athina
To execution.
The night before they gave her two oranges
But she did not eat them.
She kissed them as passionately as if
They had all spring in their juice
The entire young sap of the earth.
Later she hid them in her breast.
In the far corner of her cell

Death cowered like a frightened dog.
She called:
'Come Tiger, Blackie, Jack',
Trying to find his dog-like name.
'Come—I'll show you a vestige of Truth,
Come and sniff the oranges
In my breast.'
Dawn had broken
With ten bursts of fire they drilled
Holes in her mighty breast
They did not see
The oranges that burst
The juice mingled with blood
The pips
The ground was sanctified
The area was filled with orange trees
So many that they could not be hewn down
In Honour of the First Symphony[4]!

Shortly before the advent of the dictatorship I had started collaborating with a young poet, Manos Eleftheriou. The first fruit of this collaboration was six songs, and here at Vrakhati I was to complete this cycle with six more. Here are some of these poems by Eleftheriou. Their theme is close to that of the songs known as 'rebetika' or 'bouzoukia' which grew out of the lower depths of Athens at critical periods in our history—the Metaxas dictatorship, the civil war, and the post-war period, when men were expressing their disarray and nostalgia in the raucous tones of the underworld and were singing of a today with no tomorrow.

TWELVE POPULAR SONGS

(On poems of Manos Eleftheriou)

The Brave Young Man

The brave young man is sad
I look him in the eyes
I look at him and say no word
Tonight for he is sad.

He's had no work for one whole week
Outside it snows, the wind is blowing
He has no work, no cigarette
Tonight he breaks my heart.
The brave young man is sad
When he looks at the sky
His eyes are like two birds
Tonight my tears flow down.

The Bat in my Mind

In my mind a bat
Watches over my house
Who will tell you
So that you may learn my grief.
I send you greetings
The wind takes them away
If they fall in the sea
The waves bring them back.
I count the passing days
And those when you were near me
I find that they give pain
To my eyes and to my heart.

My Door is Open

My door is open
Should you return one day,
Unless you want to close your mind
And to forget me.
I have water for you to wash
A bed all ready made
When you are washed and combed
Lie down and go to sleep.

It Starts Again Every Morning

It starts again every morning
Our hearts have been taken away
A story in the factories
Fermented by our tears
But who feels about all that
Who will cry about all that

142

Who will speak to God
And who will write to him of it.
In the dirt and dust
In the markets and slaughter houses
Straight from the army
And in the old machine shops
But who feels for all that
And who will weep for all that
Who will speak to God
And who will write to him of it.

In This Neighbourhood

In this neighbourhood
Morning and night
We spent and lost an entire life.
In this neighbourhood
In the small narrow place
We lost ourselves and lived far from God.
In this neighbourhood—oh! in this neighbourhood.
Sorrow overtook us
Overtook us and betrayed us for a mouthful of bread.

My House is Too Small

My house is too small
To contain my love
Tell me where to come and find you.
My house is too dark
Its destiny is the night
It cannot take in the sky.
Wretched life, bitter life
Wound with the knife
Poverty gall tears
Summer and winter
The windows are nests
For the birds in spring
And for empty embraces.
My heart is alone
The house you have left
Is like a night in the rain.

I am a Stranger Passing By

Love has its sorrow
The stranger his road
The soldier his weapon
The judge his Law
But I am a stranger passing by
To those who have forgotten
And those who judged me
Who once more drink my blood.
He whose soul is black
Also has the knife
He who awaits the snake
Calls it a dove.

My Bread Tastes Good

The first year in a factory
The next in the frozen goods depot
Suddenly I found myself
Inside the machine shop
But my bread tastes good
And the wine goes to my head
Now that I have learnt
How the wheel turns.
The first day you laughed
The next you spoke to me
Without knowing how
I took the road you were taking.

During this Difficult Time

During this difficult time
I got confused trying to find you
With no consolation
And with a sick heart.
I passed through streets and alleys
The houses were dark
The bread I ate bitter as gall
Till I found you.
I lost half my life
My soul is sorely wounded

Since I must find you again
During this difficult time.

The Train Leaves at Eight

The train leaves at eight
For Katerini
In November it won't wait
For you to remember at eight
The train for Katerini won't wait in November.
Suddenly I found you again
Drinking ouzo at Lefteris's
Night will not fall elsewhere
For you to have your secrets
For you to remember who knows that night will not
    fall elsewhere.
The train leaves at eight
You alone have waited
On guard in Katerini
In the mist from five till eight
It was a knife in your heart on guard in Katerini.

God Exists

It is no Pasalimani here
No joy to be heard
Your world reaches me as a single voice
From an old unforgotten fête.
You say that time had passed
That God exists
That he does not forget us on the first of each month.

The Days and Time Go By

Troubles have come early
Nor can you even cry
Sorrow overwhelms you by day
Bitterness by night.
The days and time go by
The sky too small

145

To contain the fire
The tears, the distance.
They take our blood, our light
Our heart: but you must know
As you tread the earth
Your step grows lighter.

Also at Vrakhati I received a new collection from Eleftheriou, entitled: 'Night of Death'. At the time I was living just with Stelios the gardener, two or three worker friends, and the two dogs, Loupos and Madouvala, who adored music! I inhaled the aroma of freshly watered soil, planted flowers and did my share of the gardening. But above all I breathed the air of the sea, the beloved sea. I used to say over and over to myself: 'You're surfacing again, make good use of it, breathe as deeply as you can, for you'll be diving again soon.' We used to go fishing very early in the morning. My working hours were interrupted by visits from workers from the nearby yards, from peasants, and from students who would come right up to my place without being seen. My audience, then, was very varied: it included famous people and unknown people, and it was among them that I composed the second and third parts of 'State of Siege', 'Our Sister Athina', 'Six Popular Songs', 'Night of Death' and 'Songs for Andreas'.

I got the inspiration for the 'Songs for Andreas' while I was thinking back to the Averof prison of a few weeks before:

On my way to the toilet I peeped through the spy-hole of Cell No. 4, which was next door. I recognised Andreas Lentakis, a former Lambrakis Youth leader. I recoiled: an eye was watching me and it opened up to an inordinate size. I went into the toilet and tapped a code message on the wall, then came out. Another peep. Andreas was squatting on the ground, sketching a sort of dance. Back in my cell I squared off some paper, so we could communicate in morse. ABCD/ EFGH/IJKL etc. First you tap out the number of the row and then the number of the letter within the row. On my way back to the toilet in the evening, I threw the paper through the spy-hole. So we were able to start a long dialogue through the wall.

146

Andreas told me of his activity in the underground, of his arrest, his interrogation and his tortures. On the terrace. 'They beat me on the head for hours with little bags of sand, for they had found out that I had post-traumatic epilepsy...' Lambrou pretended to 'cherish' and 'admire' that head more than any other: 'I admire your Lambrakides,' he once told me. 'They have amazingly tough heads. Manolakos and Lentakis, for example...'

The day after I had made contact with Andreas they brought Themis, my first comrade in the underground, into my cell. Great rejoicing. Themos gave me all the news from the underground, then the news which slipped out about the Security. An endless tale. And by evening it was time for the tortures on the terrace. Andreas told me it was one of the Lambrakides. There were yells. My heart was at breaking point. When were we going to escape from this human slaughter-house? It was then that I got the idea of a hunger strike. Not just for me but for all of us. Andreas agreed. What about those who are in solitary? They are for it, as well. I warn the warders. An officer arrives immediately. I tell him of my decision.

'A hunger strike for how long?' he asks.

'Till the end.'

'You're wrong.'

'That's my look out.'

Andreas knocks. 'Drink some water and a little sugar.'

The first five days were the hardest: the body protested, reacted and writhed. Then came the giddiness. I lay on the ground. Day twelve. Between complete destruction and immortality. During a flash of lucidity I heard my wife shouting in the corridor: 'Assassins.' I remember the last message I sent Andreas: 'I am starting on my last fight for the freedom of our people.' Immediately Andreas replied, with strong and rapid taps: 'Not the last. Together we'll fight many more times before final victory.'

The cell door opened. They lifted me and took me to a car. Then it was the Saint Paul Hospital.

All these horrible memories come back to me at Vrakhati; they are still fresh in my memory. Andreas becoming the symbol of the Greek people's struggle. Yes, we Greeks are drinking treason in our milk, in our wine. A people betrayed. A people martyred. Now they are intending to exterminate you. But you'll become again what you were before. What you were during the wars of independence, the resistance and the civil war. In those days power came from the barrel of your gun.

Then the visions of the terrace. The cries. The pain which is driven in like a nail. Oh, Greek people, you have been lied to too much. You have been beguiled with false hopes. Did they know, in the East and in the West, that it was impossible for you to bring your revolution to its term? So why did they push you? Who dared do it? With what aim? To serve what interests? In any event, they were not yours. You could have made a revolution within your own means. And if you found you had gone beyond those means, you would not have hesitated to go back, to take a big step backwards, even to go back to the beginning. But today we are not even there any more: you have fallen back into Prehistory. Since your liberation the forward steps you took made you inexorably retrace your steps, stil lfarther back. And why? Because you were too trusting. You gave everything: sweat and courage, family and future. You gave your blood without counting the cost. Rivers of blood. But now the time has come: the time to reflect on the past, to take stock. The time to have faith in nobody but yourselves.

SONGS FOR ANDREAS

(Composed at Vrakhati in 1968, on four poems by Mikis Theodorakis.)

You are a Greek

What you were before, you will become again
You must become so, you must weep
Your degradation must be complete
The pillage must reach the roots of the mountains
You are a Greek, you are a Greek
You drink treason in your milk, in your wine
Your degradation must be complete, you must see it,
      you must become,
What you were before, you will become again.

We are Two

We are two, we are two, eight o'clock has sounded.
Turn out the light, the guard is knocking, they'll come
    again tonight
They strike twice, three times, a thousand and thirteen
    times
You're in pain, I'm in pain, who is most in pain
The time will come to tell us
We are two, we are three, we are a thousand and
    thirteen.
Time goes by in the rain, the blood dries on the wound
The pain abates, the leader frees us.
We are two, we are three, we are a thousand and thirteen
One ahead, one ahead, the others follow
After the silence we shall hear the same old tune.

Time to See

You have been told many lies, today they'll tell you
    more, tomorrow still more,
Your enemies tell you lies, your friends hide the truth
    from you.
The liars promise you false glory, your friends lull you
    with false truths
Where are you going with those false dreams
It's time to stop, time to sing, time to cry, to suffer, to see.

The Abattoir

At noon they hit you in the office,
I count the blows, the blood
I am a beast locked in the abattoir
For you today, for me tomorrow
This evening they'll hit Andreas on the terrace
I count the blows, the pain.
We'll meet again behind the wall
Tap tap from you, tap tap from me, this means
In the language of the dumb, I'm holding on.
Our hearts beat a tattoo
Tap tap from you, tap tap from me.
Our abattoir smells of thyme
Our cell a Red sky.

149

The 'Songs for Andreas' are completed. I finish watering the garden and then go to the studio for the recording. I breathe in the aroma of damp earth. The two dogs come and lie at my feet. Loupos, the Alsatian, looks at me peacefully: he trusts me. I sing. He closes his eyes. 'What you were before, you will become again.' Down below, the sparkling blue sea soothes me.

It is at Vrakhati that I hear the famous broadcast from Radio 'Foni tis Alithias',[5] announcing the split between the Central Committee and the Politburo of the Greek Communist Party abroad. I try to communicate with those leading cadres who were able to flee abroad. On 10 March 1968 some friends and I draw up a joint text which we send abroad so that it can be broadcast as widely as possible. This text seems to have been a voice crying in the wilderness, or to have been stifled like so many before...

TO THE MEMBERS AND LEADERS OF THE COUNTRY'S PROGRESSIVE MOVEMENT

Following an exchange of views between a number of members and cadres of the movement within the country and following the new crisis which has arisen at the top of the Greek Communist Party during and since the twelfth plenum of the Central Committee, we declare the following:

1. The movement within the country takes no part in this crisis. It recognises none of the decisions which are bound up with it. It considers the authority of the 'interior' party as the sole authority. It believes deeply that no-one else has the necessary responsibility, firmness and effectiveness to assume the leadership of the Greek Leftist and progressive movement. Before long the 'interior' party will be reconstituted on democratic foundations, its aim being to regroup, renew and develop the Greek Left and the patriotic struggle against the dictatorship, with the forces which are today organising and leading our people's fight as the main instrument.

2. Our aim is to open a new era for the Greek progressive movement and for Greece. We place complete confidence in the strength of the Greek people, in the country's fighters, and in the friends of peace and democracy throughout the world.

150

We invite our militant comrades, wherever they may be, within the country or abroad, to give us their hands and to regroup themselves around the interior centre, and, with a new dynamism and side by side with all the patriotic and anti-dictatorship forces, to join the struggle for the country's liberation from the yoke of dictatorship, for the democratic rebirth and progress of the country.

10 March 1968
A statement will soon be published on this subject.

We set to work on drawing up this statement. One of us takes charge of working out the economic programme. I am given the job of preparing the ground abroad. On 4 April 1968 we send my personal letter; but all trace of it, too, has strangely been lost.

July

On the other side of the isthmus of Corinth lives my godfather, Notis. He owns a pretty little villa among the pine-trees and overlooking the Gulf of Saronikos. While I was in the underground his villa was under close surveillance. Notis and his wife, Elli, were shadowed day and night. From time to time they were summoned to the commissariat. But Notis is a born poet. He knows that it is all temporary and all that is needed to change the world is a tear or a laugh! What's more, he's a Spartan.

After the war, when the Right imposed its terror on the people, all the progressives in Sparta were slaughtered like lambs. In fact one family—Sotiris Petroulas's—had seventeen members massacred! One night when they came to kill them, Sotiris's parents took him in their arms—he was still a baby—and escaped through the window. But fascism was not content with this bloodbath. Twenty years later it was still reigning, and all that time it had been watching Sotiris, who by this time had become a grown man. One hot night in July 1965 fascism rose up again, this time to strike him in the very heart of Athens: I had seen him only two minutes before. I was proud of him. He and thousands of other Lambrakides were going up Panepist-imiou Street, singing. He was a tall, slim, robust, unruly

151

fellow. It was impossible to imagine that one day he would stop singing, stop laughing, stop breathing.

'They've just wounded Sotiris...badly...'

I rush to the 'Evangelismos' Hospital. The corridors are full of wounded. The operating theatres are going flat out. A crowd of relatives, friends, police. I go up to where they have put the most seriously wounded:

'They've put Sotiris in the morgue! Down there!'

I run, I open the door: in the half-light of the mortuary I can just make out a bare table.

'They've just taken him away.'

'Where to?'

I leave the hospital for the offices of *Avgi,* the EDA paper.

'Over two hundred demonstrators are seriously wounded. As for Sotiris Petroulas...they've got him out of the way...'

'Good. Let's go to the headquarters of the Centre Youth. We'll make a joint move.'

'It's impossible to move in the streets. They're still filled with smoke from the tear-gas grenades.'

We rapidly form a small committee and go out with damp handkerchiefs over our mouths. The gas makes us cry and burns our mouths. We arrive at the Centre Youth headquarters. As soon as the Centrist militants see us they hurry to tell their leaders.

'Wait a moment, please.'

We wait patiently for half an hour. Finally one of the leaders consents to come:

'They've killed one of our lads, Sotiris Petroulas, and they've got the body out of the way...'

'Wait, please.'

Another half-hour wait. Then we get up and go. Papandreou's famous 'struggle on two fronts'—on the Right and on the Left—doesn't even stop for death!

I spend the whole night running from house to house. From one district to another. I feel that Sotiris lives on in me. That he is thirsty. That he is hungry. That he wants to dance. I feel a sort of animal, primitive, wild joy. I go home at dawn. I have the strength neither to get undressed nor to lie down. I slump into the armchair. Shouting: cries which for the past seventy days and nights have been raised in the streets of Athens. Twenty to a hundred thousand demonstrators each

152

evening. At times up to a million. It is a paean[6] which goes on and on echoing. At the headquarters of the Lambrakis Youth we arrange for our militants to come from their various districts. We have divided the Athens-Piraeus region into ten large sectors: of the ten, nine feed the demonstrations in the heart of Athens, while the tenth—and they take it in turn—stays at home...to rest! When the police step in the confrontation is always very violent. Each evening the hospitals have to admit a large number of seriously wounded. And yesterday they killed Sotiris.

The telephone rings.

'Come to the cemetery straightaway. Don't lose a second. They're about to bury him secretly...'

Athens is still asleep. Here and there one comes across a worker returning home, hugging the walls. No doubt a worker who still doesn't suspect anything. Who doesn't know of the sacrilege which has just been committed. Of the pain of a mother who has lost her son. Of the anger of his comrades.

I sink in a sulphurous ocean of anger and hatred. My chest swells. Beneath these plane trees in the cemetery lies Beloyannis, who was assassinated in the thick of the cold war. To the left lie thousands of members of the resistance who were executed during the occupation and the civil war. Nearby they have just dug Sotiris's grave. Our people can count their martyrs in thousands, and hundreds of thousands, and yet they never surrender. If at times they seem to weaken it is so they can get their breath back and march on. Today the whole of Greece is in a state of ferment. King Constantine, who is surrounded by crafty advisers, has deliberately provoked the people. On 15 July 1965 he called the legal Prime Minister of the country, George Papandreou, to the Palace, only to dismiss him a few moments later...He laid a trap for him and this experienced and proud politician fell into it.

'So are you submitting your resignation?' the king asked him.

'Naturally,' Papandreou replied.

If the reply had been 'No!' the fate of Greece today would have been completely different.

So there they are—the king and his advisers rubbing their hands with joy. A new Prime Minister is already waiting in the corridor in his morning suit: the Academician and poet,

153

Athanasiadis Novas. I am in the Chamber of Deputies with the other EDA members. One of our leaders, Leonidas Kyrkos, comes to tell us the news of the resignation. He says:

'We must give full support to the Centrists and the "Old Man". Above all, we must not allow them to get the initiative for they may allow themselves to be carried away by it. We must rouse the people : that is youth's role at the present moment.'

'You know that the Lambrakides have hardly any sympathy for Papandreou.'

'Exactly! We must order all militants to go out on to the streets of Athens! We must find out all Papandreou's movements and we must never miss an opportunity to cheer and support him!'

'OK.'

I go to the headquarters of the Lambrakis Youth and summon the bureau. We adopt this line, which is approved by all the members on the single condition that one of the five slogans to be used during the demonstrations will be 'PA-PAN-DRE-OU!' and the other four will be '1-1-4!' (referring to Article 114 of the Constitution which places the Constitution under the protection of the patriotism of the Greek people). 'DEMOCRACY!', 'NOVAS OUT!' and 'LEGAL GOVERNMENT!' Eventually the popular imagination created hundreds of new slogans, the most famous of which was addressed to King Constantine : 'King, Take Your Mother and Go!'

The first demonstrations are followed with sympathy by the people, and then as the days went by the vehemence of the young people ends up by winning over the masses by contagion, and to the point where all the people take up these slogans on their own account and come to demonstrate, tens and hundreds of thousands of them, outside the Chamber. It is there that an important act of contemporary Greek history is played out.

But the king's manoeuvre rebounds. It collects only the minority votes on the Right and manages to seduce only a few Centrist deputies (the people call them 'the apostates'). The majority remains faithful to the legal government of Papandreou. Faced with this unforeseen defeat, the Americans, who were in this sordid game right at the beginning, decide to take extreme measures. One by one the Centrist deputies are

154

bought out, while outside the people shout their disgust: 'How much did you get?'

This terrible struggle lasted seventy days and nights, by which time corruption had provided the few necessary votes. The third government of apostates, formed by the king and with Stefanopoulos as Premier, succeeds in getting a majority in the Chamber! The people are cruelly deceived. The king's violation of the Constitution and the barefaced methods which are then employed are a grave slur on the parliamentary institutions and the confidence the people have placed in their leaders. The ground is prepared for the colonels' putsch. That is why ever since the establishment of the military dictatorship in 1967, and in spite of their hatred for their new masters, the Greek people have only had a very limited confidence in their former leaders. So a profound crisis, affecting relations between the masses and the politicians, was created in those decisive days in the summer of 1965; the crisis lasts to this day.

I drive up to the cemetery; the forces of order are barring the way and my car is immediately surrounded. But I enjoy parliamentary immunity.

'Theodorakis, deputy!' I tell one of the police officers.

'What do you want?'

'It is for me to ask you!'

'It is forbidden to enter the cemetery.'

'What? You are now attacking the dead!'

I drive forward, bursting through the ranks of police, who leap aside. I enter the cemetery yard. A hundred policemen are barring my way. I stop, get out and walk through them. They still do not dare to touch me.

'Who's in charge?'

To the right of the entrance the parents and close relatives of Sotiris Petroulas are gathered in a large room. They spot me and want to come and meet me, but they are prevented from doing so by the police barrier.

'I want to speak to your commander.'

I am taken to a nearby building.

'Procurator So-and-so.'

'Commissar So-and-so.'

'Colonel So-and-so.'

'Delighted to meet you!'

155

'What is the purpose of your visit, Deputy?'

'I have just learned that you are preparing secretly to bury the student, Sotiris Petroulas, and that the clergy is opposed to it.'

Silence.

'Have you given the mother permission to see her son?'

'We have received a formal order not to allow anyone near the dead man.'

'And you're going to let them bury him without his own people being able to see him again? Without their being able to lay him out and mourn him?'

'Those are the orders!'

'Whose orders?'

'The Minister of the Interior, Admiral Toumbas.'

'And you're going to carry out those orders?'

'What else can we do?'

'And the other laws?'

'Which laws?'

'The laws of the dead? The divine laws, as Antigone would say. You have of course heard of Antigone, Procurator?'

'Those are the orders!'

'So, resign! That order is not only illegal, it is sacrilegious and inhuman! Anyway, don't imagine you're going to bury Petroulas like that. This dead man belongs to us...Can I make a telephone call?'

I telephone several members of the Lambrakis Youth. I tell each one loudly, so the others can hear, that they must come to the cemetery *en masse*.

When I ring off, the officers immediately telephone for reinforcements.

The mourners' laments make the cypresses quiver. We sit near them in silence. The police reinforcements begin to arrive. In a short time the yard fills up with hundreds of Lambrakides and EDA militants, and the police are ready for the confrontation. I leave the cemetery to meet the Lambrakides.

'What are we going to do?' they ask.

'Where have they put Sotiris?'

'Over there, in the chapel: they seem to be preparing to bury him because they have just laid a police cordon round it.'

'How many of them are there?'

'About two hundred.'

'There aren't many of us. Other Lambrakides are coming. Collect some stones and get ready. If we have to, we'll fight.'

The police escort me into the chapel. Sotiris seems to be still alive: he seems to be just sleeping on the bench. They have wrapped his naked body in a blood-stained sheet.

The Lambrakides keep flooding in. I warn the officers that we are determined to fight. Outside the cemetery, a crowd is gathering and can be heard chanting slogans.

The counter-order finally arrives at noon: 'The dead man must be transferred to the morgue, where he will be handed back to his relations for burial.'

The crowd now moves on to Petroulas's house, in a distant part of the capital. Thousands of students, workers and weeping mothers bring him flowers. All have their fists raised and are demanding vengeance! Sotiris's mother's cries of grief last all night.

The rest of us, at the headquarters of the Lambrakis Youth, sit around a table discussing what to do. We must solve all the problems raised by the funeral which is to take place the following day. While my comrades are discussing the matter, I am scribbling on a sheet of paper. Lines, sudden, abstract signs:

> Sotiris Petroulas
> Lambrakis welcomed you, liberty too
> Sotiris Petroulas
> Nightingale and lion, mountain and starry sky
> Sotiris Petroulas
> Be a guide to your people, show us the way!

After him come an innumerable army of heroes. Elektra, Napoleon Soukatzidis and two hundred hostages executed at Kaisariani, Vasilis Zannos, Pavlos Papamerkouriou. Over fifty thousand heroes executed. Nikos Beloyannis, Nikiforidis and many other students. Grigoris Lambrakis. And this last one, Sotiris Petroulas. This is the unending line of martyrs who show us the path to follow.

> The heroes and martyrs are our guides
> Your blue eyes
> Call us.

'I will now call on the President,' Benas says, turning to me.

'To speak is to sing. Listen to what I have just written and give me your views.'

The following day the crowd throbs in the arteries of the capital as far as the eye can see and as Petroulas's coffin comes past, borne by his comrades, the crowd roars, shakes and raises its fists. As the coffin passes, the crowd swears an oath. The young people follow their martyred brother in their thousands, singing:

> Sotiris Petroulas
> Nightingale and lion, mountains and starry sky...

I go to his house the next day. His mother is there.

'Sit down, my child,' she says. 'I was just chatting with Sotiris.'

'With Sotiris?'

'Yes. Can't you see him, sitting on the chair? I'm telling him to be careful. When I lost him the other evening, they took us to the police. "Where's my boy?" I cried. And they took me to a cake shop! You understand? A cake shop! At two o'clock in the morning. "I don't want a cake shop," I tell them; "I want my son..." Isn't that right, Sotiris?'

Petroulas's mother is still young; she has a beautiful face. She has seen seventeen of her relations massacred; this is the eighteenth—her own son. And this time it is too much for her: She is on the verge of madness.

Notis was fifteen years before he set foot again on the soil of his native Sparta. And like the poet, Nikiforos Vrettakhos, he too has sworn an oath of allegiance to Mount Taïgetos.

Notis took my boat—a caïque called 'Tsoufi'—and while I was underground and then in detention, he had moored it at the port captain's berth in the isthmus of Corinth. The bad weather had smashed her sides. Notis tended her wounds, repainted her and wrote a completely new number on her. Today we can stretch out on her. We have set course for the Peloponnese and let our imagination sail: we dream of a Greece devoted entirely to poetry and philosophy. Greece would no longer be just a hive where a free and happy people devote themselves to the pleasures of art. The people would be creator and spectator at the same time. Was it just a vision? Or did that extraordinary cultural movement in Greece in the years 1964–5 contain the seeds of this radiant socialism? Of this ideal government in which the power really belonged to the people?

'The people and the poets, or rather the *people-poet*, is one day going to take power! Greece will once again become the centre of the world. The centre of the arts.'

'We'll choose an island, Ikaria for example, and we'll make it an island of world youth. Each country will build its own temples, dedicated to art, the theatre and music. There will be concert halls and libraries. Artistic competition must be revived.'

Notis points to the isthmus of Corinth :

'That's where the Isthmic Games took place about 2,500 years ago.'

'Now the orang-outangs are watching us.' I point out, on the shore, just in front of his house, the familiar and sinister silhouettes of the Security spies.

'We will build theatres for thirty, for fifty thousand spectators!' the dramatist in him cries out.

'Or listeners!' echoes the composer.

A shark is sleeping near us, close to the surface.

'Quick, quick, your gun!' Notis shouts. 'Get your sights on him!'

But the shark had woken up and disappeared into the depths of the Gulf of Saronikos.

'In earlier days, the waters round Greece didn't harbour sharks.'

'It's the Sixth Fleet that's brought them...'

'Yes. Sharks and the dictatorship...'

But we know full well who'll be the final victor.

For thirty years we have struggled and lived every minute of this victory. We are now living this victory. But those who are dead are living it, too, and the rocks, and the trees and the vast sea which bathes our country.

Notis looks towards Mount Taïgetos and his eyes are filled with the images of resistance strugglers and andartès.[7] He climbs the mast and swears an oath to the *great victory* :

> Like the eagle he winged his way over the road
> Everyone at the windows admired him

159

He lowered his dark eyes
And went forward like a brave man.
His eyes are now clouded
Steel has entered his heart.
The blood flows, the sun is darkened
Death is on the march.
Eyes and hearts were wrong
Those in the windows were wrong
Death had mounted his steed
As he was smiling.
Who goes down to Hades today?
Why are the people thus disturbed?
Why are mountains and plains silent?
A brave young man passed by.

When we next went out in the caïque it was my turn to climb the mast and sing this new song.

But at Vrakhati my time was not devoted exclusively to dreaming. My friends insisted that I appear in public. We decided to go to a night club in the Plaka district at the foot of the Acropolis.

This kind of establishment had been started in 1963 on my initiative as a place where for a reasonable price one could hear music and poetry which were politically committed. We opened the first one and dozens followed; they became meeting places for young people.

One Saturday evening, then, we chose one of these clubs. There were only young people there: about three hundred inside and three hundred outside and on the stairs leading to the first floor.

When I was spotted no one could believe his eyes. Then some of them clapped. Others cried. The gathering was like a cornfield swaying in the wind. Singers came from other clubs (most of them were my pupils) and threw themselves into my arms. They broke into my songs. It was, of course, forbidden, but no one was thinking of that. The shadow of the dictatorship had lifted and every face was lit up.

We left at midnight. As I went through the door a boy shook me by the hand and said, in a strong voice: 'Present.' A second boy did the same. As I went down the stairs all the young people shook me by the hand and shouted: 'Present.'

The next day the police descended on the club, pulled the beard of one of the musicians and closed it down. This place, which had become free again for one evening, must exist no longer.

Meanwhile, the slander campaign against me is reaching a crescendo. Every day the Security feeds the campaign with its own inventions.

A car from the Ministry of the Presidency brings deputies, journalists and personalities to Vrakhati, all at the invitation of the junta. I am clearly regarded as one of the country's curiosities! And as tangible proof of the existence of freedom!

End of July 1968. Ladas and Lambrou arrive in Vrakhati with an impressive escort. They have come to have lunch with me...Fresh fish! The well-known photographer from the Security films the scene. I turn to him and say:

'What does this buffoonery mean? Your methods are very cheap.'

'They're souvenirs...nothing but souvenirs,' Lambrou replies, with a clearly ironic tone to his voice.

We go to a little taverna by the sea.

'Lay the table outside, beside the sea,' Ladas tells the waiter.

'But it's going to rain, Secretary-General,' Lambrou observes timidly.

'It won't rain.'

It does rain!

We are all sitting round the table.

'Read this and tell me what you think of it.' Ladas hands me a typed poem: 'Hymn of the Olympiad'.[8]

I smile.

'Why are you laughing?'

I am thinking of its singer-composer, G. Ekonomidis (the only 'collaborator' among Greek artists).

'That man had one aim in life: he wanted me to set his verses to music. He tried a number of tricks. But to use the good offices of a colonel as influential as Ladas, well! I wasn't expecting something like that!'

'Just judge him as a poet,' Lambrou interjects.

'If I understand correctly, you're trying to win me over with

161

a little song! But let's see. If I were to agree, what would I have to fear? I'd join you. How many are you in the Revolutionary Council?'

'Fourteen!'

'With me, that would make fifteen!'

'Not quite,' says Lambrou.

'No, he's right. What's more,' Ladas turns to me, 'we've come to tell you that in a few days the ban on some of your songs will be lifted.'

'And it would help a lot if you set the "Hymn of the Olympiad" to music.' Lambrou winks.

'Let's talk seriously. First, I can tell you that I no longer have the slightest doubt that your revolution constitutes a great danger to the nation and that you are, quite simply, in the service of big interests. That's why I tell you that I am and will continue to be your enemy. But it so happens that I'm also a composer; in other words, between you and me there are my songs, which our people love and want to hear. You know that perfectly well. These songs must become free again, and as soon as possible. That's why I've become a peasant and a fisherman. So, if these songs have some moral value, it's due more than anything else to the moral attitude of their creator. If I bend the knee, if my courage leaves me, if I make a false move, then my songs will lose their moral value, in other words what our people prizes most highly in them. You know that perfectly well. But so do I. So if you really want to free my songs, do so unconditionally and give up these tricks, coming to me with this "hymn" as if I was born yesterday. And you must understand that I'm not going to confine myself to songs: I shall also give concerts and make records...'

'Our life will be humanised,' says Ladas the dreamer.

I thought this was another piece of sarcasm, but no, he was sincere.

'Exactly! But the important thing is that our people profit from it, because others will follow me. Today what are you giving the people and the youth in the way of cultural nourishment? Hay! Can you see where such a policy can lead?'

'We'll give you Herod's Odeum,' Ladas says.

'Let's be serious. You must admit that there is a balance of strength between us. That's why you have released me, that's why you're not arresting me, that's why tomorrow perhaps you'll arrest me again. That's why you take the trouble to talk to me...You have tanks. I have songs. Your misfortune is that the Americans haven't yet invented a tank that can kill songs! I am stronger than you, because time wears out tanks but makes songs stronger. And as for the tortures, you've deceived me, Yannis.' I turn to Ladas.

'A good hiding for their own benefit, I suppose,' he replies, casting an approving glance at Lambrou.

'So you don't think I'm speaking behind his back, I'll repeat it in front of him.' (I point to Lambrou.)

'Secretary-General, just a box on the ears, nothing more,' Lambrou tries to explain.

'How's the inquiry into the tortures going?' I ask Ladas.
'...'

All round us there are twenty or so secret agents watching discreetly. The comedy is over. The next minute I shall be bound hand and foot again. I must react quickly.

'You know the story of the cow'—I go on in a strange tone which surprises even myself—'who kicked the pail over? Well! That story may be repeated with me. Don't wear yourselves out filling the pail with lies and false news. Just at the right moment I shall give it a kick and, bang, all will be lost!'

Beginning of August

I prepare three plans.

First. To go back underground. I fix up three circuits, each isolated from the others, so that I can pass easily from one to another.

Second. A stand-by solution: I arrange my escape from Greece for the first few days of September. We have a dress rehearsal. A friend leaves for abroad to fix the technical side.

Third. I prepare some public statements.

In the event of nothing being possible, I'll go back to prison. My relations and friends are in agreement with the third solution (the other two being known only to those directly concerned).

The Soviet Ambassador, Koryukin, comes to Vrakhati. Before leaving Greece he had asked the Greek government (and his own) for permission to come and say goodbye to me. We spend the whole of Sunday together. A concert in the evening. I record the new songs and a message to the Soviet people, Party and government, and to the Komsomol. I thank them and re-affirm the desire of our people to struggle for freedom until final victory.

14 August

'Listen, it's Moscow,' Stelios, the gardener, is shouting to me. It is my voice:

> They strike twice, three times,
> A thousand and thirteen times...
>
> ...the leader frees us.
> We are two, we are three, we are a thousand and thirteen.

(Song for Andreas)

And then: 'Dear comrades...', the complete text I had given to Koryukin.

15 August

Moscow Radio has repeated the same message in its last three broadcasts in Greek. I warn the comrades of the danger, asking them to prepare hideouts. Each circuit still lacks a link in the chain. They will be ready in seven to ten days.

Slowly but surely I feel the vice tightening on me. There are a number of signs. When I go for a swim the beach is full of suspicious characters. Their appearance and their dress, which is always black. As the threat gets closer my creative passion redoubles, along with my passion for the sea and for the land.

One day I get my son, Yorgos, to come. He is eight. 'I have to speak to you. Man to man. Soon they're going to come and arrest me again. Don't be afraid. They won't do me any harm. I shall go. But I shall come back. During that time you will take my place. You must take care of your mother and your sister.' When they finally come for me Yorgos will be there, beside me, silent and serious.

16 August

I go out for a row. A yacht passes at a distance of some three hundred metres, heading for the Ionian Sea. For the first time something pushes me to steer towards it. If they're foreigners, I'll explain...But farther out the waves are big, and my boat is small. 'Not this time,' I tell myself. When I get back to shore, I can just make out a large black car and two men in black on the beach...There they are! I am certain of it. Yes, it's them. One is coming over to me!

'I'd like a word with you.' We go over towards a pine grove. 'You are assigned to your residence. Guards will be posted outside and inside the house. Nobody has the right to visit you, except your wife. You are forbidden to go down to the sea...'

21 August

Midday. The same visitor comes back.

'You have a quarter of an hour to get ready.'
'Where are we going?'
'To Zatouna.'
'What's that?'
'A village, I suppose, near Dimitsana.'

Why this unknown place? I have since learnt that Colonel Ladas had told his secretary : 'Mikis likes the sea too much. He must be deprived of it. Find a place in the Peloponnese which is farthest from the sea and we'll put him there.'

And that was Zatouna.

References

1 Two years later I was to encounter the same atmosphere and the same lack of realism and absence of dialogue when I spoke to Greeks living in forced exile abroad.
2 A phrase taken from Theodorakis's Statement of 23 April 1967. (Translator's Note)
3 Sarafis, the chief of ELAS, Mandakas, Avgeropoulos, etc.

165

4 A year later, in Zatouna, I made the acquaintance of Athina's mother. She had two daughters; the other was married to one of the colonels. Athina was a member of the democratic army and was captured by the national army at a battle near Zatouna; she was condemned to death and executed in Tripolis in 1948. Athina's old mother had come to Zatouna on a pilgrimage to commemorate her death. She had rented a room with one of our neighbours, and one evening, with the old lady sobbing quietly on the balcony, I sang 'Our Sister Athina' to the glory and memory of her daughter.

5 'Voice of Truth', radio of the Greek Communist Party, broadcasting from Eastern Europe.

6 War song.

7 Rebels.

8 It is for the 'Olympiad of Song', a propaganda instrument of the dictatorship.

ZATOUNA

Zatouna, August to October 1968

Zatouna is in the heart of the Peloponnese, in the heart of the mountains of Arkadia. The first time I ever came to Tripolis, the main town of Arkadia, was back in 1939. It was this area which formed me. There I started writing poetry and studying philosophy. There, too, I became familiar with ancient Greece, with our history, with Christianity, Marxism and the Resistance. For the first time I felt the desire to become a composer. It was there that I knew my first love. My first friendships. I gave my first concerts there. With my friend, Argyris, I used to make long treks in the mountains; we had prepared ourselves to meet satyrs, nymphs or the great Pan in person! ('Siao', the Chinese for Pan's flute, is the title I gave my first collection of poems, which was published in Tripolis.) My friends, Grigoris, Makis, Yorgos, Takis and I used to run down the slopes of Kapsa, near Tripolis, and sit reciting poetry on a little mound we christened 'Ritsos Rock', in honour of the great poet we had just discovered.

Here I am thirty years later rediscovering these places through the eyes of a prisoner. Thirty years! Full circle. Life is unfathomable. In choosing to deport me to the eagle's nest of Zatouna, how could the military have guessed that they were bringing me back to a childhood friend, the Great Pan?

The car passes one orchard after another on the way. Before the road climbs into the mountains of the Peloponnese I snatch one last glimpse of the sea in the Gulf of Nafplion. When will I see it again? We approach Tripolis, the famous Dropolitsa.[1] Stop in front of Sekhiotis's chemist's shop. My old school friends gather round. Doctors, lawyers, civil servants, workers. They smile. I feel very proud. They have complete confidence in me. As if they had known for ages that one day I would be back among them!

I had taken this same road on 25 March 1942. I was chained to Italian soldiers and was about to encounter torture for the first time. I was to be thrown into prison by the Italian fascists who were occupying the area. Today I am taking the same road in the custody of my own compatriots (if God consents to call them Greeks). Here is the Tripolis parade ground. Elli's house. My house, near Mavroyannis's windmill. I greet you, Tripolis! They have brought me back to you. What a mistake! They cannot imagine what strength, what confidence, what certainty and what happiness it gives me. The eternal return. I repeat over and over again to myself: 'What have you done all these years? Have you remained faithful to your dreams, to the oaths you swore as a youth, to your friends? Have you really done all you should? Now the time has come for reflection, introspection, catharsis, for a new beginning.'

The road goes through the villages of Kapsa, Levidi and Vlakherna. Among the olive trees the house of the writer, Vasilis. The village of Vitina. The statue to Mitropoulos (the great conductor, who was born in Arkadia). We are now going right into the thick of the great forest of Arkadia. Night has fallen. Before Dimitsana the car turns right on to an unmade road. Deep ravines. Rocks cut by a sabre. The River Lousios, where Dias bathed, shimmers at our feet. A final, very steep turn to the top of an escarpment and here is the village of Zatouna, right before us. It is perched on Mount Menalon, which symbolically seems to clasp the village to its bosom. The mountain rises in front of us, majestic and surrounded by olive trees. I now understand the choice of Zatouna; it is a natural fortress; access is extremely difficult. I have no idea yet that many efforts, most in vain, are going to be made to reach me, by friends both known and unknown.

The car stops in front of Mantzalas's butcher's shop, which is also the only 'café' in the village. A radio is on and gives the following news: 'The forces of the Warsaw Pact are invading

170

Czechoslovakia.' I see the gendarmes' faces light up and the officer cries out: 'I'm buying this round!' The sergeant, Tsouroulas, who is in charge of the police station, turns up. Then, a little later, Colonel Mitropoulos (chief of police for Arkadia) arrives from Tripolis with his escort. I spend the night at the station. Day breaks. The sun is shining. I go outside and walk away from the station. At the foot of the ravines the plain of Megalopolis stretches out towards the south-west. To my left, the cemetery, with its centuries-old cypresses. One of my guards, Alekos, comes running up to me; 'You musn't be alone, we must always be together,' he says, breathless from running with his weight. More gendarmes arrive. Kostas, Theodoros, Nikiforos, Thanasis, and Makis, a brigadier from Pyrgos. There are to be over a hundred of them and we are going to be living together for fourteen months.

I spend the next night at Madame Tasia's inn. My wife and children join me three days later and for some time we are to live in Varkoulas's house, opposite the tiny church of Saint George, with its little garden with chrysanthemums and a goldfish pond and fountain.

To meet our immediate needs, Lambis Bitounis[2]—who was to be an invaluable friend—buys us kitchen utensils, crockery and bedclothes.

Gradually we become accepted into the little world of Zatouna: Kolokotronis, the man who runs the post office, with his shepherd's crook; Yiannis the postman; the Teris brothers, owners of two rival shops, tiny cafés which are also hair-dressing salons, as well as selling groceries, newspapers and magazines, stationery and bus tickets; Marigo and Fotini, the two old spinsters who are our neighbours; Tasos Bitounis the butcher; Helen and Golfo the two shepherdesses; Miss Vaso the teacher; and the boys and girls who became friendly with Yorgos and Margarita.

The first few times I was only allowed to go for walks in Zatouna under guard. In the morning we would drop in to the café for an ouzo. In the afternoon there was my lesson in Byzantine music in the church of Panayia, under the direction of the choir-master; my guards sing Byzantine psalms with us. In the evening another call at the café with the guards, Lambis and the postman. More ouzo. I have to sign the register at the station twice a day. Myrto is confined to the house, and the children are at school. Time for meditation, to reflect on myself. And time for creative work, but this did not come back for several months. The first problem had been to get my piano from Athens. The whole village wanted to give me a hand to get it up to my room.

However for five months—150 days—I look at my piano without touching it. It is impossible to compose anything. I am living in an iron collar which is choking me: the absurdity of these distressing measures, but above all the firm belief that Zatouna is a trap and that I am caught in it. Each night I expect someone to come for me, to throw me into a ravine and make me disappear in an 'accident'. My nerves are at breaking point. My spirit is afflicted.

Marousi (prison), November

At last! they have decided to bring me before the tribunal. Some months before the dictatorship, six EDA deputies—and I was one of them—had addressed a solemn warning to the Premier of the day putting him on his guard against a seizure of power that was being prepared by the Army. Some months after the putsch a general lodged a complaint against us for...defaming the armed forces! But the colonels hesitated to bring such a trial and kept adjourning it, giving as a pretext my physical inability to appear. Sometimes they pretended I was ill, and sometimes that snow had cut communications with Zatouna. But now they finally bring me to Athens and the hearing is to begin.

Very early one morning they came to the house and took me to the station. The Governor of Arkadia was there with the director of Security for Tripolis. My wife and children are also getting ready to leave. They lock me in a room and make me undress so I can be searched. Then we go to the square by the church, where the cars are parked which are to take us away. Beyond the church I can see my wife and the children. The Governor and the police captain go up to her and say a few words. I imagine that they are wanting to bid her farewell and give her reassurance. It is only on my return to Zatouna that I am to learn what this façade of politeness was concealing:

'Dear madam, prepare yourself and your children to be searched.'

Three pairs of eyes are trained on me. I read in their expressions: 'Are we ever going to see you again? Where are they

172

taking you? Perhaps they lied to us? Perhaps they're taking you somewhere else and not to the trial?' And this Greek officer, this Christian, who is daring to submit them to a search...

But at this moment I did not know that, so that when he comes back to me and announces our departure I look at him almost with sympathy.

The white jeep of the Dimitsana police leads the way, followed by the Governor's Austin. Then comes our car, and the vehicle of the Tripolis gendarmerie brings up the rear. The police are armed with machine pistols. After we are through Tripolis the Governor leaves the convoy. I get into the vehicle with the captain. Another stop, at Mylos. A guard goes to get us some 'souvlaki'.[3] At the Corinth Canal a jeep draws up alongside. The captain exchanges a few words with a colonel. Then more cars carrying plain clothes men come to join the line. A line of vehicles at the end of the road: another stop for another relief. After these interminable changes in the composition of the convoy we finally arrive in the capital. A long dialogue with the police captain. I tell him:

'The others don't appear to have much confidence in you...'

'They're normal security measures.'

'It's clear that they take fright at the slightest thing. They're afraid I might bribe you and that we might make a run for it together!'

'To do what?'

'To go along with Mr Karamanlis's orders.'

'What orders?'

'Hasn't he demanded of all Greek officers that they overthrow the factionists? And you're pretending not to know about it?'

'Mr Karamanlis has demanded that?'

'Sure he has!' the driver says, laughing.

'You see! And to think it's I who have to tell you what your chief has said!'

'But you, Theodorakis, you haven't exactly refrained from chasing him from power, this Karamanlis...'

'Certainly I haven't. But in the meantime another dangerous wild animal has made its appearance and its aim is to devour us both. In a manner of speaking, of course, for it is the wild animal which will end up being devoured by us.'

'On this point you are mistaken, Theodorakis. They're sturdy men and they have big patrons to protect them.'

173

'So let's form a common front: we have the people, you have the arms!'

'Whoever holds the gendarmerie holds Greece.'

'Is the gendarmerie on the side of the king? Yes or no?'

'It's the king who fucked it all up so we got in this mess!'

'His mother brooded too long on him!'

'They laid a nice little trap for him!'

'Not them. The Americans. It's the Americans who want Papadopoulos.'

'If the king forms a government with Karamanlis, then the gendarmerie will go with them.'

'It's the gendarmerie who have the power.'

'But who is at its head? For it's the head which controls everything.'

'Karamanlis has only to make a new statement and then we'll see,' says the driver.

I nod agreement.

'Don't be deceived, Mr Theodorakis. Even if Karamanlis returns to power, you'll still not get out of prison. As far as you're concerned, Greece is finished, done for.'

'And don't bank on aid from outside.'

'Not from anywhere!'

'Ha! Ha! Ha!'

'And would you be pleased with that, with an arbitrary régime? No more laws, no more lawyers, no more procurators? The people are simply told: "You are sick and we're putting you in a plaster cast..." Do you approve of all that? That generals, parliamentarians and scholars are arrested. That people are tortured.'

'Those who lead us have force on their side...'

'It's you who are handing it to them...Couldn't we agree on certain fundamental rules?'

'Which rules?'

'Respect for the Constitution, for liberties and the rights of citizens in a democracy?'

'OK. Good. But what good is it, even if we do reach agreement?'

'It's the leaders who must agree.'

We reach Marousi, which is a suburb on the Kifisia side of Athens, on the way to Mount Penteli. We enter the courtyard. Sentries and officers approach us. It is dark. The 'delivery'—of

174

me!—takes place inside the building. The register is signed and my guards leave. They are relieved by others. Once again the ritual of the complete search. We go up an interminable staircase. Wrought iron. Bars. Bolts. It is a former private house which the gendarmerie bought to instal its mobile services, 'The Hundred', as they are called. The dictators converted the whole of the first floor into a de luxe prison. They put bars and barbed wire netting on the windows. Inside, a vast hall, with a large table and chairs, off which there are five or six rooms. Off the hall to the right there are toilets and showers. Most non-communist detainees have passed through here.

I look around. I am on my own.

'Choose which bed you want,' the warder says. 'We'll bring you sheets and blankets.'

The door closes again. There's a nip in the air. I go to the window. The tight trellis of barbed wire completely blocks the view. And the nearest houses are at least a hundred metres away.

Down below, the sentries are stamping their feet to keep warm. A good moment to take a shower and go to bed.

The door opens. An officer asks:

'Have you eaten?'

'Yes, we had something on the way.'

He opens a cupboard and gets out a bottle with a little whisky in it and a tray of kourabies.[4]

'Here's a present from Mr Peponis!'

'Peponis? Where is he, then?'

'Only yesterday he was held here. He fell ill and he was transferred this morning. He had found out you were coming and that's why he left you this present...with his regards.'

'Thank you.'

'And you? What's going to become of you? Are you going on with this martyrdom for long?'

'What else can I do?'

'Who are you going to send *your* letter to?'

'What do you mean?'

'I mean a letter like the one Kazantzakis addressed to Greco.'

'Ah! Well, perhaps I could address it to Kazantzakis himself...'

'Do you like him?'

'As a Cretan, yes.'

'I adore him! Do you know his "Letter to Greco"?'[5]

'I must confess I don't.'

'I'll lend it to you. I'll go and look it out.'

I get undressed quickly and dive into the shower. When I get back to the cell, I find the officer sitting on the end of my bed, immersed in Kazantzakis.

'Excuse me. It's been such a long time since I had a good shower! Just let me lie down.' I stretch out on the bed and get warm again. A feeling of great calm comes over me. The journey has tired me a lot.

'I've underlined all the relevant passages. Do you want me to read them to you?'

'With pleasure!' I say enthusiastically, and thinking to myself: what a bloody lot we Greeks are! We kill one another, we imprison one another, we bash one another about, and yet where else would you find an officer reading passages from Kazantzakis to a prisoner in his charge!

He has a sing-song voice which trembles with emotion. He reads slowly, with a sort of fear, as if he was discovering the words for the first time:

'Achieve what it is impossible for you to achieve.'

28 November

My appearance before the tribunal has been an opportunity to see my parents, my brother and my friends, and during the journey in the Black Maria I noticed with some joy—albeit fleetingly—the bustling streets of Athens.

On the accused bench I found some dear friends. It seems the case has been adjourned again...on the pretext that the prosecution is not present.

I went back to the prison in the same car as Kanitis; he is at the Partheni camp on Leros. He asked me, on behalf of his friends and himself, to take the initiative in setting up a new party of the Left.

I am brought back to Zatouna by Egaleon[6] gendarmes. They discover the wild setting of Zatouna and it curiously seems to give them a certain admiration and respect for me: 'They must have been afraid of you to stick you out here!'

As soon as I am back in Zatouna I set to work. Since I have been in the village I have written a study of bureaucratic dogma-

176

tism, another on the possibilities for a new move by the Left, called 'The Third Way', and finally, in a search for the bases for a new anti-bureaucratic revolutionary party, I have studied the possibility of using the people's committees as primary cells.

I spoke of these works to Kanitis and promised to send him a statement on the creation of this movement as soon as I could. But meanwhile I launch an appeal to the two Great Powers.

Open letter to President Podgorny and President Nixon

Excellencies,

I understand that you are shortly to begin bilateral negotiations to settle great international questions upon whose solution the future of Mankind will to a large extent depend. I am certain that the thoughts of all peaceloving people are with you and wish you every success in taking decisive steps towards international détente and mutual understanding.

I know that the question which is now preoccupying the Greek people is of minor importance beside the great questions of disarmament, the war in Vietnam and the danger of a new war in the Middle East.

However I believe I am expressing the thoughts and feelings of all Greek people when I address this dramatic appeal to you: Think of Greece! Maybe our national question does not weigh heavily in the balance of world interests. Nobody is pretending it does, but we do consider it to be a moral question, a question of justice, in the eyes of history.

In fact, all the misfortunes which have befallen our country in the past three decades are basically a result of the fact that your antagonism has manifested itself, and is continuing to manifest itself, particularly acutely in this part of the Aegean.

Right at the beginning of the war our country joined the grand coalition of free countries which fought and defeated Nazism. But while all the other peoples have made and are continuing to make advances in the direction of progress and prosperity, the Greek people, although the first to make sacrifices in the common fight, finds itself once again enslaved and a victim of the successors of fascism. Did we deserve this cruel fate?

177

I beg you to take yourselves back to the year 1940, when Greece gave the peoples struggling against fascism their first victory in the mountains of Albania. For that victory Greece was cruelly punished by the invaders who, apart from terrible destruction and mass executions which cut down the flower of our people and ruined the country's economy, inflicted the inhuman torture of famine on the people of Athens: in the winter of 1941 about three hundred thousand Athenians died of starvation.

I beg you to remember especially the heroic battle of Crete in the spring of 1941, which again lightened the darkness of a Europe under occupation and forced Hitler to delay his aggression against the Soviet Union.

Do you remember, too, the Greek people's resistance to the Nazi occupation; the immense trials and sacrifices of our indomitable people; the great contribution of the resistance to the common struggle, if only by virtue of having made necessary the permanent stationing of eleven German divisions on our territory.

In fact, our country—like many others—fell into the holocaust on the altar of the liberty of the peoples.

I remind you of all this, Excellencies, because I don't want to go back to the very ancient titles of the Greek nation and because I also want to say that our country is not just a strategic dot on the map of the world—it is, above all, a living people, worthy of its history, since it is still defending the great human values.

I pass over what followed the Liberation, not just because what happened then is well known to you but also because my heart can no longer bear the memory of the tragedies of the civil war. Do the mistakes of that period lie only with us?

Is the Greek people incapable of managing its own affairs? Are we Greeks so undeveloped and so backward as to descend again, after so many struggles and sacrifices, to the final degradation of the evils of fascism, dictatorship and the law of the jungle?

No! The fault is not the Greek people's alone. Greece's misfortunes are due to the fact that we are situated (territorially and historically) at one of the nerve centres of the confrontation between you.

Today, after the dramatic events of three decades that have thrown our people into confusion and as a result of the antagonisms between you we are being dragged into a new tragedy. Now, you are in a position to make amends for a monstrous historical injustice for which you bear most responsibility—by helping our people recover the liberties and rights for which millions of people, Russians and Americans among them, gave their lives during the last war.

I am well aware that this appeal pays no heed to the cynical realism which is called for in international relations. But my intuition still leads me to hope. Greece stands before you. She is laden with history: covered in blood and tears. Greece, the symbol of civilisation and humanism, asks you to do something great and noble. In the name of her history and of the great sacrifices of her children for liberty and democracy, free Greece from the net of your differences and conflicts in which she is caught! Help her people to embark upon the road of democracy and national recovery! Make Greece the centre and temple of peace! And come here, to the country of the Olympiads and Delphi, and build with all the peoples of the earth, the new world peace!

Zatouna, 28 November 1968

Christmas—Appeal to U Thant

I decided to address the following protest appeal to the Secretary-General of the United Nations. I have no reason to think any notice was taken of it.

To U Thant, United Nations Organisation

From my far off exile I am following the efforts which you are making for the consolidation of world peace and respect for the rights of man. Confident that I am addressing a friend of Man and a sincere defender of civilisation, I wish to put my case before you as an example of what a free man can become in present-day Greece.

I am a composer of symphonic and popular music. Since the age of fifteen, that is in the past thirty years, I have written about ten symphonic pieces, two oratorios, a popular opera, three ballets, music for classical Greek tragedies, film music, and over two hundred popular songs.

In 1962 I founded and directed the Athens Little Symphony Orchestra and in 1966 I was director of the Pireaus Municipal Symphony Orchestra.

Between 1960 and 1967 I gave hundreds of concerts with my ensemble in dozens of countries and in front of hundreds of thousands of people. My songs, and my music as a whole, circulated and still circulates in most countries of the world in hundreds of editions and several thousand copies. In my own country sales of my records account for forty per cent of domestic production. I consider my most important work is setting to music the poetry of the greatest contemporary Greek poets, whose work thereby has become known and loved by the popular masses. I have dedicated my life and my work to the cultural rebirth of my country and I consider that in this field Greece has in the recent past been able to offer some magnificent achievements. In fact, Greek culture, which is imbued with national tradition, is an essential factor in the development of our people.

I hope that these few pieces of information will give you some idea of my work and the part I play in the present cultural life of Greece. I might add that I owe my election as deputy for Piraeus to this activity. Politically, I belong to the United Democratic Left Party (EDA).

One month after the *coup d'état* of 21 April 1967 the new régime placed a ban on all my work under Order No.18 of the Army Chief of Staff, and the ban is still in force. The sale, exchange or possession of any of my work and performing or listening (publicly or privately) to my music are punishable under martial law. Dozens of Greek citizens have been condemned by military tribunals because they possessed records bearing my name or because they were singing or listening to my songs.

Of course, I am forbidden to carry on my creative work. Furthermore, I am isolated in the middle of the Arkadia mountains, under the surveillance of dozens of guards. I know we are living in a period of great tragedy for the whole of mankind: thousands of people are still killing one another or are dying of starvation, and thousands more are being tortured or are languishing in prisons and concentration camps. In such conditions, does the individual case of a composer who is being persecuted count for very much?

But, I would like to hope that over twenty centuries of human civilisation may have persuaded at least a large part of mankind that the spiritual assassination of its political adversaries by a régime is as abject and intolerable a crime as their physical extermination.

I desire for 1969 world peace and success for your noble work.

With my greatest esteem,
Mikis Theodorakis

A little later, on the occasion of a visit to Greece by a commission of enquiry of the Council of Europe, I sent a letter in the same vein as this one and it cost me dearly, for the persecution and restrictions became a lot worse.

30 December

Yesterday Myrto and Margarita went to Tripolis to meet Nicos and Jacques Perrin, the actor who is producing the film 'Z' (Perrin has to hand over the scenario to them). On the orders of the chief of police of Arkadia, they decide to search my wife and daughter. In the evening, in front of the school, they wait in the rain and fog for the lieutenant and sub-lieutenant of the gendarmerie and five guards to undertake this search...

This evening, 30 December, I write a poem which was to become a song, 'Arkadia I'.

ARKADIA I
(Poems by Mikis Theodorakis)

1

Ancient mountains, mountains of Arkadia,
Proud unsubdued mountains, loyal mountains.
Honour has become dear and scarce, has died.
A child's in pain, my child
A prisoner, I contemplate the firs,
The trees, my only hope.

181

2

My son is nine, my son is nine.
Nine winters, nine summers. A thunderbolt his glance
He holds the seas in his two hands
They have raised his arms, pinned his shoulders to the
        wall,
They measure the sound of his breathing
And listen to his little heart
As in a Jewish ghetto
With savage German guards around
Zatouna 1968, my third place of exile.

3

The snows of Russia deep, the North Wind blows,
The fair race will come, the wretched slave awaits
They send us love songs, flowers, ardent words,
The others send us warships into Faliron Bay
Slaves groan in pain, an entire generation lost
They all promise us paradise for 1999.

4

The ears of the West are blocked, its sight cut off
The consumer's community deeply veils your soul
Your culture a smoking ruin, your words mosquitos
Flying over the marsh of industrial production
Bearing fever, lies, hypocrisy
Half a million dead in Indonesia
Concentration camps in Europe
Banishments near the Acropolis, you hear nothing,
You see nothing, in your 1969 model
You drive to your death at 120 mph

5

I'm a European with two ears, one to hear and one not.
Should Czech, Russian or Pole groan, the heavens fall
If a negro, Greek or Indian is in pain

It concerns me not, let God see to it
High up on Hymettus, a secret exists.
I'm a European, with two ears, one listens to the
     East
Fascism is once more knocking at my door,
I'm quite deaf to all that.
I've two ears, a big one and a small one
So I constantly enjoy my culture.

So on the evening of a day of waiting, in which I had to put
up with humiliating measures being taken towards my family, I
embarked on one of the most productive periods of my life; I
began the cycle of the 'Ten Arkadios'.

Meanwhile the scenario of 'Z' was being held at the police
station in Zatouna. From there it was taken to Dimitsana and
Tripolis and it ended up in Athens, where the Commandant of
General Security, a certain General Velianitis, a fanatical character, summoned my lawyer.
    'But it's the story of Lambrakis!'
    'It never occurred to me.'
    'And you have had the audacity to give this to Theodorakis!'
    'I didn't know what it was. I'm only a lawyer. I only sign
contracts.'
    'And they're to make a film of it? And they're going to elicit
the people's sympathy over the plight of a communist?'
    'I fear so.'
    'I'm going to put you in prison: so you'll never see the sun
again.'
    'Too kind! But what about the scenario?'
    'Get out, or I'll have you arrested...'
So I was not able to read the scenario. I gave my consent to
my music being used in the film, without my being involved. I
merely indicated some of the songs I had written between 1962
and 1966 which bore some relation to Lambrakis. For example
the song about 'The Child Who is Smiling', which was based on
the poem by Brendan Behan. Our people had associated it with
the memory of the deputy from Piraeus after his assassination.
The tune became the theme of 'Z'.

Some weeks before—on 5 November—when the trial of Alekos

Panagoulis[7] was about to open I had written the words of a song for which I was to write the music two years later, when I was in Milan in October 1970 on my first foreign tour.

For Alekos

When you knock twice
Then thrice, then twice again
Dear Alekos
I'll open to you
I have prepared you a meal
I've got clean clothes for you
And a comfortable bed.

When you knock twice
Then thrice, then twice again
Dear Alekos
I shall see your face.
You hide two braziers in your eyes
In your breast a thousand hearts
Hammer out your despair

When you knock twice
Then thrice, then twice again
Dear Alekos
I'll think about your escape
I see you in your narrow cell
The first to open the dance
At your own funeral!

Two productive months!
January 1969

Through underground channels I receive a new collection of poems by Manos Eleftheriou, 'The Murderer's Bazaar'. Now that inspiration has returned, I write continuously.

Eleftheriou sends me a series of his most recent poems, 'For Mother and Friends'.

ARKADIA III
(Poems by Manos Eleftheriou)

1

In an Orchard in a Garden

In an orchard in a garden
On a Sunday afternoon, a Sunday fête day
I met some friends and then we strolled along
Through the streets of Terpsithea to Pasalimani
Today the orchard is sombre as are the friends
And to stroll is but a dream for when the Sundays
     return.

2

O Sweet Celestial Mother

O sweet celestial mother of the tree of paradise
I have buried your blessing at the foot of the mountain
A spring has gushed up into the light
It has come out of the darkness like a singing bird
O sweet celestial mother, eternal dream
Once more I need your blessing to suffer my evil
     in patience.

3

Charon's Mother

Charon's mother sits on the steepest incline
Hearing her groan thus the houses trembled
The North Wind whipped the trees
She addresses a prayer to the Virgin and her
     only son
More than three hundred go to carry it
Her thoughts spur them on in their thousands
Among the silver streams the Virgin adorns
     the birds
Her son smiles at her
The mother of Charon says no more, will never
     speak again.

185

4

They Call You Mother of Christ

They call you mother of Christ, I call you Saint
Barbara
Key of the castle shut in the torment
of the struggle
Wherever you are, from wherever you come, whatever
your tongue may be
Whoever your companions on the journey, you will
never turn back
They call you mother of Laron, mother of Pontius
Pilate
But in secret you speak and weep when the hour of
death sounds.

5

O Tender Loving Virgin

O tender loving Virgin, o mother showing me
the way
Now that my heart in my breast is full of gall
You who were once a mother know the secret cracks
Opened by joy, by pain, by stubborn time
You who were a mother and now suffer, take away
this valiant son
Deep into exile, pursued by the dark moon.

6

You Were a Garden

Time is but a repetition, the world merely throbs
I have drunk every one of these mortal poisons
You were a garden—now destroyed. You were a
bird in the trees
The suffering of my heart has become a dark mass
Your words were a balm but you are now far off
And now life too has made me mad.

I am now on the look-out for other poetical texts. At this point
in my development I feel capable of moving farther along the

road opened up by 'Axion Esti'. I send anguished messages, but no text turns up. The searches increase and are now very rigorous: they keep most of my books and writings. While waiting for a new work, I take up 'Averof Epiphany' again and put it in its final form. In desperation I try to write the text for my planned oratorio myself. But my imagination plays tricks with me and in the end I write 'Exodos'.

EXODOS

'The soldiers came to arrest me while I was asleep. They made me undress and ordered me to kneel down. Then they tied my elbows behind my back as the Americans do with Vietcong prisoners. When Maria came in I felt ashamed and asked them to put my pants on. They put on my pants and my trousers. I was barefoot and I told Maria to put my shoes on. She bent down in front of me and as she was tying the laces I whispered: "Courage, Maria".'

Evangelos was in a deep sleep and he did not see the large shadows which dragged behind them microscopic soldiers.

'Hello, Georgy!' a voice said to him in the purest Greek. What news today?' But Georgy didn't hear. His ears were glued to a transistor radio which was broadcasting the movements of Steel. He recognised Johnny's strident voice... Hello, Johnny, he thought in his purest Greek, and glanced at his watch. Two more minutes and the fortress will be ours! Two minutes, a familiar voice echoed inside him. But where had he heard it before? Evangelos thought he was living through a nightmare. But it didn't stop him smiling in his sleep. Was he hearing a song? But who was going to send warning to the fortress? What were its walls made of? Nobody had ever spoken to him about it. But Johnny's voice was clearly heard: 'One minute! One minute!' But what was going to happen in one minute? Now he could actually 'listen' to his thoughts, which were saying, like a radio transmitter, and in the purest Greek: 'In one minute! In one minute!' Yes, what was going to happen? He put his hand to his ear. Georgy's thoughts were then echoed by an infernal tumult. 'Could that be the voice of

God?' he said to himself, smiling in his sleep. In fact, eight million men were snoring. And above their sleeping could be heard the shrill feminine voice of Steel: 'OK, Georgy!' Georgy threw the transistor into the air and started to dance, yelling in the purest Greek his raucous tenor could manage: Zero! Zero! Zero!

Zero! Zero! Zero! the little soldiers said and immediately fell head over heels, while their shadows were cast like heavy threats and they began to rise in the air like balloons.

'Bravo, Georgy!' the voice repeated in the purest Greek, 'you good boy!'

On 3,650 metres the voice was overlaid with background hiss, but then there was a succession of incomprehensible phrases: Bayo kanou bakavou.

The little soldiers made the sign of the cross and cried out: 'Glory be to thee, O Lord, and blessed be thy works! Thou hadst abandoned us for so long! Thou hast just remembered us. Thy Grace now comes down upon our heads!'

Unconsciously they all held their hands to their heads: their heads were no longer there and they were reassured. Life is so much easier when one doesn't have a head, they said to themselves. But they soon noticed that they couldn't think without their heads and that as a result their thoughts no longer belonged to them. Nevertheless their thoughts still existed! The transistor, now tuned to the 19 metre band, broadcast the voice of God: Bayou kanou kababé bakavou. Johnny declared: 'Georgy, the fortress is now ours' and the radio then played the national anthem.

The snoring continued until the morning, imperturbably like an interminable Byzantine psalm being intoned. But by daybreak it had stopped for ever as if the earth had stifled it. When George said to them: 'I make all you good boys!' interference rather like the throbbing of a motor bike, and then a dry cough, could be heard on 3,650 metres. Did the great God have a cold, by chance? 'Close the door! Close the door of the universe: there's a draught.' Here are the little soldiers praying to the great God Bakavou. The God of the Christian pilots who were commanding the supersonic superfortresses to fly through those very draughts which were giving the great God his cold. When God gets a cold all the little soldiers get a fever and their skin comes out in a rash. Evangelos went over towards a concrete shelter. A real concrete case. Georgy was sleeping on the blue and white flag of Greece. Steel was fanning him with a blue silk scarf, for the heat inside was stifling, although there were no flies or harmful insects, for the shelter was asepticised. Johnny had climbed up the flag pole and was licking a choc-ice with evident enjoyment. The Archbishop was kneeling in a corner, silently and continually prostrating himself. Nobody was paying the slightest attention to Evangelos. Then the march of the army of the air burst forth from the occult loudspeakers, which were bawling it out at full blast. 'I'm going to become an aviator, so never again will I touch the earth, as high up in the sky I rend the clouds asunder. And if Destiny so desires, if one day I must die, then may death's kiss come to me in my plane!' Georgy jumped up as if he was mounted on springs, and stood there. When he saw him, Johnny slipped down the flagpole and stood to attention. Likewise the Archbishop, who stiffened into a military salute. But Steel was crying with emotion. The march of the army of the air stopped suddenly and Johnny stretched right out on the Greek flag. Georgy came up and fanned him. Steel knelt down in a corner and began prostrating himself and beating his chest. The Archbishop then climbed up the flagpole, taking small, jerky licks at his vanilla ice cream as he went. Not ten minutes had passed before the loudspeakers started howling again. This time it was a wild, frenetic dance dedicated to the great God Kababé, and performed to the accompaniment of a tam-tam, a gong, a scraper, a rattle and a whistle. The Archbishop threw away his ice cream cornet, slid down the pole, lifted his cassock and joined in the holy dance. While he was dancing the Bayo-kanou the other three, enveloped in the folds of the flag, were hopping about on the spot to the rhythm of the tam-tam. Then the music gave way to an atmospheric roar which was very much like the lift-off of a space rocket; this finally gave way to the voice announcing in the purest Greek: 'You are the most lovely boys to me.' They then grabbed hold of the flag at

189

each corner, knelt down and, crying with deep national emotion, intoned the Greek national anthem for all they were worth. In the last bars—'We greet you, oh we greet you, Liberty!'—Georgy for the first time became aware of the presence of Evangelos. Then suddenly they all took on a serious and solemn air. The officer who was at the head of the guard took one step forward and gave a salute. His hand was trembling:

'Aera![8] Forward!' he cried with all his might.

'Aera!' Georgy yelled, and the air conditioning could be heard coming on with a deafening noise. The officer did an about-turn and left the shelter, followed by his men. Georgy lent across to whisper something in Johnny's ear. Johnny found himself all of a sudden astride the Archbishop's back. The Archbishop, his body lurching convulsively, began to run in large circles round Georgy and Steel. Johnny cried out like a real cowboy: 'Liberty! Liberty! Liberty!' Finally the Archbishop came to rest at the foot of the concrete wall, whereupon Johnny with a flick of his wrist dropped the switch on the air conditioning. Complete silence enveloped the overheated room. Georgy then addressed himself to Evangelos:

GEORGY'S FIRST SPEECH:

Sometimes if one confines oneself to the most general
aspect of the problem, the biggest criminals were
ourselves and ourselves are none other
than those others who are ourselves
ignoring the most fundamental duties of citizens
and consequently ignoring the duty of every citizen
every citizen must know the duties which are his
towards the community
and when I say the community in the last resort it
is only made up of each and every one of us
and when I say each one, he must know
the most fundamental of his duties
as much towards others as towards himself
he himself is quite simply just a part of the Nation
and the Nation as community what is it if not a
community marching towards the destinies of the Race,
first we must rid ourselves of the mentality of the odious past,

a past which is guilty if ever any was, a past
we must forget for ever
so that we don't go on simply aiming to destroy ourselves
as individuals—individuals who
have ignored the most fundamental of their duties
towards the community as a whole.

Evangelos wanted to step back but he was not able to
because his shoes were tied together. The Archbishop moved
across towards Georgy brandishing a silver crucifix in his
right hand. Georgy piously crossed himself. He crossed himself, and laid a kiss first on the Archbishop's clammy hand
and then on the crucifix. He repeated this seven times—in
slow motion—for the benefit of the reporters and photographers who were lurking behind the doors of the shelter.

The Archbishop, turning towards Evangelos, declared:
'Thou wert blind and thou hast regained thy sight! Thou
wert dumb and thou hast regained thy speech, infirm and
thou art walking again! Thou wert in chains and behold
thou art free!'

Evangelos tried to move his arms but they were tied so
tightly behind his back that he could not make even the
slightest movement. He felt nothing but atrocious pain.
And, hard as he tried, he could not suppress a cry. But as
he was gagged with a handkerchief (in national colours),
he could only manage a feeble whinnying. Steel and Johnny
jumped up as if he was producing an earth tremor. A
whinny! A whinny amounting to a veritable national
disaster: how had a detail of such importance been able to
escape them? They quickly opened a packet of cotton wool
which they stuffed down Evangelos's throat. But Georgy was
in gay spirits. Almost overjoyed.

GEORGY'S SECOND SPEECH:

Even the idea of the deprivation of liberty
provokes in me an allergic reaction
for I am convinced that liberty constitutes
the essential vocation of all individuals,
understood as a subordination of the individual to the
community, and I am convinced that one cannot conceive

191

of a free society without free individuals.
But what is the free individual
without the obedience which flows from his duties
towards the community the community which
in the name of the whole of mankind
has conquered the Moon and is making ready
to conquer the cosmos tomorrow
it is not a question of my authorising a return to the past,
to return to a liberty which pushed the state of liberty
so far off that in the end no liberty existed but
that of the politicians, who ignored the virtuous use
of the right of liberty which the City entrusted to them
a City which did not function as a well-managed
collectivity but was on the contrary struck down with a
very advanced malady for whose treatment I shall do my duty
as an individual and as a community
since I am myself only a part of the whole
but a part which is in the front line
so that I can the better cry with all my strength:
'Aera! Forward, Greeks!' when God gives me the order.

'Aera! Aera! Aera!' Steel, Johnny and the Archbishop cried,
enraptured. And the air conditioning started up again.

Evangelos was choking with the cotton wool which was
blocking his throat. His eyes were turned upwards. Unable
to make any other movement, he jumped up and down on
the spot in the hope that he would be able to throw up the
cotton wool which was suffocating him.

In the midst of the tumult of the air conditioning, the
Archbishop was looking contemplatively and admiringly at
Evangelos:

'A miracle! A miracle!' he said. 'Thou wert paralysed
and here thou art beginning to jump! Let's all pray to
the Lord, who is watching over Greece and has saved her
from the abyss!'

He strode with dignity towards Evangelos to bless him.
But he had to move to one side as his body was blocking
the reporters' view through the keyhole. Having now taken
up a better position, he blessed Evangelos again, changing
his expression and pose several times so as to satisfy
foreign press correspondents.

Suddenly Evangelos sank to the ground, stiff as a tree. His head hit the concrete and a little trickle of blood started to form. Then Steel read out the first official communique:

FIRST COMMUNIQUÉ

'Bloodshed has been avoided. Liberties have been re-established. The people are giving vent to their joy. We have been spared another national tragedy. This is our slogan: BAYOU-KANOU-KABABÉ-BAKAVOU, which means GREECE OF THE CHRISTIAN GREEKS.'

The voice was heard on 1,650 metres amidst atmospherics which were like machine-gun fire:
'Is he walking, Georgy?'
'No, boss.'
'Is he stuck, Georgy?'
'No, boss.'
'Is he speaking, Georgy?'
'No, boss.'
'Is he breathing, Georgy?'
'Yes, sir.'
'Can he see, Georgy?'
'Oh, yes, sir.'
'Shit, Georgy.'
'Yes, sir.'
Steel was letting the saliva dribble from his mouth. He took his whistle and blew it in accordance with the agreed signal. There followed a twenty-one gun salute. The door opened and the Regent made his entrance. The Archbishop climbed quickly up the flagpole to throw pink confetti made from Kleenex. The Regent placed his right foot on Evangelos's stomach and gently put pressure on it. Nothing happened. He decided to give him a hard blow in the side. There was a muffled groan and Johnny started his sonometer. The needle went to 0.33, well below the safety threshold!

They all sighed with relief. They got out their handkerchiefs and wiped the sweat from their faces. The Regent warmly embraced Georgy. Spontaneously they all made a circle round the flag and intoned a song specially for the occasion:

THE ZERO THIRTY-THREE SONG

When the sonometer shows 0.33
liberty exists
but when the sonometer goes beyond the safety
    threshold
then security measures must be stepped up.
So for there to be genuine Democracy
the needle must never go beyond 0.33.

At the end of the song, two green lights show up on the sonometer—then three red ones, and finally the four little blue signals which had been agreed on. Johnny announced: 0.9 on 0, 10 on 00.

More lights flick on: two red ones and two green ones at the same time, followed by six blue signals and ten yellow ones. Georgy could then say: 'Let him come in!'

The door opened and there was the Journalist. Steel handed him a scarf with the national colours which he wound around his neck. His voice then came purified, through this coloured filter which had the property of modifying the arrangement of the consonants and vowels in such a way that every word he uttered was soaked in the colours blue and white. The Archbishop fanned him with his blue handkerchief. Georgy had climbed up the flagpole and was quietly licking an ice-cream.

The Journalist spoke.

'What's he say, Johnny?' Steel asks.

Johnny acted as interpreter:

'The gentleman is a journalist and an inventor. He says that thanks to the device he has invented he is capable of controlling and describing the thoughts of this man...' Johnny pointed to Evangelos.

'A thinkometer!' Steel exclaimed.

'Exactly, a thinkometer. That's precisely what we lack.'

The Journalist bows respectfully. He takes the skirt of the Archbishop's cassock and kisses it with devotion. He does it three more times to please the photographers.

'But where is this device?' asks Georgy from the top of the pole.

The Journalist was startled and boomed out something which the filter made resonate like a tune. Georgy was satisfied.

The Journalist got a pair of pincers from his pocket.

'Pincers?' said Steel.

The Journalist leaned across and whispered something in Johnny's ear. Johnny took the pincers and went up to Evangelos. He took one of his shoes off and seized his little toenail in the jaws of the pincers. Everyone burst out laughing. Then with a sharp flick Johnny drew his wrist upward and held up a piece of blood-covered toenail in the pincers. Evangelos's body was thrown into the air as if it had just received an electric shock and a howl rent the air. He mouth threw out the cotton wool, but his eyes closed.

'He can't see any more! He can't see any more!' Georgy cried.

The Journalist leaned across again and whispered something in Johnny's ear. Johnny went up to Evangelos and yelled into his face:

'Are you free? Yes or No?'

Evangelos nodded Yes.

'Are you enchained?'

Evangelos shook his head. 'Are you angry?'

Evangelos shook his head again.

'And do we love you?'

Evangelos nodded Yes several times.

'Do we wish you well?'

Evangelos nodded Yes twice.

Steel embraced the Journalist for a long time and the Archbishop got up to give his blessing.

Georgy said:

'You have offered us this thinkometer and in return we make you a gift of the blue and white filter. You must put yourself from now on at the service of the truth.'

The Journalist boomed out something again which the filter transformed immediately into song. The Regent closed his eyes and beamed happily. He slipped his hand into his pocket and took out a medal which he threw in the inventor's face.

Johnny announced: 013 on 001 on 130-zero, and the

door opened. Evangelos's brain was now racing away so much and so well that he caught the thinkometer off its guard: its needle was reading wrong. He was obsessed by a single thought which was invading his mind: how could he send warning to the walls of the fortress, how could he join them? And first he had to find an answer to the question: what were the walls made of? Evangelos told himself that it was best not to open his eyes again. Everything was now familiar to him. He had been able to lose his liberty without feeling a thing; he had not even been aware of it. Someone stumbled on his bruised foot. He half opened his eyes cautiously and saw the Scientist, who was saying:

'To regulate the breathing at will there's only one means left for us to try, and that's to cut the blood flow to the brain. In theory this could bring about the physiological death of the subject. But it is nevertheless possible for us to keep an organism alive while it is cut off from the brain, by plugging his respiratory system directly into an IB 5 118 which provides the necessary oxygen, starts the subject inhaling and generally ensures normal respiratory functioning. From there it is possible, with the aid of a small manometer, for us to regulate the rhythm and intensity of respiratory output.'

'Which means, to put it in simple terms,' Steel interrupted, 'that it would be possible, for example, for me to place this manometer on my writing table and control respiration at a distance?'

'Right.'

'And what do you mean by "organism cut off from its brain"?' asked Georgy.

'I mean by that that the brain—and therefore the entire nervous system—is in a state of physiological death.'

'Very interesting, very, very interesting,' Johnny said.

'In that case, can one still speak of conscience?' the Archbishop asked the Scientist.

'From a purely clinical point of view, no. But from a more general philosophical point of view one could answer that in the affirmative since we are in the presence of an organism which is being kept alive.'

196

'And in your opinion this organism has a soul?'

'Beyond question, since it is continuing to live and develop in all the other parts of the body but the brain.'

'And that wouldn't be of any use to him,' Johnny felt it necessary to add.

'The most important thing for the Church,' the Archbishop then said with some solemnity, 'is the soul, which constitutes the immortal part of human existence. It's the soul which must one day stand before the Lord when the brain has become vacant. Therefore, what does it matter if a perishable element—like the brain—is destroyed AFTER or BEFORE final death? In my view, the problem doesn't even arise. And that's why the Church blesses this act which our brother is going to perform. He is our fellow-creature and we are all just his most humble and devoted servants.'

'Well, doctor, what are you waiting for? What's holding up the treatment?' Georgy asked with some impatience.

'First, the prisoner must be transferred to the surgery block.'

'Prisoner? Prisoner?' the others all cried out in unison.

'Where have you seen a prisoner here? We simply took the necessary measures—the most vital measures,' Georgy roared at the Scientist, 'to protect him from himself. For his life was in danger from his own strength. If he had had free use of his legs he would have fallen from the top of a building. If he had had free use of his hands he could have stuck a knife into his heart. If he had had free use of speech he would have been able to say idiotic things which would have damaged his brain. And if he had been left with the free use of his own thoughts it would have led him to commit a crime against himself. Suicide, in fact. But unfortunately he is continuing to breath in a senseless, wild way and this may turn out to be very bad both for himself and for our work, which, as you say, is aimed exclusively at saving him. That's why we've called you here. For, and you're perfectly aware of this, the free use of the breathing function can bring all sorts of ills like pneumonia, pleurisy, aerophagia and other dangerous complaints. So our work is profoundly liberating. However I admit that certain details may lead someone who is not very mature politically to draw wrong conclusions. That's what's happening in your case

197

and I cannot accept it, for you are a scholar, an individual who dedicates his life totally to abstract meditation and who is very far removed from the problems which beset ordinary mortals. You constitute a social élite and I invite you to remain up there with your noble preoccupations. It is up to us to look after everything else. And when we need your services again we'll call on you.'

The Scientist coughed discreetly, as he was already absorbed with the technical details of the operation he had to perform on Evangelos, to cut the blood flow to his brain. This enslaved body before him caused him no concern at all. He observed by his clothes that he was an inhabitant of a working-class suburb. He had once had to go and look after people in such an area, years ago. At this moment he was thinking of the thirty or more patients who were waiting for him in his consulting rooms, as they did every day. Thirty at five hundred, that's fifteen thousand drachmas a day. Or 450,000 drachmas a month. Not counting the extras. He really must buy himself a new yacht. He's thinking of a Dutch one which has just come on the market.

Then he noticed for the first time the little pool of blood which was forming under Evangelos's head. He shuddered. He noticed a sort of flash between the half-closed eyelids of the poor, unfortunate Evangelos. The Scientist recoiled involuntarily. Is it possible, he asked himself, that this look could have such force when I've just been told that this man no longer has any thoughts? And it's not the look of a madman. It reminds me of something, but what?

His thoughts then left the yacht and went back several years into the past, to a day when he had encountered a similar look. Near the university. Flags were waving in the wind. Songs and cries were coming from every side as the Germans threw grenades into the crowd. But that didn't stop the crowd surging forward. The Nazi soldiers were hiding behind the tanks.

Beside him a young girl was marching with a Greek flag. One of the tanks came towards her. Everybody fled. The young girl did not move. He saw her staring at the tank. It came towards her and her body was crushed beneath its tracks. But the expression stayed on her face.

It was exactly the same expression in this man stretched

198

out in front of him. Had nothing been lost, then? 450,000 drachmas a month, that is 5,400,000 drachmas a year. Not counting the rest. And to think he might himself be in the same position as this man. But it was not so—the thought comforted him. To each his own fate, he thought to himself, almost aloud. He thought of the operation with less enthusiasm.

Evangelos had fainted. And from then on he could remember nothing and did not know anything of what might have happened up to the time when he found himself inside a car.

This is what had really happened:

As soon as the Scientist had left, Georgy and his group were seized with frenzy. They all started dancing and jumping on poor Evangelos's body. The Regent dealt him a fearful blow with his boot on the base of the skull. Evangelos lost consciousness. The Voice was heard again on 3,650 metres and it was still as satisfied with the news it was receiving from Georgy. It gave the order that Evangelos be sent urgently to get surgery. But the problem was that the surgery department was inside the walls of the fortress. So nobody, literally nobody, could see Evangelos or, naturally, find out the object of the operation. Deep down Georgy and his friends were pathologically afraid of the walls, although outwardly they boasted of having built them. This amounted to saying, in other words, that these walls served their own purposes.

This summer the air was rather icy. Night came and Evangelos felt his heart twinge with the cold. He sat down on the edge of his bed and without thinking put on his heavy boots. He slipped his pullover on over his pyjamas and went out into the garden. He sat down on a stone, looked up at the Pole Star which was overhead and dreamt that he was in the middle of a vast plain. In the east the sky took on a pink tinge. He then noticed a black line on the horizon: it was the walls. He heard neither the crowing of the cock nor the twittering of the birds. But as day broke, a rumbling sound emerged from the ground like a murmuring from a thousand mouths at once, but each with its own distinctive timbre. The walls were singing. He turned his back on them and saw his shadow stretching out and slipping rapidly away like a snake into the yellowish plain. Suddenly he heard a noise like something catching fire or a bomb exploding, and he knew that his shadow had just smashed the walls. He did not cry. He was content simply to lift his head to the sky. But, strangely, the sky was not there any more. He turned round to the east to see the sun. But, strangely, as the sun rose, so the walls did too and the rumbling sound now became crystal clear. The sun's rays were aiming at a definite target in the centre of the vault of heaven. Evangelos began to run, dragging his shadow behind him. He must have been running for over five hours when a voice like a piercing cry swept down at his feet and opened up a very deep pit. He stopped dead and when he raised his eyes he saw thousands, millions of hands waving as if in greeting. Then he realised that the walls were alive. But when he tried to jump over the pit and go towards them, all the hands fell suddenly like so many dead leaves. A frightening noise rent the yellowish air and he saw the walls shrinking and forming once again that black line which was like a strap around the neck of the horizon.

He was still in front of the pit and his shadow was resting against an oak tree at the other end of the plain. Then, strangely, the shadow started to move independently. He thought the time had come when Man's shadow was to guide Man, and he prepared his body and his thoughts accordingly. He fell so heavily to his knees that he felt a sharp pain. Then he saw his shadow turning round him like the hand of a watch, but at top speed. He worked it out that each complete turn took ten seconds. He stood absolutely still. In his guts he felt something beginning to turn at the same speed but in the opposite direction. That held his attention for some time. He tried to think and he noticed that his thoughts were no longer indistinguishable from the shadow. The certainty of this calmed him down. He then noticed for the first time the thousands, the millions of eyes which were looking at him all with the same expression. They were all round and their white pupils were the size of green peas. They had no eyelids and could not open and close. But they were very lively eyes and one could see reflections in them like butterflies. Their force of expression was reminiscent of the brassy sounds of a trumpet.

Evangelos got up to vomit. He leant over so as not to see all those eyes and held his stomach. Suddenly his shadow turned to stone and in spite of himself he heard the Voice saying: 'EXODOS'. The eyes disappeared. Evangelos had learned that walls can see.

> 'The soldiers came to arrest me while I was asleep. They made me undress and ordered me to kneel down. Then they tied my elbows behind my back as the Americans do with Vietcong prisoners. When Maria came in I felt ashamed and asked them to put my pants on. They put on my pants and my trousers. I was barefoot and I told Maria to put my shoes on. She bent down in front of me and as she was tying the laces I whispered: "Courage, Maria".'

At last! I get Porfyris's anthology. It has been examined by the gendarmerie for two days and then sent back to Dimitsana for further examination, and from there to Tripolis. I still have to wait a week before they send me it. But most of the texts I am looking for are there. To start with, Kalvos, an epic poet of the last century, whose language is robust and grandiose. His call to arms must strike a chord in sensitive Greek hearts.

ARKADIA IV
(Poems by Andreas Kalvos)

Third Ode
The Volcanoes

Morning rays of the sun
Why do you proceed?
Does the eye of heaven
Like to see the work of robbers?

Greeks, divine souls
Who in great dangers
Have shown tireless strength
And lofty nature,

201

How during these trials
Of the homeland have you not tried
To protect the crown of laurel
From the wicked hands of such robbers?
They are many of them
Fearful to behold

But one Greek, one brave man
Can scatter them!

Fourth Ode

To Samos

All those who feel
Fear of the mailed fist
Must stay under the yoke of slavery
Freedom demands merit and daring.

Freedom—for the myth conceals
The mind of truth—gave wings
To Ikaros—if he fell
The winged one drowned in the sea

He fell from high
And died free
If you become the wretched victim
Of a tyrant, you will find an ignominious grave.

Sixth Ode

The Vows

It will be better if
The swollen waves of the sea
Drown my homeland
Like a desperate deserted boat.

On the mainland, on the islands
I would sooner see
A flame spread everywhere
Consuming cities, forests, peoples and hopes.

It would be better
If the Greeks were scattered
Throughout the world
Begging their daily bread.

Greeks, seize the sword
Raise your eyes
Here in the heavens
God is your sole protector.

If God and your weapons
Are lacking, it will be better
For you to see once more
The Turkish cavalry on Mount Kithairon.

It would be better, for
The crueller and blinder
Tyranny today
The sooner salvation!

I draw up the Statement which is quoted below. I decide that
Holy Week and Easter must be the occasion for a large demonstration on the part of all prisoners which will serve as the basis
for wider action by all resistance workers in the country and
abroad. When I send this statement to Athens I send with it
the following instructions:

1 The statement must reach into all the camps, prisons and
detention centres.
2 Committees of support, both Greek and international, must
be formed abroad. They will undertake to approach and
intervene with governments and mobilise public opinion.
3 Greeks and their foreign friends will go on hunger strike outside all Greek and American embassies and consulates
throughout the world.
4 Hundreds of black flags bearing a large X will be unfurled
outside the United Nations building and the White House.
5 Black flags will be raised in the concentration camps.
6 A massive contingent of foreign journalists must be brought
to Greece for the occasion.
7 When the hunger strike reaches its height the Resistance net-

works will move on to dramatic actions in support of it. Hundreds of black flags will be raised from one end of Greece to the other. A demonstration must be organised in the centre of Athens, with the help of students and young workers.

I considered that to prepare the ground for activity of such dimensions a state of psychological 'shock' would first have to be created. Two thousand prisoners going on hunger strike at the same time could be an important event for the Resistance and could help to rouse the 'silent majority'. The results would be well worth such a sacrifice. Naturally, I discussed this project with my wife.

'What will become of the children?' she asked. 'Could they watch you die?'

'I think they'll take me away from here...'

'In which case what will become of us? Are you going to leave us alone in their hands?'

'You won't be alone. The Greek people, the whole world will be with you.'

'But you won't hold out. The other time you were at death's door after thirteen days.'

'That's why I'm fixing a time limit of three weeks.'

'I doubt if you'll make it...And if you're left alone?'

'I have no choice in the matter...Each day that passes strengthens their power. We must create a shock...It's not a desperate act but a clear political act. Think of the effect of a hunger strike which united over two thousand prisoners of the Left, the Centre and the Right. And then, if you like, it's a way of prodding our compatriots into action. It's a way for us who are in the grip of the junta to take up the leadership of the fight again. We're risking our lives to do that...Do you think we won't be able to persuade a hundred young people to give us their support and follow our example?'

This question of time had become a nightmare. Right from the beginning of the dictatorship I felt we had to act as quickly as possible. Regardless of the cost. Before the people grow weary. Before the junta manages to establish itself everywhere. Now, during my detention in Zatouna, I watched the junta gaining ground every day. The Panagoulis affair had been a painful 'trial' for me. Here was a young student who had dared to defy the hangmen. Who was brought to the military court like a

204

lamb to the slaughter. Who was knocked about so much that he had to be given support so he could stand up. And he had insulted his judges with a sovereign contempt for death! He had even provoked them! This act of heroism was inspired directly by our national traditions. I was sure there would be at least ten or a dozen young people ready to follow this example and avenge Panagoulis. But once again intimidation gained the upper hand and I could see that the malady was very far advanced. That is why I said to myself: 'Your turn has come. What do you have left to offer? It's now or never. Maybe the abscess will burst...'

I have found among my papers my draft statement and I reproduce it here: 'I declare that I am going to begin a long HUNGER STRIKE on Easter Monday as a protest against my continuing detention and that of thousands of my compatriots. I invite all political prisoners and all those who have been exiled to the camps to follow my example. During these holy days of Easter let us take the road of sacrifice to Golgotha to alert world opinion to the tragic plight of our people.

'I invite all Greek patriots, and especially all young people who are working or studying abroad, to give us energetic support by organising hunger strikes to show that they associate themselves completely with our struggle.

'Let us receive inspiration from our heroic traditions and let us suffer further trials in the certainty that we are going to render great service to the cause of liberty and democracy which is so intimately bound up with the history of our country, with its present and with its future.

'Finally I invite our indomitable and proud people to stand resolutely beside us and to see that by undertaking this action we are placing boundless confidence in its strength, which will ultimately sweep the tyranny from power and open up before our country the path of liberty, democracy and progress.'

Myrto and I spend the night finding ways of disseminating this statement. Our imaginations are working at fever pitch. Once more we must distract the attention of the monster in whose cluches we are held. And as each time in the past, we spend anguished days and nights awaiting confirmation that the 'goods' have arrived 'safely'.

Before sending the last message Myrto says:

'So the die is cast! You have decided!'

'The die is cast.' I smile.

'Well, I'll tell you of my own decision.'

'Tell me...'

'I think that if you undertake another hunger strike you won't survive.'

'Why do you say that?'

'I am absolutely certain of it. And that's why I have decided to kill myself and the children.'

I shudder. I know Myrto is not in the habit of speaking lightly. She doesn't say much but she always does what she says she's going to do. What am I to say? I search my mind for a purely formal answer:

'After all, they won't be the first children to find themselves without a father.'

(That is exactly the reply Myrto was to make some weeks later when the Governor of Arkadia came to the house.)

I went into the little room where our children were sleeping. They were smiling in their sleep, unaware of what great horrors were being prepared for them by the very people who had brought them into the world. My heart sank and from that night on Zatouna became a hell on earth. The only weapon left to me with which to rise above it and find the light was writing music. But that was no easy matter. For I had to fight my own spirit in order to see just a little light, a little blue sky, and to hear the birds twittering as they built their nests under the balcony...You who will one day hear the 'Song of Zatouna' must think of all this and make sure that these dreadful things never happen again...The song you are going to hear will get you in the guts...

(What became of this statement? A year later, in January 1970, I was to send the same text from Oropos, announcing a hunger strike for Easter Week. I managed to get it into the camps and prisons. We had taken this decision together with many comrades, some in Greece and some abroad. No doubt they still have the different texts of these statements, along with other messages I have now forgotten. I beg them to make known to the Greek people what became of all those messages I sent at different times and what use was made of them. Did they really reach their destination? This must be looked into and they must be published all together. Surely today is the Hour of Truth?)

206

February

Seferis has broken his silence. So has Anna Synodinou. Could this be the heralding of the dawn? 'Forward, creators!' I hear the brassy voice of Angelos Sikelianos. I see him floating back and forth through the clouds like an enormous angel. I see him advancing along noisy roads. 'Forward! Help us raise the sun over Greece!' This verse of Sikelianos carries me along like a whirlwind. It is snowing. I am alone. The guards are shivering with the cold. I call them in. It is warm indoors. I offer them some Marc, some nuts and some dried figs. They take their greatcoats off. I sit down at the piano and compose. They stare at me. 'Let's start again...' I take up Sikelianos's poem again from the beginning and get right into the music. Another round of Marc. The walnut trees are covered with snow. I stop writing. 'What about going down to the café?' They would rather not. 'No, go on playing!' I cover a sheet of music. The bottle of Marc is empty. It has stopped snowing. We leave the house with crimson faces, with alcohol and music coming out of the pores of our skin. We clear the snow from the road. We go into the café. 'Yannis, I'm buying a round for everybody!' 'What's happened, are you getting married?' says Khronis. 'Exactly! I've just married my music to Sikelianos...' And one of the guards, who was watching me closely as I was writing, cries out: 'Forward! Help us raise the sun over Greece!' Lambis butts in: 'It's my turn to buy a round! Let's go and get some *mézés* from the grocer's.'

But I am only at the beginning: I stay indoors the next day and the day after that, and this goes on for over a week. The guards wonder what is happening. They show interest in the work's progress and come up the stairs to get tit-bits of information. Lambis brings me food so I don't die of hunger. They all understand that I am in another world and it makes quite an impression on them. The snow is now a metre deep. I open the door on to the balcony. The air is crystal clear. The guards have lit a fire in front of Madame Fotini's house, next door.

'Well?' they ask.

'It's finished!'

'March of the Spirit' was born.

ARKADIA V
(Poem by Angelos Sikelianos)

As I threw the final torch into the hearth,
(Torch of my life closed in time),
Into the hearth of your new freedom, Greece!
My soul suddenly lit up as if
All space were copper or as if
The holy cell of Herakleitos were around me,
Where, for years,
He forged his thoughts on Eternity
And hung them like weapons
In the Temple of Ephesus...

Gigantic thoughts,
Like clouds of fire or islands of purple
In a mythical sunset,
Lit up in my mind,
Suddenly my whole life flared up
In concern for your new freedom, Greece!

So I did not say:
This is the light of my funeral pyre...
I said, I am the torch of your history,
So let my abandoned body burn like a torch.
With this torch
Marching upright, as at the final hour
I shall light up every corner of the Universe,
I shall open the road to the soul,
To the spirit, to your body, Greece.

I spoke and went forward
Holding my burning liver
On your Caucasus,
Every step of mine
Was the first, and was, I thought, the last.
My naked foot trod in your blood,
My naked foot brushed against your bodies,
For my body, my face, my entire spirit
Was mirrored, as in a lake, in your blood.
There, in such a scarlet mirror, Greece

A bottomless mirror, a mirror of abyss
Of your freedom and your thirst, I saw myself
Moulded out of heavy red clay
A new Adam of the newest creation
That we plan to create for you, Greece.

And I said:
I know it, yes I know that your gods
The Olympians have become an earthly foundation
For we have buried them deep, lest foreigners find them.
The foundations have been strengthened twice and thrice
With the bones our enemies have buried above...
And I know that for libations and vows
For the new Temple we have dreamt for you, Greece
Days and nights more brothers have killed each other
Than lambs slaughtered for Easter...

Fate and your Fate is mine threefold
And from Love, the great creator Love
Now that my soul has hardened and penetrates
Right into the mud and on to your blood to mould
The new heart needed for your struggle, Greece.
The new heart already enclosed in my breast
Today I call with it to all comrades:
'Forward: Help us raise the sun over Greece
Forward: Help us raise the sun over the whole world.
Look, its wheel is deeply stuck in the mud,
Look, its axle is deeply sunk in the blood.
Forward lads, the sun cannot rise alone
Push with knee and chest to get it out of the mud
Push with chest and knee to get it out of the blood.
Look how we blood brothers lean upon it
Forward brothers, it has surrounded us by fire
Forward, forward, its flame has engulfed us.
Forward creators...Your burdened thrust
Support with heads and feet lest the sun sink.

Help me as well brothers, lest I sink too.
It is already on me, in me and around me,
I have been turning in a sacred dizziness with it.
The cruppers of a thousand bulls hold its base

209

A two-headed eagle above me
Shakes its wings and its scream
Resounds in my head and in my soul,
The far and near are one for me
Unheard heavy harmonies surround me.
Forward comrades, help raise the sun
So that it may become a spirit.

The new Word approaches. It will colour everything
In its new flame, mind and body, pure steel.
Our earth has had enough human flesh
Fat and fertile, we must not let our soil
Dry up after the heavy blood bath
Richer and deeper than any first rains.
Tomorrow all must go out with twelve pairs of oxen
And plough this blood-drenched land.
The laurel must blossom and become the tree of life
Our vine must spread to the ends of the Universe.
Forward lads, the sun cannot rise alone
Push with knee and chest to get it out of the mud
Push with chest and knee to get it out of the blood
Push with hands and heads that the sun may shine on
    the Spirit.'

Thus as I threw the final torch into the hearth,
(Torch of my life closed in time),
Into the hearth of your new freedom, Greece.
Suddenly my cry was strongly raised, as if
All space were copper, or as if
The holy cell of Herakleitos were around me,
Where, for years,
He forged his thoughts on Eternity
And hung them like weapons
In the Temple of Ephesus...
Just as I cried to you, comrades!

March

I am happy to have set Kalvos to music. This poet's speech is
like a torrent of lava which will submerge the Greeks and burn
its mark into their skin. That is why I have received so much

210

nourishment from the works of Rigas, Solomos and Kalvos. I felt within me a quasi-physiological need to liberate their cry and to submit to their *élan*. I was driven by this breath of inspiration from the very first hours of the dictatorship, and felt I was capable of bringing this dragon down. In my mind's eye I saw the great multitude of young Greeks storming the streets of Athens and Salonika and chasing out the tyrants.

I also saw the great mass of our brothers living abroad flowing across our borders like a river and impulsively joining the new fight. But what I did not see...

Now I am counting the days and the hours which have passed since we sounded the assault and since our bugle call has been hanging over our heads. The only ones to have heard it were the Lambrakides, the avant-garde of our youth. They went in groups to the sacrifice, and confronted the wild rage of a steel-clad adversary.

As for myself, a composer of the people, I went underground, into the world of cellars and cupboards, hunted like game by the enemies of our people, while around me the ocean which should have swept away and drowned everything in a tempest was content just to lap gently, in little waves, on the sand...

A great historic opportunity has been wasted. The tyrants would have panicked and all that would have been needed to precipitate their downfall would have been slight pressure, a brief struggle and a few sacrifices. But no party and no leader took part seriously in launching this struggle.

The people couldn't feel other than deceived and disoriented. And now we're all going to have to pay for this mistake.

The junta has got through the critical first few months. And to make it fall we shall now have to wage a long battle. From now on the changes will be slow. From now on our tactics will have to take account of this new state of affairs.

April

My wife and children are back again. The north wind has dropped. The clouds have withdrawn to the mountain tops. The trees clothe themselves in green. Makis, the only man in the village who's still young, gives me a hand in the garden. I plant carrots, beans, cabbages and sunflowers.

Zatouna is getting ready to celebrate Easter. At the foot of the big walnut tree which blossoms in front of my balcony they are going to kill three hundred baby lambs.

Daras, the shepherd who plays the violin at the café Teris, has got his instrument out:

'Theodoro Kolokotronis is waiting
for the cuckoo to sing...'

When he has finished this heroic song, which is about the Greeks' resistance to the Turks, he turns to me and says:

'When I go to sleep, my goat comes and lies down beside me. No doubt we both have the same dreams.'

Athenians who originally came from the village begin to return to spend Easter with their families. My presence in the village creates an exceptional atmosphere: furtive smiles and looks. I re-encounter the characteristically tense atmosphere of the capital. Whom can I talk to?

Kyra Lenio, the unfortunate goddess of the mountains, comes down from her hideout. She has her own story. About thirty years ago, when Kyra Lenio was young, beautiful and rich, she went up into the mountains with her animals because her mother and her sister had died; ever since then she has stayed up there, locked within her sorrow and her solitude. In the winter she comes down to sleep in the village (and without saying anything, she would leave some milk at our door each evening) and in the summer she sleeps in the mountains. This old shepherdess's faithfulness to sorrow, her pride and her dignity remind me of the quality of our Greek people, and that thought comforts me more than anything.

She stops for a moment at our door:

'How solid the oak trees are on their roots!'

'The oaks are still going strong!'

'You can speak openly. I'm not afraid of anyone. Look after yourself. I'll bring you some milk. That'll keep your strength up.'

In the church the lights and the candles are shining brightly. The Virgin is smiling at the Christ child. As I pass him in the parvis, the priest asks:

'Have you written a canticle for Easter?'

'No, a PAEAN!'

ARKADIA VI
(Poem by Mikis Theodorakis)

Paean

The majestic mountains embrace
The rocks, precipices, people and fir trees.
They have seen armies of Turks and other conquerors.
They have received the bodies of heroes
The curses of the brave.
The trees remain that shaded
The sleep of Perdikas
The cuckoo that Kolokotronis did not hear
Has come and nested in Zatouna.
In vain do my guards try
To cage his song.
The ravines take it on their shoulders
Swiftly to the olive groves
The mountains of Arcady are lofty
They control the seas
And the flute of Pan
Drowns the grunts of the barracks.

Boa constrictors, orang-utangs and monkeys
Wearing togas
Holding sceptres
Archbishops and generals commanding
Shout: 'Aera!'
Behind them are raised
Birds' feathers.

Frightened heroes abandon the marbles
Run from the poets' verses
Again seek refuge by the banks of the Lousios,
By the springs of Mount Menalon
Sharing the shade with the lark.

Guardian mountains of my homeland's valour
Your dream is the paean
Your song the gun.

Rigas Ferraios, I call you!
From Australia to Canada
From Germany to Tashkent
In prisons, on the islands and mountains
The Greeks are spread.

Dionysios Solomos, I call you!
Jailers and prisoners,
Beaters and beaten
Those ordering and ordered
Terrorisers and terrorised
Possessors and possessed
The Greeks are split.

Andreas Kalvos, I call you!
The most brilliant sun is amazed
So are the mountains and fir trees
The sea shore, the nightingales
My homeland, the cradle of beauty and metre
Today a place of death.

Kostis Palamas, I call you!
Never has such light become darkness
Such bravery, fear
Such strength, weakness
So many heroes, marble busts
My homeland, birthplace of Digenis and Diakos
Today a country of subjects.

Nikos Kazantzakis, I call you!
If the mortal forget
Who still speak the language of Androutsos
Memory lives behind grilles and sentry boxes
Memory lives in stones
It nests in yellow leaves
Covering your body, O Greece!

Angelos Sikelianos, I call you!
The soul of my homeland
A river of many shapes
Blinded by blood

214

Deafened by the groans
Paralysed by the great hatred
And great love
In equal control of your soul.
The soul of my homeland
Consists of two handcuffs
Tightened on two rivers
Two mountains
Bound by ropes
To the bench on the terrace.

The Argive plain
Swollen by whipping
Mount Olympus
Tied and hanging
From the mast of the aircraft carrier
To make it talk.

The soul of my̆ homeland
Is this seed
Laying out its roots
On the rock
You are mother, wife, daughter
Perceiving from afar seas and mountains
Secretly painting in blood
The red eggs of the Resurrection
To be hatched by time and men
May my sad country one day enjoy
A Greek Easter.

Unknown poet, I call you!

Notes on 'Paean'

'They have seen armies of Turks and other conquerors'
After the Democratic Army's retreat to the north of Greece at
the end of the Civil War in 1949, the rebels—'andartès'—who
found themselves to the south of Athens, in the Peloponnese,
were surrounded and completely wiped out by the Royalist forces.
The number of victims rose to over twelve thousand men, massacred in the space of a few weeks.

215

'The trees remain that shaded the sleep of Perdikas'

Perdikas was one of the 'Kapetanios' in the Peloponnese during the Civil War. He was well-known for his technique of surprise attack and for the extraordinary speed with which he moved his men from one region to another. He fell into an ambush and was decapitated by the Royalist army.

'The cuckoo that Kolokotronis did not hear'

Theodoros Kolokotronis was one of the heroes of the Revolution of 1821. Popular tradition has dedicated dozens of songs to him. The shepherd of Zatouna was a self-taught musician and accompanied himself on the violin. He had a particular affection for a famous song which told of the cuckoo whose song greeting the day Theodoros Kolokotronis awaited: it was a symbol of the fact that liberty was not something that could be put off. But it was obvious that the old shepherd was attached to this song chiefly because it showed he was opposed to the junta and belonged in the resistance camp.

Each time he sang it and came to the word 'Theodoros' his voice swelled enormously and everyone on the café terrace started clapping in time with the song and their faces lit up. Most of the gendarmes who were present laughed into their beards, for they too, in their heart of hearts detested the tyrants. So this song about Kolokotronis seemed magically to create a sort of national unity on the scale of this little village, a unity rooted deep in our national traditions. I ought to point out that the police had forbidden all the inhabitants of Zatouna to approach me, talk to me or even greet me. And without exception all the inhabitants of the village, every time they passed me when I was out walking with my two guards, would look me straight in the face and say loudly and boldly: 'Hullo, there!' Immediately they would summon the offender to the police station where they would threaten him. But this did not stop him saying 'Hullo, there!' next time he saw me.

'In vain do my guards try to cage his song'

I composed ten cycles of songs at Zatouna, the 'Ten Arkadias', as I called them. And I managed to get all these works secretly to Athens, and from there abroad. By what means?

First I ought to say that postal communication was impossible. Every parcel I was sent—whether it contained food, books

216

or clothes—was examined. The few things they allowed me to send were subjected to innumerable controls and all ended up with the KYP (Central Intelligence Service) in Athens. Everything which entered or left our house was the object of a thorough search by the guards. They reduced bread, cakes and biscuits to crumbs; they examined our refuse by hand, and item by item. However, all these precautions did not stop communication in both directions, which went on without interruption. I was called one day to the police headquarters in Tripolis to be told:

'They're announcing recent songs of yours again on the BBC. Songs you've managed to get out, and we're going to get into trouble for it.'

'Listen,' I tell the officers, 'I'm doing my duty. You have deported me and my family. That doesn't stop me fighting. And you, what are you doing?'

'Well, we're only puppets...'

'Well-armed puppets...'

'Yes, but... With this BBC business what are we going to look like?'

'This is just the beginning. You can expect much worse things than this.'

Where did I get such confidence? It is difficult at the moment to say, because if I gave the facts I would be endangering a large number of honest people who are at the mercy of the junta in Greece. But I can say that at Zatouna this spontaneous assistance on the part of so many people broke our isolation. Ninety per cent of the people around us were supporters, patriots, democrats and implacable enemies of the military dictatorship.

So in this way very valuable information always reached our isolated village, cut off from everything, in time to warn us that the junta was preparing to get the police to move in on us.

When the police confiscated our transistor radio one day, we discovered two others which had arrived mysteriously...On another occasion I learned that they were preparing to take my piano and my tape-recorder away and to throw me into the cell under the police station with the aim of intimidating me. So I prepared to go on hunger strike. I drew up a statement[9] in several copies and gave them to a firm friend to pass to the foreign press. It was agreed that as soon as this friend heard me utter the sentence 'I'd like some rusks' in the café he would

217

immediately go and post the texts to Athens. It was the signal that I was going to start my hunger strike the next day. Having prepared everything carefully, I had only to wait for the first offensive before going on to the counter-attack.

One evening the sergeant told me that the director of police in Tripolis had just arrived in Zatouna and wanted me to go and see him at the station. I replied that it was too late and that I couldn't go...Half an hour later the director arrived in person. I had won the first round.

'Why didn't you answer when I called you?'

'Would we have come to any agreement?'

'Is it true that you asked the sergeant to tell me that I ought to be wearing a turban because in your opinion I am neither a Greek nor a Christian nor a man?'

'That's right.'

'Is it true that you told our officer, Liberis, that if he laid a finger on your daughter you would take vengeance on his whole family?'

'Precisely. And I'd like to say again, to you and to your subordinates, that I shall not tolerate any act or indignity against my children or my wife...'

'The orders...'

'Does your uniform and your insignia permit you to hunt down and beat up innocent and defenceless children? And I give you my personal assurance that if you lay a finger on my wife again I shall tear your wife's clothes off in the main square in Tripolis...'

I gave free rein to my fury. I also wanted to show off my strength. And all of a sudden I yelled at him:

'And don't you dare make a move. It's all fixed: at a sign from me the whole world will know I'm beginning a long hunger strike...'

The naïve lieutenant-colonel was thunderstruck. He was not a bad fellow, just an official. But the result is the same when one is serving a bad cause faithfully. In the end they did not dare either to take my piano or to put me in the police cell.

'(They) shout "Aera" and behind them are raised birds' feathers...'

At the beginning of 1969 Papadopoulos made a speech to scientists. He said: 'You're the infantry and I'm your leader.

218

When I shout "Aera!", "Forward!", you will surge forward behind me!'

'And there they seek refuge by the banks of the Lousios...'
This river bears its name because Zeus bathed in it (the Greek for bath is 'loutro'). It flows between Dimitsana and Zatouna and into the plain of Megalopolis; its source is in the heart of the Peloponnese.

Letter to friends abroad

To the English section of the Patriotic Front (PAM)
(please communicate the following to the Greek Committee against the Dictatorship)

Zatouna, 23 April 1969

My dear friends,

On 21 April 1969 eight months had passed since I was exiled to Zatouna. The village is small; barely twenty families live here. It is hemmed in on three sides by mountains. On the fourth side there is a 300 metre ravine, through which the River Lousios flows. Opposite Zatouna rises Mount Menalon, which is covered with fir trees.

Our house is in the centre of the village and faces a little square. There is one fairly big room and another small one where the children, Margarita and Yorgos, sleep. They both go to the local school, which has only 25 pupils.

We spend the day indoors. Sometimes I play the piano. Sometimes we read. The children don't bother us. Myrto, my wife, hardly ever leaves the house. Throughout the autumn and winter we had rain, snow and fog. The snow here sometimes stays around until 20 May.

I have to go to the police station twice a day. Our house is under guard night and day. Two guards are at the door. A third guard paces up and down the road. At night, when the village is plunged in darkness, our house is lit up with powerful arc-lights. The state, or rather the Greek taxpayer, is spending 20,000 drachmas a month on this illumination.

Every time I go out I am escorted by two guards. I do not have the right to speak to anyone. Anyone who greets me is risking a lot: he is summoned to the police station and is submitted to close interrogation and a search...They have even undressed the women.

At the beginning I was free to go out at any time of day, but later I was forced to stay indoors for twenty hours out of twenty-four. A short time before Easter they stepped up this restriction to twenty-two hours out of twenty-four. Now I am once again able to go out for two hours in the morning and two in the evening. My walk has to be within the village. I do not have the right to go even ten metres outside it. But sometimes it happens that this timetable for my outings is not respected. I am locked in my room without any explanation. My legal position is like that of a slave in the time of the Roman Empire. I have no means, legal or otherwise, of defending my person and the members of my family against arbitrary power. Apart, of course, from our firm determination to sacrifice our lives if our honour and our ideals are at stake. 'Every time I look at you,' I said one day to a police officer who had come to visit us, 'I think I can hear the sound of jungle tom-toms.'

I am not allowed to correspond with anyone. In eight months I have sent two letters which have reached their destination (Athens), and then with a delay of two months. All correspondence from the village is opened at Tripolis. I have obtained permission to telephone my parents once a week. But even then I am not allowed to speak freely. If I say anything but 'How are you?' 'We're well...', etc, they interrupt the call. It goes without saying that the call is made in the presence of my two guards and it is certain that I am under the surveillance of at least three different departments. My 'guard' is made up of a brigadier, a captain and fourteen gendarmes. The TEA (batallions of national security)[10] of the area have been given a special task: to make a rigorous search of all vehicles, drivers and pedestrians entering the village. No foreigner is allowed to go through Zatouna. If he insists, he is given a rough time; this happened to some Germans who were brutally maltreated at Dimitsana, Vitina and Tripolis because they insisted on entering the village.

Each time my wife or my children have to leave Zatouna they are subjected to a humiliating search by a woman in the presence of the brigadier. When we first arrived one of

220

the guards forced my son, who is nine, to raise his arms and he then pushed him against a wall right in the centre of the village and stripped him. The little boy suffered a terrible nervous shock, and when he got to the house he was having convulsions; these have returned subsequently. He is now getting special treatment by a psychiatrist for his nerves. At school there are formal orders that my children shall be kept apart from the others.

But life is stronger than orders. On 25 March,[11] my Margarita played the part of 'Liberty' in a sketch put on at the school fête.[12] The whole village likes us and helps us. Even our guards try, in one way or another, to show us their sympathy. It is only the orders coming from Athens which are inhuman and barbaric.

When it was announced that the commission of the Council of Europe was about to arrive in Zatouna exceptional measures were taken. I had to be transferred to another village. Under no circumstances would I be presented to the commission. It was the same with my trial before the Court of Appeal in Athens, which was adjourned three times.[13] A team had been given the job of blowing up the road to stop me getting to the tribunal, because they knew, of course, what I was going to say. In the end the snow came to their aid. This was the excuse for them to declare that reasons of security had not permitted my transfer to the tribunal. So the trial was put off for the third time. Now it is adjourned until 25 June.

On Easter Monday we sent our children to Athens: Yorgos was showing signs of serious disturbance. On the Wednesday after Easter Myrto wanted to phone to find out how he was. They stopped us. So I shouted out from the balcony to our guards that they were not Christians, not Greeks and not men. After this incident we were permitted to use the telephone.

The first restrictive measures were applied after the visit in November 1968 of a West German television crew. They reached their height after the admirable report by John Barry in the *Sunday Times*, which started mobilisation, arrests, interrogations, etc...and for several days created great nervousness throughout the region.

At the beginning I was not allowed to use the telephone,

221

to go out or to receive books and periodicals. They confiscated my transistor radio and so our last link with the outside world was cut. Now they even stop the local bus as it enters the village and search the passengers. Needless to say, these measures, far from inconveniencing us, give us some joy, not because we are masochists but because we know it means that the action of friends is producing a powerful echo abroad. How can we express our love and gratitude to people like the West German television reporters or John Barry, who made so many sacrifices and laid themselves open to so many dangers for us?

And there are many other people, more unfortunate, who were not allowed to get to us: French, Italians, English, Germans, Dutch, Americans, unknown friends. Our gratitude is no less towards them. Also we express our thanks for the Greek-language broadcasts from all countries which are helping us in our struggle. In this atmosphere energy, far from dwindling, gets stronger and broader, as does faith in the overthrow of the tyranny and in the triumph of liberty.

As a composer, responding to my vocation, I have written here in Zatouna six song cycles which I call Arkadias. These songs—the ones I have just written, the ones I wrote yesterday as well as the ones I shall write tomorrow—are dedicated to all of you who believe in man, in life, in justice, in democracy, in liberty, and who have made the struggle to defend them the aim of your lives. They are dedicated in particular to the Greek fighters for liberty and to the friends of our people abroad who are helping us in our difficult struggle.

Having sent my music, which cannot be silenced, to the four corners of the earth, I know that I myself am invincible. Nothing can be done against ideas or against those who heroically defend them. Against the Greeks nothing can be done, and this is what I sing about.

Exactly two years ago to the day I was saying in a message that the new fight would be long and hard but beautiful. Yes, it is beautiful, this fight for liberty. The sacrifices are beautiful, the laments, the tears, the hardships, the bitterness and the deprivations are beautiful when everything is done for the people and the motherland.

Two years have already passed and a lot more time will pass before we reach the blessed moment of victory. How can one not rejoice when one knows, as I do, that with each minute that passes our people is more united? That internal divisions are becoming less sharp? That more and more people are becoming aware of the rottenness of the oligarchy, and, at the present moment, the dictatorship? That the Greek patriots who are defending freedom are becoming more and more numerous? Can one be in any doubt that the Greek people will emerge victorious from this painful experience?

Differences of view, moral failure and weakness, disputes, egoism, suspicions, and mean, calculated deeds will be lessened by the feelings of duty towards the nation. I see here the profound recognition by all political prisoners, all fighters and the entire Greek people of this unprecedented wave of panhellenism which is so good for our country and which is now emerging elsewhere in the world, especially in Europe. We shall regain our liberty united with all peoples who are lovers of liberty. Let me end with this exhortation:

Forge patriotic unity!

Organise the struggle for liberty on solid bases!

There is no path to final victory but the path of merciless struggle!

And let us never forget that Liberty is not a gift but something one wins by fighting for it!

Mikis Theodorakis

Contact with the outside world
5 May

COLOGNE RADIO: Anna Synodinou's appeal. Resolution passed by the Foreign Ministers of the Council of Europe on the Greek question.

In MOSCOW the organ of the Young Communists, *Komsomolskaya Pravda*, reproduces the *Sunday Times* article.

Nikitas Venizelos takes a stand.

COLOGNE RADIO: An SPD[14] deputy demands clarification from the Greek government of rumours about my deportation! According to the deputy, he had been told in Brussels by an official of the Greek régime that Mikis Theodorakis was completely free to travel within Greece!

There are also new irritants, one of them being the article the Athens correspondent of *Le Monde*, Marc Marceau, wrote on the second anniversary of the putsch, on 23 April 1969, and of which this is an extract:

In two years the new régime has brought in a Constitution which in principle offers a more democratic legal framework than the previous one. They have undertaken a Herculean task in reforming the State and installing a modern technical and administrative apparatus. They are doing their utmost to loosen the anachronistic links which often pervert the relations between Church and State.

Furthermore, the new leaders have managed to keep the national economy under control, to preserve the machine, and to pursue a policy of productive investment. They are endeavouring to bring together under one national flag a powerful merchant marine which is sailing under various flags of convenience. Also, they have put a stop to tax evasion, and this increases State revenues. Measures have been taken to help wage-earners, public officials and retired people. The peasants continue to be the government's main concern. The government can also take credit for its measures in the field of education: the building of new schools, the appointment of teachers, scholarships for poor students, free school books.

Le Monde, 23 April 1969

I could not restrain myself from dedicating this song to Marc Marceau in gratitude:

Marc Marceau

I may be in exile
I may obey my guards
I have every freedom
Monsieur Marceau has said so

I may be gagged
I may utter moans
I am a mighty fortress
Monsieur Marceau has said so

The Academy in Bouboulinas Street
Helps the development
Of our national economy
Monsieur Marceau has said so

Servant, slave, pariah
Have you seen another people
A slave of freedom
Monsieur Marceau has said so.

VOICE OF TRUTH broadcasts the *Sunday Times* piece.
The BBC put out the third special broadcast comprising the
'Seven Songs of Zatouna'; they had also been demanded by
radio stations in Denmark, Canada and Munich.

Yorgos's birthday. Myrto has made a Halva cake.[15] We have
put nine candles on it. Yorgos is very excited.

6 May

STRASBOURG : The European Council of Ministers addresses
a warning to the Greek government.
BRUSSELS : Statement from the Secretary-General of the
International Confederation of Free Trade Unions.
CANNES FESTIVAL: Diplomatic incident between France
and Algeria over the film 'Z' (a co-production of the two coun-
tries which France was presenting as her own).
STOCKHOLM: Twelve students go on hunger strike in
front of the University to secure the release of Panagoulis.
COLOGNE: Broadcast of a message I had sent them on tape.
Article in the *Frankfurter Allgemeine Zeitung*. A deputy in the
Bundestag asks the Greek Embassy in Bonn to provide him with
explanations for the deplorable conditions of detention.

7 May

I drank wine with the two officers who are guarding me at
Mantzalas, the butcher's. The wine is excellent but it goes to my
head. Can't sleep. I read Solzhenitsyn.
PARIS RADIO: protest from the widow of the writer,
Theotokas.

Protest by the former Premier, Kanellopoulos, before the Athens Academy.

Statement by General Akritas, the head of a resistance organisation called the National Resistance Movement.

MOSCOW RADIO: Amnesty International demands the release of the Greek deputies who are in prison. Twelve English poets demand the release of Yannis Ritsos.

The Panagoulis brothers protest at the conditions under which Alekos is held.

8 May

Presence in the region of four (Dutch?) journalists.

Rain and cold. The morning ritual of signing the register at the police station. In the evening 'accompanied' walks and a tour of the cafés. Lambis offered me an ouzo. Margarita is listening to Tchaikovsky's Fifth Symphony on the radio. In the evening Myrto comes over faint. Tasis is organising a reunion at his place. I am reading *America's Burning*.

MOSCOW RADIO: Broadcast 'Genesis' from my oratorios 'Axion Esti'.

9 May

The cold spell continues. At midday there is a downpour. The bus service, which has been withdrawn because of the bad weather, is resumed after a break of seven days. We have received a parcel for Yorgos's birthday. Magnificent Kataifi.[16] Lambis offers us a blow-out at Yannis's, with 'Patsa'.[17] A present from Takis Veriopoulos.

'Yorgos is making progress at school.' 'We've found a buyer in Athens for our DKW!' (Code phrases for our clandestine broadcasts).

11 May

COLOGNE RADIO: A listener asks for my music.

ZATOUNA: Report of a Pullman arriving with foreign tourists.

VOICE OF FREEDOM: Broadcast devoted to Ritsos and Theodorakis, with 'Romiosini' performed wonderfully by the singer, Schültze. Broadcast of a message I had recorded on tape.

BUDAPEST: A work by a Hungarian composer entitled 'You Are Not Alone', based on some of my tunes.

ZATOUNA: Three Germans are roaming round these parts. Journalists? Lieutenant Papadimitriou orders that our children be searched every day.

Two reporters from *Paris Match* have made known through radio messages that they are prepared to risk sneaking into the village and then into our house to spend an evening doing a photographic reportage.

Our hope would be that this report on our living conditions might have the same impact as the *Sunday Times* article or the West German broadcasts, that it would attract the attention of the free world to our fate and to the situation in Greece. We wanted to try every way of making this visit possible (whatever the risk of reprisals). I was asked only to provide a detailed plan of the village. Alas! This was impossible to do under the eyes of my guards, who never let me out of their sight.

But Margarita (who was ten at the time) has a phenomenal memory. So she went out to play with her ball in a different part of the village each day and brought back precise details which I drew: here there is a fountain, then the road bends, there there is a tree, and three houses, and so on.

Gradually the pieces of the jigsaw were fitted together and we had a complete and very accurate map.

But Margarita's work was not finished yet: she had to commit the whole plan to memory, for we could not take the risk of sending the piece of paper...which would certainly not reach its destination.

Then she left for Athens on the pretext of a visit to the doctor. As she had to be sent on her own, and as there was nothing visibly the matter with her, we had given her strict instructions: 'If at a bus stop they want to take you off, don't wait for them to start questioning you...Yell out very loudly who you are...The police won't dare to carry on in front of the people in the bus and they'll let you go.'

But all went off well. Margarita got to Athens, telephoned friends with a secret code, and then at their house carefully drew out her plan. It was sent to the *Paris Match* reporters, who set out. The next thing we learned was that they had been spotted a kilometre from the village and driven away. There was no reportage in *Paris Match*.

Reflections
May

The Resistance is making no headway...This must be frankly admitted and it must be stated that the opposition that has been encountered is not the only reason for it; the real obstacle is subjective—our people feel powerless and have no confidence in their own resources, because they have been betrayed by their leaders.

For my part, I refuse to subscribe to this view: I want to find the means of rousing this inert mass and, to do that, to find the way to their hearts.

I don't want to evade my own responsibility in this. I am trying to understand what is happening. This text which I found among my papers reflects the thoughts which were preoccupying me in May 1969:

> The military dictatorship is the logical consequence of the moral bankruptcy of the Greek ruling class. The aggressive scorn with which the present régime is crushing moral values is only a continuation of the contemptuous attitude which the Greek ruling class displayed to precisely the same values: hence this relentless struggle against the intellectual and scientific élite of the country.
>
> The soul of a dictatorship is never imported from outside: it is a national product (even if it is imposed and supported by foreigners). It is not a new wound but an abscess which comes to a head in the weak organism of power. The dictators are conscious of the bankruptcy of this ruling class. They rail against the corruption of political mores but they were themselves born of this process of decomposition.
>
> Having been betrayed by their leaders, the Greek people have only themselves to rely on. To give another chance to their leaders would be a tragic illusion. Our honour cannot be content to find refuge in the depths of the soul of that 'anonymous Greek' of the time of the 1821 Revolution.
>
> The dictatorship is the death rattle of a decadent society in agony. To the people's exasperation the dictators have added disgust. They have killed off the old sick animal repre-

sented by the *ancien régime* but sooner or later the whole
bleating flock will be led to the slaughter.

Let us take stock of the extent of our responsibility. It is
our own fault entirely if we have allowed ourselves to be
made fools of.

In order to be able to save our country let us at least
have the courage to acknowledge our shame.

A survivor in June

Summer makes its solemn entrance. The air is still cool. The
chrysanthemums are blooming. The trees are once again covered
with thick foliage. During my daily walk with Makis, the
adjutant, we go beyond the 'frontier'—the cheese dairy—and lie
out on an overhanging rock, with a view of the great mass of
Mount Menalon. Down below us shines the village of Dimitsana. Above, the village of Zygovitsi, resting lightly on the
shrivelled up shoulder of the mountain. It was in the deep
ravine that the centre of the underground was situated during
the period of Turkish domination. We watch the torrent of the
Lousios roaring down.

We felled two rotten walnut trees and carried the wood to
Lambis's house. Myrto has ordered some donkey saddles to be
used as seats. The framework is made of wood and then Lambis
chooses the skins and gives them to Khoulias, 'the boss of the
factory', who covers the frame. In former times Zatouna was a
flourishing town with large shops, taweries and weaving work-
shops, and it took in two parishes. Today the only things to
remain of this past are the memories and the wholesale grocer,
Sotiropoulos. This man doesn't leave his shop until almost
midday, when he goes out for lunch; he eats standing up as if
he didn't want to waste any time and as if he were used to the
style and rhythm of work of an earlier period; then he returns
quickly to his shop for his siesta behind an almost empty
window, sitting on a chair, waiting for customers long since
gone.

I flick through the pages of my anthology. I keep the
book open at Takis Sinopoulos: his poem 'The Survivor' has
something which appeals to me and which concerns me!

ARKADIA VII
(Poem by Takis Sinopoulos)

The Survivor

What place then is this?
On what slope is the head
Wide open to the sun?
The arms and legs
Devoured
By the fire of the sun?
What place is this my children?
You so tall so white
You my father so tall so white
You my mother so tall so white
What place then is this?
On what slope is the head
Wide open to the sun?
Where am I then?
In what country, in what land?
Under the buried earth
In what mountains that burn?
The watchful and hunted look
Among the dried up stones
Now that I hear the steps
And the murmur
And the imperious order
I hear the obstinacy
The boasting
The repentance and I hear
That other more serene voice
More assured
What place then is this?
Scattered pieces of glass
Here and there among the mountains
Rotting rags and paper
Here and there among the mountains
So high and white
A mute cry
And where am I?
Oh where am I?

Passing by a forest of spiders
Endlessly fleeing
Wandering in a forest of drums
Trying to make my voice heard
And all the time
Knocking again and again
Against the doors and windows behind which
These times are enclosed
The peering face announcing night
Lodging in the bosom of night
Just as the seed lodges in the earth
The coke in the brazier
Fear and despair
In the voice of men
What place then is this?

Reflections and an Interview
5 June

One might be tempted to think that life in exile flows along calmly and monotonously. It does nothing of the kind! First, there are the anxieties and the irritating difficulties the 'authorities' cause us from time to time. For my part, I try to impart an air of routine to the relations we are forced to have with those who guard us. The walk, the station, the café, the house. However, different orders come at every turn to cause us disquiet. At one moment I am confined to the house; then, gradually, the orders become less strict again and we get back into the usual routine.

Of course, we have other incidents with my jailers, who show that they are particularly irritated by the fact that I don't recognise them as my jailers, a legitimate authority, but as accomplices of a band of gangsters, and that I quite often tell them as much. 'Now everyone knows that they are in the service of Illegality,' one of my guards told me, or that they are 'just robots', as another said. So they do what they are told without thinking. There are even some who think the opposite, but they comply with their orders out of fear or because there's nothing else for them to do. Because they are 'too small', and because 'there are informers everywhere', and so on.

7 June

Seferis[18] has spoken. It was expected that the intellectuals would then speak out *en masse*. In the end sixteen intellectuals—and not those most in the public eye—followed Seferis. Then—silence. But then the great actress Synodinou speaks out and hopes revive. But time passes. Nothing...Today the front has moved elsewhere: to the Council of State! The 'revolt' of the magistrates is bringing judicial chaos. In fact, it is a powerful blow to the heart of the régime. Hopes are rising again. Who will be next? The clerics, the men of science? The workers, maybe? Or even the students? No!

Shortly before the magistrates' demonstration there were arrests of generals in the Army and Air Force. This was also a terrible blow for the junta: it lost its last friends among the officers. These things took place in the past two or three months. A lot? Perhaps! But they seem very slight to us.

We think Greek society is gravely sick, that it is suffering from a social malady, the most serious there is—'indifference'. For these are certainly problems which can be analysed and explained politically, but there is also personal dignity, and it is this which is really lacking, because it is eaten up by indifference.

One cannot demand too much of the ordinary citizen who is unarmed in the face of violence and arbitrary rule and whose only strength is to be able to take part in an organised struggle. So long as the organisation is lacking—and the parties are responsible for this—one cannot expect acts of serious resistance on the part of anonymous and isolated citizens.

But what about *well-known* citizens? The case of Seferis and Synodinou proves the moral collapse of all distinguished Greek intellectuals and artists. Like the case of the three professors at the University of Thessalonika who cancelled out the moral authority of hundreds of other university teachers. And the behaviour of the members of the Council of State is a lesson for all those magistrates, senior officers, civil servants and other individuals who continue by their authority to stand as guarantors of those who have seized power.

And the students. Profound as their theories may be, they will never convince me that the conciliatory attitude of the student youth towards the régime is justified. I freely admit that the weakness of the parties and the organisations, and the mistakes that have been made, and so on...are partly to blame for this. But still, beyond that, there is the student, the Greek student, with his well-known tradition of heroism. What does the student need in order to act? Just courage! Is there any lack of contemporary examples? Kiaos, Dariotis and Panagoulis. And the hundreds of heroic students who have preferred the rigours of illegal activity and tortures and who are still in prison or exile. A group of three students can become a terrible force. Ten such groups can shake a university. A hundred can shake the dictatorship. A thousand such groups can overthrow the tyranny.

What can we say, though, about the 'free Greeks'? Those who are abroad. One wonders what they are doing. There are certainly many obstacles, but more than twenty-five months have passed since 21 April 1967. I know what I am talking about and my judgement is a hard one.

...In my view, for a certain period, forms of *collective* struggle against the dictatorship have to be found which do not expose the ordinary citizen but which do teach him the art of struggle, especially by organising him in groups, so as to strengthen his will and his faith, and by making him see the extent and importance of his power when he does act in a group, shoulder to shoulder with people who detest the tyranny. There is no need for complicated analyses and statements to achieve this effect. What is necessary, though, is to discover the appropriate form the struggle should take in each situation and to decide how to present it clearly and systematically in the form of instructions and orders.

We envisage a boycott, first of the press and then of all the junta's propaganda media.

Then we must gradually move on to active resistance, with specific instructions being given to individuals and groups.

Instead of this, what is happening? There's a lot of talk, there are quarrels, general statements and promises. That is why it is impossible to remain 'calm' here in exile.

12 June

Today is a great day: at nine o'clock this evening the BBC broadcast 'Paean', which I wrote on Easter Day. But even pleasurable moments are not without their anguish: we are waiting for the reprisals which will follow! What will it be this time?

17 June

'The mountains of Arkadia are very high and the tunes from

Pan's flute drown the grunts of the barracks.' The grunting is becoming louder : a good sign ! The resignation of another eight members of the Council of State has been announced today : Stasinopoulos is under police surveillance. His telephone has been cut off; his house is surrounded...The régime is devouring itself. Was it not you generals, ministers, magistrates and state counsellors who held to your bosom this viper which is now biting you? It was the same with Hitler. The capitalists had fed him so he would eat Stalin, but eating gave him an appetite and he ended up by wanting to devour everything!...Until Churchill and Stalin joined forces and destroyed him. It is only by banding together that the Greeks will save themselves and their motherland.

18 June

The idea of a new Greece never leaves my mind. I am in continual contact with my most faithful friends. I send them all the texts I write so they can draw lessons from the past and the present, so they can prepare for the future.

15 July

At the beginning of June I had been told that the Italian journalist, Nerio Minuzzo, was going to move into the neighbourhood under an assumed name and, of course, concealing his profession. We had our work cut out to arrange a real interview under the noses of my guards. It took us almost a week to get through it... one question at a time.

In a parcel I got from my father today there was the reportage in a Greek periodical, cut up and rejigged. The alarm is sounded immediately; there is just enough time to take a quick look at my photograph...and they drag me off and put me under arrest.

I am dying of curiosity. I should love to know what accusations the reportage makes. Some days later the foreign radios begin to give extensive extracts from it. I have never been more grateful for my little transistor radio, which has been an invaluable companion, defying all orders to silence.

INTERVIEW (written) granted to Nerio Minuzzo (published in the Italian weekly magazine *Europeo*, on 3 July 1969)

QUESTION: Now that the dictatorship has been in power for two years is it possible to see any end to it?

ANSWER: My answer to that question depends on a number of considerations. First, it must be realised that the Left in Greece is going through a profound political crisis and that this has direct, negative consequences for the organisation of a strong resistance movement. The other political groupings, the Right and the Centre, are no better off. Furthermore, the international situation, which is based on a balance of fear, gives no assistance to the Greek people. This is particularly so as far as the Soviet Union's attitude towards Greece is concerned. It is the same attitude which was shown very clearly in December 1944 and then again during the Civil War: an attitude of rigorous neutrality.

Another consideration is that although the present dictatorship is a product of the Right, its actions and aims have got out of the control of those who are the political representatives of the Right. One could also say that the Americans' plans, too, have been overtaken—and it was the Americans who prepared and supported the dictatorship, and they are continuing to do so. It's easy to see that the present Greek régime is doing more harm than good to American policy.

QUESTION: Will the colonels be able to hold on for long?

ANSWER: I think that Mr Averof, the former Foreign Minister and an eminent spokesman of the Right, has expressed better than anyone the fear aroused by the disintegration of the so-called nationalist bloc. Averof is convinced that the dictatorship's heavy burden of oppression is producing deep discord among the Greek people: the young people, in particular, are turning towards the Left. That's why he's suggesting a 'bridge' policy to Papadopoulos: this is the formation of a transition government made up of 'nationalist' politicians and members of the military junta. The 'bridge' government might, within the limits of the possible, save the Right, which is in a bad way, but this solution is unacceptable and, what's more, impossible. Anyone who wished to collaborate with the dictators today would be placing himself outside the nationalist fold and would find himself isolated. At the present moment there is nothing that can save the dictatorship. Averof's solution merely expresses despair and panic in the face of the Greek people's desire for democracy, progress and a new deal. The dictatorship has been a fatal mistake for American policy and for NATO's interests in Europe.

Looking a little farther ahead, I can say that it will be the dictatorship itself which will give birth to the free Greece of tomorrow. Even the immediate future is black for the military régime. This time the Greek people will not be able to forget.

QUESTION: Can the present opposition transform itself into a real armed struggle?

ANSWER: I think that the Greek people will only decide to engage in armed struggle when they are convinced that there is no other way of delivering themselves from the dictatorship.

QUESTION: Are there other genuine opportunities for opposition?

ANSWER: There is one, an ideal one: the union of all democratic forces, the creation of a common resistance front, under unified leadership, and finally the strengthening and broadening of this struggle.

But there is also a second solution: the formation of a national front, consisting in the main of those representatives of the Centre and the Right who are opposed to the régime; the main object of this would be to lead the country back to parliamentary democracy.

The first solution would require a lot of time and many sacrifices. On the other hand, it would lead to radical changes. The second would lead to the end of the dictatorship, but then it would open up the way to new political struggles and mass movements to consolidate democracy, so as to bring about vital historic changes.

QUESTION: What is the immediate objective?

ANSWER: To overthrow the dictatorship. That is the real objective. To achieve it, it is necessary to regroup all the available forces: from the extreme Left to the extreme Right. I might add that we must take advantage of those American political circles which are favourably disposed to us, in so far as they exist. I do not consider it possible to contemplate the first solution before we have exhausted all the possibilities for overthrowing the dictatorship without bloodshed on the basis of the second solution.

QUESTION: What made the *coup d'état* so easy in 1967?

ANSWER: The Crown, the upper cadres of the Army, the people who managed the state apparatus, the politicians of the Right and Centre who succeeded in creating, with American economic aid, an abnormal military and police organism, an instrument of oppression, which they finally delivered into the hands of Papadopoulos. All the men of the dictatorship had to do was push the buttons of this monstrous apparatus, which—according to a French sociologist—had cost the American people 1,489 million dollars. This money was spent simply so that thousands of people could be oppressed and gagged, so that thousands of civil servants, and members of the military and the police could become cogs in the machine, so that those Greeks who constituted an opposition force could be arrested: thousands of men of the Left, hundreds of men of the Centre and several dozen monarchist generals. In other words, the monstrous machine has its own logic: it has ended up by turning against the people who built it.

QUESTION: What are the responsibilities of the Greek political forces?

ANSWER: It is certainly not Colonel Papadopoulos who created this chaotic and disastrous situation. He only

237

brought it to fruition. Those who are really responsible are us Greeks—all of us, without exception. But more specifically, the fault is that of the parties, the politicians, the intellectuals, and those who belong, so to speak, to the élite.

At the present moment it would be a mistake to make accusations and look for individual cases of responsibility. For example, let us take the three principal Greek political forces one by one. Let's begin with the Left. Its responsibilities go back to the period 1943–9. In these years the Left committed a series of grave political errors which were in a sense at the root of the present split. Then the Right: it remained on its own in power from 1952 to 1963, without solving a single one of the great national problems. The only answers it had for the growing demands of the people were sterile anti-communism and police repression. That was how the popular explosion came about in Greece in 1963 and 1964 and brought the Centre Union to power. However, even this party, which had obtained 53 per cent of the votes in the 1964 elections, showed it was incapable of governing.

Something happened in our country which in my view has not yet been correctly assessed abroad: the Greek bourgeois parties, chiefly the Right, thought they were able to ignore the people's will. They refused to concede even the most elementary political and social reforms. In fact, they maintained the conditions of the Civil War intact throughout the period 1950–67. For them it was a question of preserving the privileges of an economic oligarchy, at the expense of the majority. This anti-national and anti-people tactic, applied for seventeen long years, had only one effect and that was to wear the bourgeois forces out politically. The popular forces were awakening. Being unable to oppose the feelings of the nation or to put pressure on them by raising the bogey of communism, and seeing, in the end, that they were in the process of losing even their traditional electoral support, the conservative forces got out their last weapon: dictatorship. The great remedy of those who feel they are lost.

QUESTION: To what extent have outside forces, albeit indirectly, influenced developments in Greece?

238

ANSWER: In spite of all our shortcomings, faults and errors, if we had been left alone we would in the end have found the path to progress and happiness. The whole tragedy of Greece has to be seen in this light. In fact, from the period of the occupation to the present day our country has never been independent, not even relatively so. Greece has been a sort of 'dominion', a new type of colony. You Europeans cannot understand that it is here in Greece that all the 'moral values' and all the ideals of the famous 'free world' are stripped of all their meaning. This has cost us very dear. But if Greece, by sacrificing herself in this way, does in the end succeed in enlightening the consciences of the peoples of Europe, then perhaps it will all have been worthwhile. On one point, however, nobody in Europe must be in any doubt: the volcano which is called Greece *will erupt* and its lava will destroy a lot of your illusions.

QUESTION: Why did the Left in Greece break up just at the moment when unity was so vital for making a common front against the dictatorship?

ANSWER: The split in the political forces of the Left was inevitable, and the crisis had been building up for several years. It is distressing that it broke out at such a difficult time for our country.

The Greek Left had won over the great mass of the people during the Resistance. Then came the Civil War. And for us, defeat. The Communist Party was outlawed; its members were physically eliminated in their tens of thousands, its cadres destroyed...And there was the exodus: sixty thousand went into exile. For the others it was for years a question of prison, deportation and persecution.

From there we come on to the EDA, the regrouping of the Left under one roof, and the recent struggles. In a word, we have never experienced normal activity. We all said the same things but deep down we were different, because our personal experiences were different.

At the present moment, I consider that the creation of another Communist Party was a mistake: we now have two

239

parties with the same programme and the same name, and this means in fact that we have no party. Each is trying to isolate the other until one of them ends up by triumphing over the other.

QUESTION : Everyone in Athens is wondering what your position is at the present time.

ANSWER: The two fragments of the Communist Party are made up of friends to whom I have been bound over long and difficult years of struggle. They all love me but they have not had the chance of keeping me in touch with what is going on. My personal position on this issue is truly dramatic.

I cannot disown men like Antonis Brillakis, with whom I set up the Patriotic Front in the early days of the dictatorship. In the same way, I cannot deny the fact that at the moment Brillakis is representing the Front abroad. For me Brillakis, Drakopoulos, Votsis and the other representatives of the Left with whom I have worked remain true friends and companions in struggle. I have the same feelings towards the cadres of the Lambrakis Youth organisation, men like Misios Khronis, Aristidis Manolakos, Andreas Lentakis, Sotirios Anastasiadis and Khristos Reklitis, who took part in the struggle from the very beginning and who have been arrested and tortured for having done so. I could not pass them by now because they are not in agreement with the Politburo of the Greek Communist Party and have set up another Greek Communist Party.

On the other hand, there is a man like Grigoris Farakos, a member of this Politburo, whom the others have ceased to recognise. Farakos is a great fighter. He is now in prison and will soon be brought once again before a tribunal on matters which go back to the period of the Civil War. His life is in danger. Everyone should act to save him.

Takis Benas should also be helped and protected. He is an able and devoted comrade. He was arrested a few months ago. But no one speaks of him. Why? The radio broadcasts from abroad don't give any news of Benas, either. Tortures and suffering should be unacceptable to everyone, without exception. Now Benas, too, probably belongs to the new Greek Communist Party.

I am convinced that the setting up of a new party has been a mistake. But as far as my personal position is concerned, I shall belong to the Patriotic Front for as long as this dictatorship lasts. I have launched and I shall continue to launch, appeals for unity, though I don't have great hopes of their being heeded. But I remain in the Resistance. At the moment partisan discussions don't interest me. I see only one enemy: the dictatorship. And I have only one aim, its overthrow. I am prepared to collaborate with anybody to this end, regardless of his political convictions.

My future, after the fall of the dictatorship, will depend on several factors. I want to dedicate myself wholly to my artistic activity, to my music. I shall return to political life only if I see I cannot do otherwise, as I do at the moment. I belong to a progressive movement, the Greek Left, but after the dictatorship I shall strive to collaborate only with progressive forces which are completely new and which have a programme which is as ambitious as it is realistic.

Kharis 1944
29 July 1969

Today is my birthday. At present I am forced to stay indoors all day. The only time I get out is between eleven in the morning and noon to sign the register at the police station. In the evening Myrto and I sit out on the balcony. Opposite us, on her balcony, Madam Marigo is knitting. On the balcony to our right Madam Fotini is knitting. These two old neighbours detest one another and were at daggers drawn long before we arrived. We are the audience for their implacable enmity. We hear them calling their respective hens when they wander beyond the (of course, invisible) demarcation line which marks off their territory on the square.

Between the square and us: the guards. People walk about in the square and in the street, which constitute the 'promenade', the well-defined itinerary one finds in every Greek town, where all the townspeople meet at the end of the afternoon. They look up at us and greet us furtively. With great caution. Then the street empties again.

'Sing us your song "Kharis", Mister Mikis,' the younger guards implore me.

I oblige and go out on to the balcony again to explain to them: 'Kharis is not dead. He is still needed. We who are here, locked in this house—besieged. You who are locked in this village—besieged. The Greeks who are locked in military decrees—besieged.'

'We're all in the same boat,' they say.

Before I completed 'The Survivor' I had begun work on two poems by Manolis Anagnostakis, 'Kharis' and 'I Speak'. For so many years I have been thinking of this particular collaboration and now the moment has come.

I play my new composition to a sergeant who arrived recently. He is an old man and the music encourages him to talk:

'To think that during the Civil War I hunted you everywhere to try and kill you. And today I have to keep watch over you and not let you out of my sight even when you go to the toilet! Now I know you I am disgusted to think that I have to treat you like a dangerous animal.'

I give him a glass of Marc; he listens to the music with great emotion. When I finish playing he clasps me in his arms and tells me out loud, without fear of the other guards:

'How can they dare to lock you up in this village! You have made our hearts sing.'

He then went to the station and asked to see his chief to make a report.

'I was serving as a guard at Mikis's,' he says. 'He played the piano to me. I can no longer stay in that post.'

He is put under close arrest for a month. He has a wife and child.

Non-commissioned officers and ordinary gendarmes come up to listen to me playing and singing. They are frequently deeply moved. As for the villagers, they send messages: 'Leave your window open when you're playing. We stay out in the garden waiting for your music.'

I open my windows wide and sing 'Kharis'.

ARKADIA VIII

(Poems by Manolis Anagnostakis)

1

I speak

I speak of the last trumpet call
Of defeated soldiers,
Of the final rags,
Of our festive clothes,
Of our children,
Selling cigarettes to passers-by.

I speak of the flowers,
Fading on the graves
Rotted by rain,
Of the houses agape,
Windowless
Like empty helmets,
Of the girls begging
Baring their breasts
Showing their sores.

I speak of the barefoot mothers
Wandering in the ruins,
Of the cities ablaze,
The heaps of bodies in the streets,
The prostituted poets,
Who tremble by night
On the doorsteps.

I speak of the endless nights
With feeble lighting
Early mornings,
Of the loaded lorries
And footsteps
On damp paving stones.

I speak of the forecourts of prisons
Of the tears of those about to die.

But I speak still more
Of the fishermen,
Who left their nets
To follow His steps

And when He tired,
Did not rest
And when He betrayed them,
Did not deny Him
And when He was glorified,
Turned their eyes away
And the comrades spat on them
And crucified them
Yet they serene,
Take the endless road
Without a glance
Of woe or hesitation
Walking alone
In the fearful desert of the crowd.

2
Kharis 1944

We were all together
Tirelessly passing the time.
Singing softly
Of the days to come
Laden with vivid scenes.
He was singing
We were silent
His voice aroused
Small fires.
Thousands of small fires
Set alight our youth
Night and day
He played hide and seek
With death
In every corner and alley.
He desired,
Forgetting his own body,
To give the others
Spring.
We were all together
But you might have thought
That he was all of us,
One day someone
Whispered in our ears:

'Kharis is dead'.
He had been killed—or something like that.
Words that we heard every day.
No one had seen him
It was at dusk
His fists must have been clenched
As always.
In his eyes
The unquenchable joy
Of the new life.
But all this was simple
And time is short.
No one has sufficient time
We are not all together any more:
Two or three have gone abroad
Another has gone far away
In a vague manner
And Kharis was killed.
Some left, others came,
New streets filled up
A crowd surges forward uncontrollably
Flags wave again in the air
The wind whips the banners
Songs rise up in the chaos
If among the voices
That pierce the night
Echo against the walls,
You distinguish one, it is his.
It rouses fires
Thousands of little fires
That set our untamed youth alight.
It is his voice
Sounding in the crowd
Like a sun around
Embracing the world
Dissolving bitterness
Like a sun lighting the way
A shining sun lighting up the cities
Clearing the way before us
For the truth and its serene light.

How far can a voice carry? How far can a song travel?

Our imagination is working at fever pitch: we must at all costs carry on getting the material out clandestinely. We hide messages in bread, in rubbish, in clothes, in shoes. With the collusion of various people. Using a thousand subterfuges. I cannot reveal some ruses without compromising people, but I can tell how we went about getting my songs over the walls of our 'fortress'. I cut the tape after each song had been recorded. I rolled the piece of tape up very tightly; this made a little disc about two centimetres across and Myrto cleverly made a little casing of the same size for each one, which she then sewed on to Yorgo's coat as big buttons. When he went to Athens, of course, he was thoroughly searched from head to toe, but the buttons aroused no suspicion and he walked on, proudly wearing my songs on his chest.

On three occasions the BBC broadcast songs I had written here only ten days before. The whole village was listening in; and we would get our tiny transistor radio out from its hiding place.

They deliver a registered letter, covered with administrative rubber stamping. First it did the journey Zatouna-Dimitsana-Tripolis-Police headquarters and then back again Tripolis-Dimitsana-Zatouna. A letter full of caution and restraint and very circumspect. With it are two collections of poetry. The signature: that of Kostas Kalantzis. I am called to the station to be handed official notification that my deportation to Zatouna has been extended by one year. More in fun than anger I added the high-sounding phrases of this piece of information at the end of my new composition.

ARKADIA IX

The Outlaw's Mother
(Poems by Kostas Kalantzis)

If the barbarians have closed the gates to you
And crowned you with a crown of thorns
The same fate will await them, my son
At the hands of an unknown god
In this dark city
I do not want to die, my son

Pitiless despair strikes me
The better to kill me as I go on
Do not worry me so much, my son
My eyes must stay open
You are my last son and your absence weighs
It will weigh on for centuries
I shall become darker than night
And wander about like a spectre
Outside I hear a noise like a whine
The sorrowful whine of our dog
I shall wander through mountain and valley
The plains and torrents will question me
The springs will be silent as I pass
Fires will kindle in my breast
The sun, the moon, the stars will ask me
I shall not have the heart to reply
Alas! You will have taken all with you
And my body will no longer find peace
In this despair and this wandering
I received your most bitter letter
How sad your news is
Come back my child, I await you
Come back and I shall open my wings
And take you in tenderly
My heart will feel an infinite solace
When you are close to it, my son
How many times shall I have tasted death
Tasted it until I am sated
To comfort me in my old age
I only want one sign from you.

Letter to comrades
September

THE HISTORIC TASKS
OF THE GREEK LEFT
Open letter to my comrades

What is happening at the moment in the imperialist camp?
Let us first point to the main facts: (a) growing social
agitation in the capitalist countries and (b) the peoples'
struggle against pro-American dictatorial régimes.

247

The periodic monetary crises, the massive strikes and the student unrest are shaking the 'consumer society' to its foundations, and in the eyes of bourgeois economists and politicians it is this consumer society which will bring the final solution to all social problems.

However, the figures show that 'the rich are getting richer and the poor are getting poorer'. This means that the basis of wealth in the advanced industrial countries of the world lies in the increasing exploitation of the under-developed countries by the great international monopolies. Thus, for example, the United States in the period 1959–65 received profits from Latin America which amounted to 4,046 million dollars, from Asia amounting to 5,154 million dollars, and some of this, some 4,823 million dollars, are invested in Europe (see Claude Julien's *L'Empire Améri-cain*, p.230). This is how the poor people are helping the rich to become even richer.

In their efforts to raise their economic and military strategy on to a world scale, the United States has had recourse to two methods: as far as the advanced indus-trial countries are concerned, they have used economic penetration in depth to an extent that guarantees them absolute control over the economic lives and consequently over the political lives of these countries. Western econom-ists rejoice to see in this an achievement of the capitalist world, notably in having succeeded in overcoming its inter-nal antagonisms and in marching forward to the integra-tion of the capitalist system.

In fact, it is a question not of integration but rather of the absorption of the various national economies by the United States economy.

We said above that the United States has made and is still making colossal investments in Europe. It is therefore quite normal that the countries of the Old Continent which are 'profiting' from this should be experiencing a period of economic boom. But the question is: on what basis are these capital investments made? Certainly not on the basis of developing the national economy in accordance with a programme corresponding to the social interests and historic needs of the country concerned, but on the basis of the programmes of economic expansion of the American monopolies and of the interests of those who are investing their capital, the American plutocrats. The result will be that this type of growth of the national economies of these countries will sooner or later come into conflict with the fundamental interests of the working masses.

With regard to the under-developed countries, United States policy follows one very simple principle : to guarantee absolute control of these states economically, politically and military, by making them into new types of colony. Let me draw a parallel here. The old type of colony corresponds to the system of slavery; the new type to the system of serfdom. The slave people have been transformed into serfs. In my opinion it is not hard to see that American policy has made a grave mistake here and that sooner or later it will pay dearly for it : it has underestimated a series of historical values, it has not taken account of the people. It thought that to guarantee dominion over a country it was sufficient to control all its mechanisms : the administrative apparatus, the Army, the police, the national economy, etc., if necessary by the usual means of martial law, repression, censorship and brainwashing.

However many soldiers, politicians, psychologists, detectives and other experts must have worked to reach the conclusion that when a people (especially an 'under-developed' people) is manipulated with all the modern means of intimidation, repression and blackmail, all it can then do is to submit absolutely to the wishes of those exercising power.. In other words, they considered and treated the people like a herd of animals and tried to find ways of leading this human 'herd', just as one does a herd of animals, with whip and the lasso. The question as to who would be the 'shepherd' is a secondary one. It is enough that the 'shepherd' (a) obeys his masters' orders and (b) makes good use of all the abundant means of repression which American 'aid' puts at his disposal. The Americans have valued highly the virtues of the military. Discipline, yes! Imagination, no! And above all there must be not too much concern for the political, cultural and social demands of the peoples.

The fact that this same sequence of events takes place in many other countries proves that there is a plan which the elected officers of the CIA and generally of American policy in our country are called upon to put into effect.

How can the progressive forces throughout the world, and the progressive movements in a country which is under the control of the military, turn this perverse way in which the United States has treated a number of peoples to their advantage?

A prime characteristic of this paranoiac policy is the destruction of all political and social forces, with the single exception of the most reactionary and oligarchic circles. This tactic leads objectively, by the reactions it provokes, to all the viable forces of the nation uniting, regardless of political allegiance.

This creates a valuable historic opportunity for the progressive forces which are in the forefront of the resistance to unite all the national forces on the basis of a programme of national independence, democracy and social progress.

So this unity must be considered the essential condition of the struggle for the liberation of a people.

I now come to the specific problems which concern the Greek progressive movement.

In the years which followed the Civil War we had to face all the consequences of the victory of the counter-revolutionary forces. We had to deliver the Greek people from the reactionary ideology, to fight against internal divisions, to unmask the régime of national resignation and political agents, to bring an end to the isolation of the Left, to show the people the need for change, to organise the workers, to defend our popular culture from the assaults of cosmopolitanism from the other side of the Atlantic, to rally the masses under the banner of democracy, to isolate the anti-people and anti-national forces, and to ensure the victory of democracy.

Since the Civil War we have written a real epic into the history books: its main stages are well known and the result can be seen in the 1964 election figures—democracy 65 per cent, national resignation 35 per cent.

From 15 July 1965 the enemy went on to the counter-offensive and achieved several tactical successes, though without managing to alter the essential relationship of the political forces to his advantage. On the contrary, if the

250

elections of 28 May 1967 had taken place, democracy would have emerged even stronger, with 75 per cent of the vote.

It was to cheat the Greek people of this tactical victory that, out of panic, it was decided to apply in Greece, the famous technique of dictatorship, which the brains in the United States had worked out for the under-developed countries. However, although from the tactical point of view the militarists managed to seize power and have kept it right up to the present day, from the strategic point of view the results have been precisely the reverse! It is true beyond any doubt that the paranoiac tactics of the dictators *are strengthening the unity of the people all the time* and that they are, moreover, making the people dynamic and determined, and strong enough to achieve national liberation through struggle.

Today, after thirty months of dictatorship, the Greek people are more united than ever. The more the Americans exert pressure on the masses, the more they turn them into a volcano. But this gives us, the representatives of the Left, special historic responsibilities. For each time a revolutionary situation presents itself, the revolutionary forces must assume leadership of the struggle if it is to be profitably exploited. This task devolves entirely upon us.

The outlook is bright. At the moment there are two sorts of solution to the crisis which is raging in our country:

(a) There is still the possibility of overthrowing the dictatorship 'from within' and of forming a government of pro-American politicians (Karamanlis, Mavros, Mitsotakis, etc.). This government would then do away with martial law, free political prisoners and declare elections. Now the Americans dread this unknown quantity—the state of mind of the Greek people. They know only too well that anti-Americanism has now even reached the conservative sections of the population. By accepting such a solution (under pressure from our people) they would take care to permit only a very slender measure of liberty so as to maintain, on the one hand, their control over the public life of the country, and on the other hand, a semblance of democratic rule to fool world opinion. This solution would nonetheless in my view be an important step forward.

(b) But if this 'flexible' solution is not adopted, then the struggle must go on. A large proportion of the Greek people still believe in this 'normal' solution of our internal crisis. So it follows that the development of our resistance movement is directly linked to the Greek people's decision to abandon this illusion and to rely simply on their own strength.

I see three stages in this development: (i) consolidation, (ii) extension and (iii) the final assault by all the popular forces on the dictatorship. In my view, the first stage is the most difficult but it is also decisive. Today, after thirty months of dictatorship, this first stage is still not complete, and the responsibility for this rests very largely with us, with the Left.

Now, we must be capable of leading these popular forces in any situation that might arise.

Our internal activity will soon enter a critical phase, as we are not yet ready to respond to the greater and more complex tasks which lie ahead.

So it is essential that all members and cadres of the Left view the present state of affairs in a spirit which is not defeatist and that they behave as victors with new, historic tasks to fulfil, rather than as vanquished for whom a superficial defeat conceals a greater reality—that the Greek people is on its feet and waiting to be led to more decisive victories.

That is why I consider it to be a historical imperative that all adherents and representatives of the progressive movement unite immediately in a new social and political resistance bloc, based on a common programme of struggle.

This union corresponds not only to the historic needs of the Greek people but also to a broader requirement of the world movement. In fact, the key slogan for all partisans of the Left throughout the world is in the Political Testament of Ho Chi Minh : Union of all progressive forces on a common line of struggle.

It is really odd that we should be wasting our energies quarrelling when such great objectives lie ahead.

In my view, the surest and most practical way of unifying our progressive movement is to call a conference as soon as possible in which the best known figures on the Greek Left would take part, not as representatives of parties but as representatives of all the various trends which have emerged recently in the Left. The aim of this conference would be to create a new political organism, modelled on EDA, which would group all the forces on the Left behind a programme which was restricted to the common struggle as we have defined it.

In the present period this new political organism would be the backbone of the Patriotic Front. So all the resistance forces of the Left, which are dispersed and frequently in conflict with one another, would rally under a new single leadership and would carry our resistance movement on to a more intense phase of the struggle.

I have been hoping that someone or some people would be found to take this initiative. But time is passing and we risk missing our rendezvous with history. That is why I have decided to take the initiative myself, through this message which I am addressing to all responsible cadres of our glorious progressive movement without exception and without distinction.

At the same time, I believe I am expressing the deep longings of all our comrades and friends who are now in prison and unable to make their voices heard.

The first condition which must be fulfilled if our people are to take advantage of all the opportunities offered by international agreements, is still that the Left be united. This will make it possible for our people once again to carry out its burdensome historic tasks.

Zatouna, 10 September 1969

N.B. This letter left Zatouna like the others. Did it arrive? I still do not know.

Last Days of Zatouna
September

The nuts have been beaten down from the trees. The leaves are yellowing and falling. I ask permission for my family to leave here and for my father to come and join me for a few days. Myrto is but the shadow of her former self. She is worn out. When she has no more housework to do she sits for hours at the foot of the bed. She never goes out, although everyone, the villagers and the guards, beg her to take some air.

I give her some tranquillisers to cure her depression. She makes a little progress and agrees to go out on the balcony.

The conditions here are hardly any better for the children. They see me all the time in the company of the guards. One day one of the guards starts chasing Margarita, whom he has received orders to keep under lock and key. I see my daughter rush up the stairs four at a time and throw herself on the bed. She is still sobbing in the evening. It is therefore a matter of some urgency that all three of them leave. I shall spend the second winter here alone.

I am already preparing for this; I mend the chimney and collect some wood. I place an order for a whole barrel of sheep's milk cheese. I have just made a start on a new oratorio on a poem by Pergialis (the only manuscript, apart from those of Eleftheriou, to have reached me). I have planned a work schedule. I want to perfect my English and start learning Russian and Italian. I read everything I can lay hands on, and from cover to cover. The important thing is to gather as many elements for my work as possible.

Finally they grant permission for my wife and children to leave. On 21 September I go for my last walk with Myrto. We are allowed to go as far as Saint Eleousa, on the edge of the village, under guard, of course. We want to look at the countryside for one last time together, and to sit on the stone bench behind the chapel, looking down on the village and the little pine wood. We have spent so many hours there! The guards keep a modest few metres from us. On the way back, a farewell round of the cafés. An officer turns up on a motor cycle:

'Lieutenant Kostas Stergiou has ordered that your wife and your children are to be searched at the station at nine o'clock in the morning.'

I give free rein to my anger and the officer takes fright. He goes off to report back to Lieutenant Stergiou, who in the end agrees to the search taking place in the house.

All night we try to keep our thoughts and feelings to ourselves as much as we can. The children are sleeping soundly. And I cannot stop thinking of the morning, when I shall be on my own again.

In the morning the village is sealed off, the house surrounded and the guard reinforced. A jeep pulls up in the square. An officer gets out and walks like a conquering hero towards our house. I give my wife a strong dose of sedative and so as not to make any violent outburst I take some myself. I tell Myrto: 'Be brave. It's nothing. Maybe they'll put you in prison. We must both be patient.' They lock me in the kitchen. The hours pass. The search is not over. I hear cries. Then silence. I control myself as best I can: I know I am capable of fixing that officer. He is doing the search with the help of two acolytes. I would only have to grab him by the throat, and before the others had time to step in...But what's the use? Who'd pay for it in the end? There is a more elegant solution: to kill him through his honour, to make sure that tomorrow his name is covered with shame and that people spit in his face in the street. I take a paper napkin and jot things down to take my mind off it. The door opens. 'Not allowed to say goodbye to your family!' the officer yells through his nose. Myrto waves from a distance, in tears. The children manage to slip out through a window but the guards rush round and catch them; they grab them and put them in the jeep. I go out on to the balcony. I can feel the compassion of the whole village. The jeep drives off I am unable to stifle a cry:

'Myrto!'

I stare at an officer. He is unable to look me in the eye and quickly turns on his heels. He must have seen a murderous glow in my eyes. The gendarmes lower their eyes.

I leave the house, without my usual guard. No one dares to stop me. Shame paralyses them. I go to the Café Teris. I get drunk on ouzo. Back at the house I flop on the bed and fall sound asleep. When I wake up, I go over to the piano and write a song, 'My Name is Kostas Stergiou'. I tell the guards to come up and listen to it. As I sing it to them I see their faces light up. Now everyone in the village—including the police—hates and despises Lieutenant Kostas Stergiou.

ARKADIA X

My Name is Kostas Stergiou

My name is Kostas Stergiou
Descendant of the Visigoths,
The Ostrogoths, the Mavrogoths.
I live in caves,

255

I fashion clubs,
I drink water out of skulls.
My profession is death.
But for the time being I am serving
The big Dragon who has sent me to Arcady.
Over my body I wear a uniform,
I carefully hide my club
Under my greatcoat.
My name is Kostas Stergiou
Descendant of the Mamelukes,
The Mavrolukes, the Susulukes,
I am a cross
Between Neanderthal man and wolf,
For the time being,
I ride in a jeep.
I terrorise women and children
My speciality is searching people
I search children's souls
And I spread fear,
I impose the Law,
The Law of the great Dragon
Who has sent me, for the time being,
To Arcady.

I Had Three Lives

I had three lives
The wind took one
The rains another
And my third life
Suddenly imprisoned
Was drowned in tears.
I remained alone
Lifeless, abandoned
The wind had taken one
The rains the second.
I was alone, I and the Dragon
In the big cave.
I have a club, I have a sword.
I shall strangle you, I shall kill you,
I shall extinguish you, I shall shake you

Out of my life.
For I have three lives
One to feel pain,
One to have desires
And the third to conquer.

My father has arrived. He is coming up the path from the police
station, escorted by two guards. They had made him go there to
be searched.

'You don't even have any respect for the wounds he got
fighting the Turks at Bizani,' I tell Colonel Mitropoulos, 'no
more respect than you have for his white hair. You debase
everything!'

'We are robots, we carry out orders.'

My old father manages a smile, with some difficulty. He is
worn out by the journey and by the extra irritants.

'They behaved very properly,' he keeps saying, for fear that
I might do something.

Thanks to my father being here I can now breathe more
deeply. I have new strength. We go out together. We go and
sit in the cafés of Zatouna. We buy rounds. And we are bought
rounds. We eat together. We relax and talk together for hours
on end. When my father leaves I shall really be alone. Alone
with Great Pan, the man-goat whose bleating can be heard
coming from high up in the mountains above this house. The
cold spells return. I play my music to father. I read him my
notes, my reflections. When I have to stay indoors, my father
can only go out if he is escorted by guards. I have just got to
the heart of 'Arkadia XI', which I am writing to a poem of
Notis Pergialis.

Arise, My Sun

Three brave men decided
To escape from Hell.
To escape one spring morning
One Saturday evening.

They put on their best clothes
And waited for nightfall

Yet suddenly on high
The sun rose up.

Out of respect for my father, I employ Cretan rhythms for the first chorus:

Arise, my sun
Arise, my sun
My brave sun!
I want my youth back
My strength, my charm
To lift up two mountains
And go to meet you.

Then I begin the women's chorus:

Resist!
Resist!
Resist the chains of bronze, the claws of the cruel
    murderer
High, higher, still higher raise your head against
    brute force
Deep, deeper, still deeper swell the rivers with
    your blood
Forward brothers all together set the world alight!

They call my father to the station again. Another search, as he is leaving.

I shall not see him again except in the distance, at the end of the jetty, from behind the barbed wire of Oropos, and one last time, on a Saturday evening, in the Sotiria Hospital in Athens, two days before I leave for Paris.

References

1 Old name for Tripolis.
2 Lambis Bitounis had worked all his life as a driver of lorries and buses. He was about sixty and had retired to Zatouna. He lived in the family house which dominated the little vil-

lage square. At the time of the civil war he had for a time been a prisoner of the partisans. Ideologically he belonged to the extreme Right. His brother, a commissar of police and commander of the armoured section of the Athens Police, had distinguished himself by his fanaticism and by the ferocity of his charges against strikers and demonstrators. He had been disgraced by the junta, like all pure-blooded royalist officers. He had stayed for a time at Zatouna. Lambis had had a hard struggle and had suffered a lot in his life. He was proud and hospitable. That is why although he always considered me his ideological adversary, he, and the whole village, was on my side. He knew that he had himself been a victim of violence and that was sufficient for him to forget our differences and to show deep humanity towards me on all occasions.

3 Greek kebabs.
4 Sweetmeats of flour, butter and fine sugar, made into small circular pieces. (Translator's Note)
5 *Anafora Ston Greco*, a posthumous autobiographical novel translated into English, by P. A. Brien (1965), as *Report to Greco*. (Translator's Note)
6 Suburb of Athens.
7 Accused and finally condemned to death for attempting to assassinate the chief of the junta, Papadopoulos.
8 Aera: the war cry of Greek soldiers, literally 'Nothing can stop us'.
9 Text of the statement:
To the police superintendent in Zatouna:
As a sign of my protest at the fact that for a long time I have been deprived of all personal liberty—like thousands of my compatriots—and at the barbaric, inhuman and revolting treatment you have inflicted upon me, I have decided that today I shall begin a HUNGER STRIKE lasting three weeks.

In advance I hold you—yourself, your superiors and the government—responsible before the Greek people for anything that might happen to me and to my family.

Mikis Theodorakis

10 Paramilitary corps set up during the Civil War (1946–9) in the rural areas of the north.
11 Greek national holiday.
12 It does not seem that the irony of the situation worried the

authorities: Margarita chosen to represent liberty before her father who is surrounded by a dozen gendarmes.

13 Theodorakis was the subject of three trials, one of which had passed a judgement he had appealed against.

14 Social Democratic Party.

15 Sweetmeat made of almonds, honey, etc.

16 Honey cake.

17 Tripe soup.

18 Greek poet who won the Nobel Prize for Literature in 1963. Under the name of George Seferiades he was Greek Ambassador in London from 1957 to 1962. (Translator's Note)

OROPOS —The Camp

October 1969

Some days after my father had left, they call me to the station. I am received by Stergiou 'the Visigoth'. 'You're going to be transferred to the camp of Oropos. From now on you'll be under penitentiary régime. From tonight you'll sleep in your cell.'

I am thrown into an underground cell and given a blanket. Two days later I move to the first floor and then on the fourth day I am taken into the house and searched before leaving. I sort out the things I must take with me. At dawn on the following day, the last Sunday in October, a cortège of cars comes to take me away. At Tripolis my guards are relieved. The same procedure at Corinth, and then again at Athens. I see the Gulf of Nafplion again. The Isthmus of Corinth. The Sacred Way. In Athens we take the motorway to Salonika. A right turn through fir trees, and there before us the island of Euboea. Oropos faces the island. We enter the camp. A door of one of the huts opens. Comrades hurl themselves into my arms.

At the beginning I feel strangely 'free'. I can walk and move about without having a guard on my heels. The sea shimmers in the distance. There is a garden with flowers and vegetables. Oropos seems like paradise! In the refectory I sit next to Andreas Lentakis, Toundas and Polyzos. I sleep in the room nearest the sea, with Thanasis, Mikhalis, Theodoros and Dimos.

After meals I sing them my new songs. After a few days I

have a little choir. Then, fairly quickly, the climate, the horizon, changes. The sea becomes a frontier. A barrier. The camp contracts before my eyes. The barbed wire grows higher. Two visitors, once every two months. Correspondence is restricted. Forced labour and sickness. The average age of the prisoners is fifty-six. The average sentence twelve years. And to crown it all there are our partisan quarrels, the fanaticism of the clans.

November 1969

The visiting room. The loudspeakers are calling my name:
'Theodorakis to the visiting room!'

It is my wife and my father. With visiting rights as they are, it is impossible for all the others who would want to see me. My mother? My children? Perhaps in another two months. I jump over the garden gate, which the guard always takes care to lock (the big padlock has 'Made in Poland' on it).

I go into the administration building. My wife and my father are waiting in the first room on the left. They get up and kiss me. Then we sit down, face to face. The officers and guards listen carefully to every word. If we say something which does not strictly concern the family, they shout:
'You're forbidden to say that!'
'And that, too! Forbidden!'
Myrto smiles.
'I see you're smiling. Why?'
'I'm happy. You can't imagine how everybody is showing us such affection, respect and devotion.'
'Forbidden!' the officer shouts.
'What is forbidden?' I ask. 'Affection?'
My father steps in angrily.
'You cannot forbid such a sentiment!'
'You know,' Myrto goes on, 'nobody wants to take our money. "No," they say, "you'll offend us! You have given us so much! Let us offer you something in return..." It's the same everywhere we go—in the shops, in taxis and at the cinema. Everywhere!'
'The people are with us,' I say.
'Forbidden!'

The composer, Yannis Khristou, has been killed in an accident.

264

The news shatters me. A blind, mad death. I am inspired to write a song based on a poem by Seferis. On 15 January 1970 I finish setting 'Raven' to music. My walking companion, Toundas, and I organise the 'première' in the empty kitchen. On the table a bottle of beer which we drank at the end of the 'concert'.

RAVEN

(Flow-song for singer, chorus and orchestra, composed between 7 and 10 January 1970, on a poem by George Seferis, written in 1937.)

Dedicated to Yannis Khristou

Years like wings. What does the motionless raven
    recall?
What do the dead near the tree roots recall?
Your hands were the colour of the falling apple,
That voice, that low voice kept coming back.
Those who travel set the sails and the stars,
Listen to the wind, to the other sea farther than the
    wind
Near them like a hollow shell, they hear
Nothing else, they search not in the cypress shadow,
For a lost face, a coin : they do not wonder,
Seeing a raven on a dead branch, what his thoughts
    may be.
He sits motionless, hour after hour, a little higher,
The spirit of an eyeless statue.
A crowd is gathered in this bird,
Thousands of forgotten men, smoothed out wrinkles,
Broken embraces, suspended laughs,
Unfinished tasks, silent stations,
A heavy sleep on a golden couch.
He is still. He looks at me. What does he recall?
There are so many sores on those invisible men,
Passions suspended till the Last Judgement

265

Crawling desires mingled in the ground,
Dead children, women too weary at dawn.
Who knows what he ponders on that dead branch,
On the roots of the yellow tree, on the shoulders
Of other men, on those unusual features swallowed up
    by earth
That dare not touch the slightest drop of water.
Who knows if he ponders at all?
Your hands had the weight of the hand in the water
Or that in the grottoes of the sea, a light relieved weight,
Skimming across the sea up to the islands,
With the gesture warding off a dark idea.
The plain is heavy after rain. What recalls
The dark straight flame in the grey sky,
Caught between man and his memory,
Between the wound and the dark sword inflicting it?
The plain has darkened, drunk the rain, the wind has
    dropped.
My breath suffices not—what will replace it?
Between the memory—a mantle—a frightened breast
Between the shadows fighting to become man and woman
    again,
Between sleep and death, a stagnant life.
Your hands have always moved towards the sleep of the
    sea
Caressing the dream gently approaching the golden spider,
Pulling the cluster of stars towards the sun,
Eyes closed, wings folded.

The camp governor has handed me back the complaints
which were addressed to the Red Cross in the name of all the
prisoners. He stubbornly insists that the requests be made to his
office, one at a time, and signed by the prisoner concerned—
and not collectively as we are determined to do. On the dossier
he has made a note in the margin: 'Returned for not conforming to the regulations'. In the evening I take this note into the
refectory and make up a song on the spot called 'For Not
Conforming'. I also wrote other songs for the camp chorus:
'Do Not Forget Oropos', 'To Oropos' and 'Our Best Years'.

266

For Not Conforming

Beyond the sea
The azure sky
A mother waits
I haven't seen her for years
'For not conforming'.
Time goes by and by
I walk within the barbed wire
Many dark days will go by
Before I see your face
'For not conforming'.
Halicarnassus, Partheni,
Oropos, Korydalos,
The hero awaits
The sun of freedom
'For not conforming'.

Do Not Forget Oropos

The father in exile
The house with no master
We rot in tyranny
In deep darkness
And you tormented people
Do not forget Oropos
The abandoned mother weeps
The trees and birds weep
Night has fallen on our homeland
Bereft of all caresses
And you tormented people
Do not forget Oropos
Although trapped in barbed wire
Our hearts do not give in
We shall be faithful to our oath
Progress and freedom
And you, tormented people
Do not forget Oropos.

To Oropos

What is there at Oropos

Other than this Greek land
Bathed in the proud tears
For interminable hours
Of all those who for freedom
Have renounced the sweetness of home
Oh companion Greeks of Rigas
Sing the songs of freedom
May despair be overcome
And our homeland delivered
Enter the fighting lists
And our country will flower again
Our Greece will flower again.

Our Best Years

All our best years
That portion of our life
We are spending behind barbed wire
My mother so tender
For a dream, an idea
How many days and nights
What thousands of sobs
Yet we retain within us
A radiant free homeland
Like a hovering multitude
In the blinding sun
The brotherhood of men
Are creating a free future
One day the mighty torrent
Will submerge the oppressors
Sweep them into oblivion
In wrath and shame.

When I came to Oropos, the ninety-one prisoners were divided
into two large groups: those who followed Koliyannis—about
forty of them, and those who represented 'chaos', twenty-three.
The others, who supported EDA, were not organised. There
were two different questions I had to face. The first: to analyse
the past and decide on the future, on the party's plan. The
second: to consider the present, especially in the camp.

On the first point I was essentially in agreement with some of the 'chaos' leaders, because they were seeking a new way and were rejecting the old labels (it was this *negative* quality which earned them the epithet of 'chaos').

On the second point I was in agreement with the supporters of Koliyannis. But with the friends on the Interior Bureau I was more or less in agreement on both questions.

The 'chaos' group showed complete indifference for the organisation of life and the struggle in the camp. They did so as a reaction to the 'Koliyannistes', who made it the focus of their interests. The Koliyannistes permitted no discussion, however amicable, of questions concerning the movement's past, and still less its future. When I tried to start a public debate they provoked incidents and 'ordered' their people not to speak to me any more. Almost all put forward the same argument: 'We support that fraction of the party which enjoys the support of the international movement.' And there were those who simply said: 'We are the party.'

I was obsessed by a feeling of shame with respect to the camp administration and of responsibility towards my comrades, because we had no representative to defend our interests in the camp. In my view, whatever our differences, we had to adopt a common attitude towards the common adversary. For almost a month I sounded out opinion and held discussions in an attempt to set up a single committee for the whole camp. Meanwhile some comrades arrived who were supporters of the Interior Bureau, and they immediately started to organise themselves.

I had a talk with their leader:
'Why don't you accept my plan?'
'Because it is against principles.'
'What principles?'
'Those of *my* party.' (He stressed *my*.)

The leader of the Koliyannistes, in his turn, said the same thing. He was a former leader of the Lambrakis Youth. He told me: '*My* party has decided this...*My* party has stated that...' So the rest of us are left without a party! Dimos, for example, who has served nineteen years in prison and three years' deportation and who has sacrificed himself for the cause, is now 'without a party', because he thought the Party should be worthy of its name and not be reduced to what its successive 'proprietors' have made of it.

The talks have failed. I decide to go alone to the huts. I begin with the Koliyannistes:

'I think it's out of the question for the camp to remain without representatives. My efforts to set up a joint committee have failed. That's why I'm standing before you. I am putting myself forward as your representative. If I'm elected, I shall appoint the various committees. Each hut will elect its own representative to deal with its own affairs. I make just one condition: that I get at least 90 per cent of the vote. If I don't, I'll retire to my corner and it'll be up to you.'

'And who are you, my friend, to ask to represent us?'

'I've been your deputy and I believe I have greater responsibility for having held that post.'

'It's we who take on responsibilities, we who belong to the Party.'

'Very well, in that case vote against me!'

In the end I was elected with 99 per cent of the vote!

We set to work immediately: we whitewashed the kitchen and the canteen, cleaned the windows, installed a shower, swept the yard, organised literary and artistic evenings and study courses, laid out a tennis and volleyball court, knocked up a table, bats and a net for table-tennis, and organised a chess championship. We now had one committee to deal with immediate problems and another to deal with the International Red Cross. At last we had our own representation to the camp authorities. The camp was united, at least on this level, for thirty days.

I found myself in regular contact with those outside. In the camp I had shared out my jobs and chosen people to work with me. On questions concerning the daily life of the camp I worked mainly with the supporters of Koliyannis and the supporters of the Interior Bureau; on political and ideological questions mainly with those who belonged to no particular group and who wanted, as I did, to move towards something radically new. As their researches had reached no firm conclusion and as they gave utterance to the most extreme views, the 'chaos' got themselves a second name: 'the cosmics'!

Some friends and I had worked out afresh the point of view represented by the 'flexible' solution, the Karamanlis solution;

270

this position was very widely held in the prisons and the camps. We had agreed that I should send Karamanlis a personal letter in which I would develop our views on what needed to be done at some length. A comrade was given the job of drawing up the final text, which was to reflect a collective and not just an individual view. The letter left normally but I have still not found out if it arrived and if so what response it had.

To the Honourable Konstantin Karamanlis, Paris
President,

Although it is somewhat delayed, due to the conditions in which I find myself and of which you are certainly aware, I believe it is my duty to present some thoughts on the subject of your statements of two months ago, thoughts which are prompted by concern—similar to your own—for the fate of the Nation and are very timely in the light of recent developments.

I should first like to assure you, Mr President, that I consider your statements to be an important and positive contribution to the general efforts which are being made by our people and the entire political world to deliver our country from the colonels' dictatorship. I also consider them to be capable of providing a basis upon which to regroup the anti-dictatorship forces which are struggling for a return to normal political life and for the establishment of a new, democratic course.

You quite rightly denounce and draw attention to the dangers and catastrophes which lie in store for the Nation if the dictatorship lasts any longer, and I fully understand that it was with a deep sense of responsibility and regret that you were led to take this decision and appeal to honest individuals and to the Army to overthrow the dictators.

Nevertheless, allow me, two months after your appeal— two months in which it has had no response, in my view because of the specific difficulties that exist in the Army —to express the view that it was too cautious; it tended not to take in all those forces which are capable one way or another, of playing a part in this enterprise and it ignored the decisive importance, weight and effectiveness of

271

mass participation by the people in the fight to suppress relentless tyranny.

I must assure you, Mr President, that this observation does not stem from our philosophical differences, the differences in our views of the world and ways of thinking; it is the lesson given by the history of all people and all periods.

In fact, never has a tyranny which is supported by Praetorian guards and employs well-tried techniques of oppression and intimidation, been suppressed by such methods *without* the support of the popular masses. Only a vast movement, employing the vital sources of popular strength and imbued through and through with the spirit of sacrifice and heroism of a people which feels the effects of the tyranny in its bones and understands instinctively the imperative demands of history, can be in a position to undertake the struggle with single-minded devotion until final victory is won.

I should like to make another observation on the text of your statements. It concerns the transition period which is to follow the fall of the dictatorship and which must, according to you, see rule by a government with reinforced powers. Far from wishing to criticise and question your thesis, I should, though, like to draw your attention to the fact that this way of putting the problem risks arousing fear among a section of the people that it is a veiled plan to replace the present dictatorship with a similar structure, or might even provide the pretext (and this has already happened) for negative criticism, which could obscure what is essential and positive in your statements.

I am firmly convinced that the definition and statement of a clear objective (in the spirit, for example, of the recent statement by a number of men of letters, political personalities and others of every persuasion), which gives expression to the aspirations of our people and establishes the essential conditions for democracy to function, will give the most decisive impetus to the people's struggle for the suppression of the dictatorship.

Mr President, I understand the profound reason for your appeal for energetic action against the colonels' junta being limited to officers and soldiers and I also understand your hesitation in addressing yourself to the broader sections of the population. Permit me, though, not to share your fears. The Greek people have proved many times that they can assume their responsibilities in the darkest hours of their history. Today, strengthened by the painful experience of the recent past and endowed with extraordinary political sense, the Greek people are ready to fight for the re-establishment of sound democracy against any seditious attempt, provided that they have before them a programme which represents their aspirations and which guarantees respect for their basic rights and interests.

Mr President, I appreciated the significance and decisive importance of your statements from the very first. Especially after the international isolation of the junta by the decision of the Council of Europe. Your authority as a former President of the Council and as a political personality with influence over an important section of the Nation will be a valuable contribution to this struggle. By taking on the leadership of this struggle you will have deserved well of the Nation.

I am sure you will agree with my observations, which are those of an intellectual and leader of Greek youth who is working in the service of the people and the Nation; I am at your service. I have one single ambition: to make any sacrifice that may be needed for a democratic and free Greece where one will be able to laugh and sing again.

Please accept, Mr President, this expression of my profound esteem and greetings on my own behalf and on behalf of my fellow prisoners in Oropos.

Mikis Theodorakis
Oropos Camp, Christmas 1969

N.B. Of course, you may make use of this letter in any way you wish and I beg to be allowed to do likewise.

At various times we sent similar letters to other politicians and personalities.

Christmas is approaching. I feel that the camp must make its presence felt in a fighting manner. The 'independents' hesitate: they are not prepared to take part in demonstrations with the supporters of Koliyannis.

24 December I call the hut representatives to tell them that I shall not be eating any meals or going out for a walk on Christmas Day; I make it quite clear that it is up to each man what he does. I have already made an agreement with those who are outside. Reporters and photographers will be coming to see the camp and take photographs. We were going to try to hang black flags on the trees and on the barbed wire. In the end the 'independents' refuse to take part in the demonstration.

On Christmas morning our relations come to visit us. They are sent away. Heavy, dark clouds hang low over a rough sea. On the jetty I can just make out the silhouettes of my wife and my father. The gendarmes are in pursuit. But, there they are again, on the beach. I am gripping on to the barbed wire and biting my lips until they bleed.

In this 'Graeco-Christian' atmosphere we see a bishop, a deacon and the commandant from the Security, a hooligan who came originally from Nafplion, entering the camp. We are beside ourselves with anger. We all run to the first hut. I can hardly get the words out of my mouth. I am followed by Zouzoulas... a former cantor. And Tsokas makes the closing speech. He is terrific! So we force the bishop and the man from the Security to stand for two hours hearing our charge. Our hearts are lighter after it...

How can we tolerate this provocation on the part of the civil and religious authorities when our children are sitting round the table eating Christmas lunch without their parents, like orphans. And our parents without their children. Our wives alone, without their husbands. At this particular moment we are all as one, all ninety men, comrades, fellow-prisoners, united by our sorrow.

But after a while some go back to their huts and others to the canteen. Twenty-three refuse to go on a hunger strike as a protest against our internment. However, when the man from the Security comes in to count them, they get up and make their protest. They get up as one man and assail him: 'Above all, don't go and think we're not protesting. You can put us on the list of hunger strikers, too...' But partisan fanaticism finally prevails over joint action.

'We are in a sense welded together,' Dimos later explains. 'When the Koliyannistes go one way, we automatically, go the other...'

'So, your policy is always determined by opposition to others?

So you are not "independent"...'

'You can't understand us: you haven't lived in Lakki camp.'[1]

The same day the 'independents' stop saying hello to me. Some exhibit deadly hatred. They make it quite clear: 'We no longer recognise you as our representative.' I am even forced to change huts. All that because I agreed to take part in a demonstration with Koliyannistes.

Those who remain faithful to me decide, with me, to prepare a big demonstration. I explain my point of view: 'We must orientate the camp towards well-organised and coordinated combative action which will arouse some emotion. The results will be manifold: We'll awaken the interest of world opinion. We'll create around us an atmosphere favourable for unity. We'll give an aim to our activity. We'll contribute to our own liberation.'

I draw up a text. We decide that I shall sign it on my own, because it is more difficult for the enemy to strike at me than at someone else. We send copies to all the camps and prisons. The aim: to set in motion a unified and coordinated hunger strike movement (the duration to be decided by each detention centre, but for a minimum period of 48 hours). The first replies begin coming in a month later. One prison decides on a 48-hour strike, another a 3-day one. Farakos, for example, comes out for a 7-day strike.

Then I think again about my idea for a unified Patriotic Front. A valued friend, a leader of the Lambrakis Youth, has just arrived in the camp. There is complete agreement between us. I am able to have constructive discussions with him in complete freedom. I breathe again. It is a great source of strength to have a friend and comrade beside one whom one understands and who understands oneself. Together we sketch the outlines of the Patriotic Front, united against the dictatorship.

We invite the representatives of the three groups to discuss the details. The representative of the supporters of the Interior Bureau accepts our idea enthusiastically. The representative of the 'independents', with reservations. The delegate of the Koliyannistes rejects it violently and out of hand. I announce that I am going to talk to the huts about it. The same evening I begin with the comrades in the first hut: four of them agree

275

with me. One recent supporter of the Koliyannis faction asks me :

'What's the good of having the unified PAM when there's already the camp organisation?'

'Our life here has shown that we can unite for a higher objective, the Resistance. Sure, we have discussions on our own engagement in the party, but doesn't the PAM admit Centrists and even supporters of the Right in its ranks?'

'Who's going to determine the political line?' he asks.

'All of us here, through our elected representatives. It will be the same in each camp and in each prison, according to rules we shall establish together; the rules must aim at adopting positions and taking action jointly.'

'That can never happen. Only the avant-garde party, ours, can determine the line.'

The speaker has only recently become a communist. He was recruited last month by his son-in-law, one of the leaders of the Koliyannistes. And whom is he addressing? One of us has done nineteen years in prison, plus three more he is serving now. Another has done sixteen years, and so on.

I go on to the next hut. I speak. One of the 'audience' is pretending to be reading. This is Barbastathis, and he suddenly interrupts:

'Listen, my dear Theodorakis. I am very keen to listen to you. You tell me to offer you my hand. But my hand is clean, you see...'

'And by giving me it you're going to sully it?'

'I don't know,' he says, mockingly.

That's enough. I go back to my hut to write my letter of resignation as camp representative.

From the next day the Koliyannistes no longer acknowledge me when I greet them. Strange! Soon after I find out that they received an order to stop greeting me from five o'clock in the afternoon! I should have guessed as much: solidarity between prisoners and organised political groups is solidarity between two irreconcilable elements. The 'independents' were right. We are once again divided into two parties. Now, on the one side there are the Interior Bureau and the 'independents' and on the other the 'Koliyannistes'. It took me months to understand the Koliyannistes. They pretend to want an organisation for the whole camp, while keeping control of it in their own hands. In other words, they do not want a single, unified organisation,

276

which would be effective; they say No to the fight. But they sabotage the camp's unity of action.

Spring

Spring is undecided: sometimes it rains, sometimes the wind blows, sometimes the sun breaks through. Today the weather is marvellous, the sea is shimmering and the new leaves are shaking in the breeze.

After lunch, a walk along by the barbed wire fence, facing the sea. The ferry boats which do the round trip from Oropos to Euboea seem to be dancing on the sea. Two hundred metres away they turn sharply and disappear behind the jetty. We did not see any 'visitors' today—those friends who take the risk of coming out on to that jetty to wave to us. Just a few groups watching us out of the corners of their eyes. The walk begins to drag. I go back to the hut and lie down, enjoying the gentle warmth of this spring day.

I must have been dozing for a good half an hour when some-one comes and wakes me:

'There are some people on the jetty singing your songs and looking in this direction. They must be friends of yours.'

'And the guards?'

'They seem happy enough. They're not making any move.'

I dress quickly and go outside. The familiar words of one of my songs are carried on the breeze:

> 'I gave you rose-water
> You gave me poison...'

I can make out two or three voices. Voices I know. I walk over and grasp the barbed wire. One of the singers waves. I climb the barbed wire to see better.

A guard asks:

'Is it one of your songs, Mr Theodorakis?'

'Who can that be?' a prisoner asks.

'I know that voice. Wait! I recognise his walk: it's Manolis Khiotis!'[2]

The gendarme officer who has the grisly reputation of picking up our visitors now goes out of the camp and walks towards them. We signal to them to go away. But they carry on singing

277

and he is going to take them to the administration building and
then off to the station in Nea Ionia.

My comrades on this side of the barbed wire start humming
Khiotis's song:

> 'Eagle of the winter cold
> Falcon of solitude...'

I shudder. Those friends on the jetty seem to be performing a
solemn and sacred act. They move slowly away. They stare at us
rigidly and intently. Then they come back towards us. They
are singing beautifully together and the breeze swings their song
back and forth.

I recall my first meeting with Khiotis. It was in the little
Columbia studio in Lykourguou Street in 1959. He got his
bouzouki out of its case with great care. He held it tenderly like
a small child. And then!

Then the little studio was filled with crystal springs and many-
coloured suns.

I played him my 'Epitafios'.

'At that point the rhythm can't be as you play it,' he said.

'What do you mean?'

'It's a zeïbekiko rhythm, a very strong zeïbekiko rhythm.
Listen...'

He played various parts of the work—'A Day in May', 'You
Have Ruled, My Star', etc.—and beneath his magical fingers
they all revealed their real soul, the authentic zeïbekiko rhythm
he has given them. And after 'Epitafios' we had other big
successes together: 'Deserters', 'The City' and 'Epiphany'. The
musical genius of Khiotis is linked with my work for ever.

When we worked together we communicated with one another
from the very beginning in such a close and deep way that one
could have sworn we had grown up together.

And today Khiotis has come to see me! Here! In this camp,
where I am caged behind barbed wire like a wild animal, a
criminal, or a bird. He has come to sing me the songs we have
played and sung so many times together in the past and which
everyone had taken to their lips and hearts. That is why at this
particular moment the guards have given up using their arms
and prefer to let their hearts roam free with the poignant
melodies of these songs—the flesh and the voice of Greekness:

278

'Take a twig of osier
A head of rosemary
And change into the cool of the Moon
To rise up as midnight chimes
In the middle of the thirsty garden...'

The officer goes up to the little group, but as soon as Khiotis gives his name, he just remonstrates; however, the little group has to go away. They move off slowly and solemnly, like priests. Just before they go out of sight behind a white fishing net which is drying on the shore—they wave and bid us farewell.

I walk back from the barbed wire. My heart is heavy and I feel that my soul has literally been 'drained' and that I am left as just skin and bone. I can look neither at the sky nor at the sea. My eyes are fixed on the ground.

Next day we read in the papers of the sudden death of Manolis Khiotis. 'Manolis Khiotis went yesterday to Oropos and had a heart attack immediately he got home.' I then knew why I was looking so fixedly at the ground when the spring was shining so splendidly around me.

We are organising the hunger strike for 21 April. We hold a meeting: the Interior Bureau and the 'independents'. We decided that I shall start a seven-day hunger strike, starting on Easter Monday. My strike companions would be three young Lambrakides. We learn that the Koliyannistes are to go on a 24-hour strike. The others will begin a 48-hour hunger strike on Easter Day because their disagreements prevent them from going on strike together...So that there is some sort of unity about the strikes I shall strike with everyone, making seven days in all for me, and we shall all finish together.

We now had to set about defining our programme clearly. With no illusions. I prepare a text and put it forward for discussion. We meet again, all together: the Interior Communist Party and the 'independents'. There is a big debate on the text. Amendments are made to it. In the end we all agree on the final text. Copies are made. On 25 March all the Evangelos[3] are in the visiting room with their parents and near relations... The first copies leave on 25 March. When will they arrive? They arrived in Paris at the same time as I did, in April.

I have changed huts. Andreas Lentakis has given me his place.

I now have Rambavila, Mikhalis and Vayopoulos for neighbours. From my bed I can see the observation post above the window. Manolis is on guard duty up there. It was he who guarded me at Zatouna: there I had him below me, now he is above. The roles are reversed. I shall encounter him again as a guard in the corridor at the sinister prison hospital of Sotiria. There is a Cretan song which goes: 'Manolis, you turn and turn again like a swan.'

I lie on my bed for hours. I write an essay on my music. I read a lot. And when the weather is fine I go and sit looking at the sea. I have begun to set to music a poem by Léopold Sédar Senghor.[4] I am planning to write a new cycle of twelve songs. I was to write only three of them, as I was transferred to Sotiria; I am not to return to the camp.

For some time the humidity, the bad accommodation and food, and, more than anything, the nervous tension, malaise and bitterness resulting from the difficult and delusory relations in the camp have had a bad effect on my health.

At Zatouna, before, the sudden change of climate (the village is at an altitude of 1,100 metres) had given me bouts of dizziness and fever. From time to time I had inexplicable attacks with very violent abdominal pains. I was confined to bed for almost a week. This was attributed at the time to stomach trouble. The sergeant at the gendarmerie, Tsouroulas, who ran the 'chemist's', vied with the efforts of the country doctor in Dimitsana to give me the most effective purgative. (Since then, in May 1970 I had a similar attack, when I was travelling between Paris and Rome, where I had to take the floor alongside Santiago Carrillo,[5] at a meeting organised by the Italian Youth Against NATO. The Italian doctors who examined me took me straight into the operating theatre. They diagnosed chronic appendicitis as the cause of my frequent attacks. It seemed it was an advanced stage. Inflammation of the appendix had spread to the liver and during my speech at the meeting peritonitis broke out.) The progress of this infection perhaps explains the sudden swelling of my body during my detention at Oropos. In fact, my features became gradually deformed, to such a point that my wife literally went crazy when she saw me during one of our rare meetings.

Haemoptysis started up again. I decided not to say anything

about it, and to wait for spring and the sun. I feared they would take me away from my comrades and isolate me in some prison hospital room. However, my condition got worse. One evening I spoke about it to three comrades from my hut: Vayopoulos, Mikhalis and Andreas Rambavila.

(Rambavila arrived in Paris after I did, a free but sick man. He was got into hospital through the good offices of our dear friend Professor Milliez, who told us: 'He has very acute leukaemia. He hasn't got long to live.' Since 1937 he had been deported from one camp to another. A writer and journalist, a man with a comfortable income, he had offered his life to the movement and to the people. I did not think it possible that he could die. He had left Oropos a week before me, destined for a prison hospital. He had lent me his 'office', his lamp and his chair. Before falling into a coma he insisted on seeing me. But at the time I was not in Paris. He died before I got there. What did he want to say to me? Still a militant of the people: he went with modesty, no fuss, and confident until his last breath that our people would be free.)

'There's the question of protecting the hut. My illness is contagious. I ought to go away...' I tell them.

They protested:

'Don't worry about us...Go and lie down. We'll save you.'

We had agreed to keep the matter a secret so that I am not taken away.

I remember that at that time we were living with an additional source of anguish. We had learned that an army unit was near the camp. Now, this unit, which was commanded by Papadopoulos's brother, was composed of fascist extremists who wanted to organise a commando unit to break into the camp and take some of us off and kill us. We had taken protective measures: we barricaded the doors and windows and built a rampart behind, made of beds and mattresses; we also intended, in the event of an attack, to shout to alert the village...

The commandant must have noticed that something was up. In vain I was going out into the cold and wind, muffled up to show nothing was happening. One day the camp doctor called me to his office.

'It would be useless. If I'm sent to a sanatorium and watched over by guards, I'd die within the hour. Better to give me medicines. It'll soon be spring, it'll be getting warmer, I'll pull

281

through alright...'

The news of my illness had leaked out. The junta was worried. They sent reporters who took secret photographs of me.

We were discussing the organisation of the unified PAM and the hunger strike for 21 April when the commandant called for me.

'You're going with Vitalis to the general state hospital for a check-up. You won't be kept in.'

'If we're kept in, we'll go on hunger strike.'

Because that meant total isolation, far from one's comrades and at the mercy of the guards.

'You have my word of honour...'

The next morning he calls us again.

'Take nothing with you. You'll be back this evening.'

The black English cars of the Gendarmerie's Special Service roll up with our guards; they are also in black. Four cars. Vitalis gets in one with five guards. I am in the other, with five guards. The other two cars are there to escort us.

We soon arrive at the state hospital. While we are waiting, I show my guards the marble plaque on the wall which says: 'Founded during the presidency of Konstantin Karamanlis.'

'Why do they keep that plaque?' I ask. 'He's a traitor. Didn't he call on you to rise up against the junta?'

Silence.

I whisper to the gendarme next to me:

'Tell me, be honest, what photo will one be seeing up there?' (It was the gendarmes at Zatouna who taught me this phrase.)

He looks round furtively and says quietly:

'The man you've just mentioned.'

The officer who is in charge of the expedition comes running down the stairs. We are off again. The cars tear off.

'Where are we going?'

Silence. We get out on to a country road leading towards Mount Hymettus. Cypresses on both sides...

'You're being taken to the firing squad,' a gendarme says, laughing. I shudder. I remembered that about a month before, during a similar trip, we got lost in the back alleys of Agia-Paraskevi, near Athens. I was sure then that I was being taken to some secret and 'special' place. But now I see in front of us the vehicle carrying Vitalis.

'You're no match...' I say, after a brief silence.

282

'Ah! They're stupid, our people!' the gendarme goes on. 'In their place I'd have killed the lot of you...'

'Eh! Eh! Eh! I'm scared of blood,' another says, and they all roar with laughter.

We turn right. An impasse! On the left there is a large prison door. The 'Sotiria' prison-sanatorium! They are waiting for us. I get out. I protest to the major, whom I recognise as having searched me once before. No reaction. They take me to the office. I have my hands up. A gendarme sub-lieutenant searches me under the armpits. 'Shoes off!' 'Your money!'

I protest.

'This is what gangsters do. The camp commandant gave me his word of honour...' They smile. '...Anyway, from now on we're going on hunger strike. I hold you personally responsible,' I tell the major.

No reaction. They keep our money. They establish our identity. As usual, we are just objects to be recorded: debit and credit. Then we are taken inside the prison. The cells are closed. In the passage the guard who is escorting us puts his hand over each spy-hole we pass to stop the prisoners seeing us. Doors, stairs, more stairs, more doors. A huge cell, freshly roughcast. Barred windows all around: a real hen coop.

'They put the stiffs in here,' Vitalis says.

'We've prepared it specially for you,' the guard commandant tells me, politely.

'Much obliged,' I reply, with equal politeness.

We are locked up. The windows overlook the garden. About twenty sick prisoners are doing their daily exercise. They have spotted us and smile and make gestures behind their backs. Many of them run their hands through their hair: a sign of greeting. Two or three ignore us. All the others show surprise, joy and emotion. They make it quite clear that they are sympathetic.

The doctor, the director of the hospital, comes in. In his spare time he paints. He praises the climate of the area, the beauty of the landscape, the bird song in the morning! He waxes lyrical! In just a few moments he is going to get into his car and drive into Athens. Us inside, him outside. It is in the nature of things. He does not seem too bothered with our troubles. But he can't dissociate himself from it...after all, I'm an artist, too.

'I need three days to do a complete examination,' he tells us.

283

'That means we'll be able to leave on Saturday.'

We accept the delay and suspend the hunger strike until then.

Someone threw a piece of paper wrapped round a stone through our spy-hole: 'Dear friends, all of us here are ready to help you! We're at your service. Anything you want. Any mission. We're in contact with the outside world. I beg you to give me your confidence...In the afternoon you'll find me sitting in the shade of the big tree. Send me a note in the same way...We are 'common law' prisoners. At the other end of the building there are three of your comrades from Leros. They're in a very bad way. They've been told of your arrival. They embrace you. Greetings!'

We prepare our reply: 'We've been treated here like real gangsters. If we're here after Sunday we're going on hunger strike. The signal will be: our sitting in the window with our backs to the bars. Tell our friends. Telephone number —. We greet you. We'd like details of our comrades. Greetings!'

On the next two days we are taken to the laboratory for examination. Saturday is visiting day. In the visitors' room—my father and Myrto. How many years have I seen them coming to visit me in prisons and prison hospitals! They bring fruit, books, a little chess set, paper and pencils, two plates, one toothbrush, some soap...A new stock of equipment!

Papadopoulos spoke yesterday.

I ask my father:

'What are our chances of being freed?'

'Not more than one in twenty!'

However they are both calm! For us the torture of prison is the suffering which our ordeal causes others, our relations and friends. If they were to make the best of it, then internment would be just a game for us!

'All the orders of the Chief of the General Staff of the Army have been cancelled, except two, those which ban your works,' my father says with evident pride.

I talk to them excitedly about the camp. I want to think and make them think that the camp was marvellous. Spring is on its way. Our roses will be blooming. I shall sit under the fir trees and devote myself to my work. The study I call my 'artistic credo' is going well. Creative work, I have in hand. I am euphoric, lyrical even! We say goodbye. When shall I see them again?. . .

That evening we apply to the commandant to let us out for walks. The garden is out, but there is a long balcony.

Sunday. Midday. The door opens. An hour's walk. At one o'clock on the dot the doctor comes back. He asks us to wait until the next day, Monday, to give him time to have the X-rays developed. We say yes. Sunday seems interminable. I read *Vol de Nuit*. We play chess. At midnight a walk out on the balcony. The cells are empty. How many hundreds of comrades have breathed their last here? It was here that Ploumbidis[6] was 'looked after'. And it was from here that he was taken to be executed. 'We deny that Ploumbidis has been executed,' Zakhariadis, the then Secretary-General of the Greek Communist Party, had said, even adding that 'the agent Ploumbidis is safe and well in South America'. Next day the newspapers published a photograph of his corpse, riddled with bullets. Oh exemplary bureaucracy, how many crimes were committed for your greater glory!

Monday, 13 April 1969

No indication that they are going to come and take us away. We decide to start the hunger strike. In the afternoon we will be in the window with our backs to the bars...

At midday we are taken out for a walk. The guard who escorts me tells me his troubles. He had hired a car and it had been in collision with another car. He paid for the damage but the owner of the hire company is blackmailing him. Did he and his friends have some girls with them in the car? Wasn't he a bit tipsy?

'But does he know you're a gendarme?'

My question seems to irritate him :

'But...Why this "but"? He's got influence, that fellow has.'

'Is he a protégé of the junta?'

'I reckon...'

'Why didn't you beat him up? Are you or are you not a gendarme?'

'I fear the consequences...a transfer.'

'And are you still going to pay up?'

'I don't know what to do.'

The head guard comes in.

'Mr Theodorakis, get ready. You're leaving. You, Vitalis, you're staying here.'

285

'Impossible!' Vitalis shouts. 'If I'm not leaving as well I'm going on a hunger strike.'

I take him to one side. He is very weak. He is spitting blood. 'It's just an administrative detail. Tomorrow or the day after you'll be back with us. Be patient! Now they're taking me away, they won't be long before they come for you as well, I'm sure of it. If they haven't moved you by Thursday the whole camp will be on its feet. I'm going to get the volleyball teams ready,' I tell him, laughing (Vitalis was an excellent volleyball player). We embrace one another...

A corridor...a staircase...a door...more stairs another door. Strange! The head guard is alone. Usually he is with his men. We go out into the yard. Surprisingly, it is deserted. Where is the guard? We go on. A man in black is coming towards us. He holds his hand out and introduces himself.

'Colonel Ioannidis.'

I think perhaps he is the station chief. The big gate of the prison hospital opens a little...Myrto! What's all this? Good news or bad news? I have no time to think. My wife comes up to us, smiling enigmatically.

I try to tell by her eyes. Is it sadness? Hope? Despair?

'Don't you see who's with me?'

Her voice seems to be singing. It is only then that I am aware of the presence of J.-J. Servan-Schreiber.

'Mr Schreiber! What's he want here?'

'He has the Premier's permission. He wants to speak to you.'

'Where?'

'In the car. He is in a hurry. He has to get to the airport.'

I ask to go to the 'office'.

'What for?'

'The money. I want to leave it for Vitalis.'

'Leave the money!'

'Am I not going to be searched?' (I had got used to being.)

'Let's go,' the colonel says.

'Mr Schreiber, what a coincidence! When I get back to the camp I must tell my friends about your book, *The American Challenge*.'' Suddenly my joy disappears...He has the Premier's permission. He has no escort. So, it's a big trap. Watch it!...

Myrto is holding a poppy. As we go through the big gates, she whispers:

'It's symbolic.' She nods strangely at the red flower.

Another surprise! The impasse is deserted. No guard here, either. Just a black car. The colonel opens the rear door. 'Sit next to your wife,' Servan-Schreiber sits on the other side. The colonel is in front, next to the driver. We move off. The police must be hiding a bit farther on. At the first turning we're going to meet the other cars...A turn...Nothing...We are alone. Strange! I wait for the 'interview' to begin, but Schreiber stays silent. He is wearing a large pair of dark glasses. I look at him out of the corner of my eye. His thoughts seem to be elsewhere. He is tired and stretched out in his seat.

'In Paris I was a regular reader of *L'Express*.' I try to break the ice. Myrto knocks me with her knee. She nods towards the colonel. What's up? We are passing the Hilton Hotel. The statue of Truman. (Funny! How many nights have I spent blowing that statue up in my imagination!) My wife whispers:

'You're leaving!'

'Where to?'

'Paris!'

'And you?'

'Later.'

'How?'

'He'll come back.'

'Who?'

'Schreiber.'

Was this going to be a master stroke of kidnapping? And we had made so many plans for escaping! Maybe one of these plans has been put into effect. I begin to get uneasy. But then, the man in front of me can't be a real colonel. I look around. Instinctively I crouch down in my seat as far as I can... Vouliagmeni Avenue.

'I'm kidnapping you,' Schreiber says finally, as if he had been reading my thoughts.

No, I think to myself, that's unlikely. We'll be arrested at the airport. Then the interrogators of the Security again. Prison. It will start all over again.

Schreiber is talking with the colonel! Arranging some technical details. No! It's not a kidnapping—I thought as much. The colonels have found a way of getting rid of me. And what about the camp? And spring? My companions? My study? I am overcome with a deep sense of sadness. So I am going to be a free man! FREE! I feel dizzy. I tell myself: 'Keep calm!

Don't let yourself be caught off balance! Any minute you'll be up before the Military Police (ESA)[8]...Be prepared for more pain and more ordeals...' We're now at the airport, by the sea. We stop in front of the terminal for international flights.

Schreiber passes me his dark glasses. 'It would be better if you weren't recognised.' He gets out of the car. I ask the colonel:

'Are you by any chance the commandant of the ESA?'

'No! He's my namesake. I'm the Premier's *chef de cabinet*. I have orders to take you to Mr Schreiber's aircraft.'

I remember the other Ioannidis in the camp at Makronisos; standing on a chair 'haranguing' us. It was 26 March 1949. He was then a lieutenant or a captain. I was right in front of him. I was standing up and he was on the chair. Our faces were quite close and his breath smelt of alcohol. 'Those of you who are Greek, who aren't Bulgarians, leave the ranks. The others are to die!' There were about three hundred of us. Only thirteen walked out. We were then beaten up for three days and three nights.

We move off again and follow a black car. Stop in front of the VIP lounge. A waiter in tails asks if we would like 'to take something'.

'A whisky!' I tell him, as if I were a head of state.

We settle in comfortable armchairs. I suddenly think of Vitalis. How could he imagine what was happening to me...Is he eating his meal or has he started his hunger strike?

The colonel is making a telephone call:

'Yes, Mr President...He is with me here...No, he hasn't got a passport...The aircraft is ready...In ten minutes...'

He puts the phone down. 'The Premier sends you his greetings...'

At last we leave. We get back into the car...The aircraft. A pretty stewardess ('If only Toundas could see her', I said to myself, thinking of my Oropos comrade who was constantly tormented and obsessed by his exuberant youth...). Schreiber and his escort follow on foot. I shake hands with the *chef de cabinet*. I kiss my wife. I get into the aircraft. I put on my seat belt. The little jet takes off like a toy.

On the ground my wife and the Colonel watch us climb into the sky. The pilot puts the aircraft into a dive as a final farewell. The journey towards freedom begins with a pang of heartfelt anguish. All that I love, that I have loved, I am leaving behind.

I am leaving. But *my life* is staying behind. I shall fight so that we can become one again, my life and myself, myself and my very beautiful homeland which is twinkling beneath my feet and which is receding into the distance with the merging of the blue sea and the grey mountains.

I turn to Schreiber. I feel a deep sense of gratitude. I look into his eyes. He's a friend!

'Thank you!' I am unable to say anything else.

After a long pause I ask:

'What will become of my wife and children?'

'I'll be coming back for them on Saturday. Papadopoulos has promised.'

All my music, too, I have left it behind, at Oropos. A river of music. A river of dreams, of hope and despair.

Some days after my arrival in Paris I get a letter from my comrades in the camp. A simple letter. A priceless gift.

Dear Mikis,

It's now ten days since you left us and we haven't got used to your not being around. It seems that the door will open at any minute and that the whole hut will be lit up with your smile. If we go out into the yard we believe we are going to see you on the other side of the barbed wire, sitting, deep in meditation, contemplating the sea and the jetty. We often go to your bed to be closer to you. As we go into the refectory your songs are still resounding in our ears. We still see you raising your arms to direct the choir.

Dear Mikis, we miss you tremendously. But we are so pleased to know that you are breathing the air of liberty again. We have faith in you. We know that you will not stop fighting for a single moment for the deliverance of our people who have suffered so much and for the release of all political prisoners. We have learned recently that newspapers, radios and news agencies throughout the world are speaking of nothing but you, and our emotion and pride are immeasurable. Your fight for the happiness and dignity of men, for the noblest ideals, will always inspire us on our difficult journey. All of us here in this outpost of Oropos will keep on our feet, thinking of our people, with your songs on our lips, and concerned for all who are dear, our comrades, for all mankind.

Dear Mikis, we greet you and we have only one wish: to celebrate all of us together, and soon, the RESURREC-TION—in the cities and the villages of our motherland, with you at our head directing the concerts of liberty and democracy.

Greetings, Mikis
25 April 1970
The political prisoners of Oropos

References

1 On the island of Leros there were two camps: Partheni and Lakki. In the second the Koliyannistes were in an overwhelming majority and literally terrorised their opponents.
2 One of Greece's most popular singers and bouzouki players.
3 The Day of the Annunciation of the Blessed Virgin Mary (Evangelismos), 25 March, is the name day feast of the Evangelos.
4 President of Senegal and Secretary-General of the Union Progressiste Sénégalaise; President Senghor is a poet, a sponsor of negro art, an advocate of a French-speaking commonwealth, and an advocate of joint economic action by the Third World towards the industrialised world. (Translator's Note)
5 General Secretary of the Spanish Communist Party.
6 Nikolas Ploumbidis, member of the Politburo of the Greek Communist Party. Arrested in 1952 and sentenced and executed in the following year. Zakhariadis, the then Secretary-General of the Greek Communist Party, had accused him of being an agent of the Security. This accusation, which was made over the radio station 'Eleftheri Ellada' (Free Greece), was untrue and a complete fabrication. He was rehabilitated in 1956 by the new leadership of the Greek Communist Party.
7 Le Défi Américain.
8 Elliniki Stratiotiki Astinomia.

CHRONOLOGY OF EVENTS

29 July 1925   Mikis Theodorakis is born on the island of Chios. The previous year (25 March 1924) Greece had become a republic following the Greek royal family's sympathies for the Germans during the First World War and the failed invasion of Turkey. Theodorakis's father, a budget official in the Ministry of the Interior, is frequently moved from post to post and so Mikis spends his youth in several provincial towns.

1932   Ioannina. Theodorakis learns to sing Byzantine hymns and, since his father is from Crete and his mother from the Greek colony in Asia Minor, he also gets to know the very varied tradition of Greek folk song.

3 November 1935   The Army organises a rigged plebiscite in which 97 per cent of the electorate opts for the return of the monarchy. King George II comes to the throne.

1935   Argostoli. A town of seven thousand inhabitants and one piano. At the bishop's request, Theodorakis performs the 'Passion' in church on Good Friday.

9 May 1936   The police and the gendarmerie kill thirty people and wound hundreds of others during a demonstration in Thessalonika. This prompts the young poet, Yannis Ritsos, to write a series of poems, 'Epitafios'—a mother's lament over her dead son. Twenty-two years later Theodorakis sets eight of these poems to music.

4 August 1936 King George II grants dictatorial power to General Ioannis Metaxas. Metaxas tells the Greek people that he has taken over the leadership of the country to counter 'the communist threat'. The communists hold 15 of the 250 seats in Parliament.

1937 Theodorakis begins his secondary education in Patras. His family later moves to Pyrgos, south of Patras. He gets his first violin and his first accordion, and forms a small band; he writes his first compositions.

1939–43 Tripolis. It is here that Theodorakis writes 'The Song of Captain Zacharias' (1939, from a poem by A. Valaoritis). (During the Second World War this becomes the song of the Greek maritime resistance.) Theodorakis directs choirs, forms an orchestra, and gives his first concert, at which his Byzantine ode, 'Kasiani' (1942), is played.

7 April 1939 Italian troops occupy Albania. September 1939: outbreak of the Second World War.

28 October 1940 War between Greece and Italy as a result of the Greek 'No' to Mussolini's ultimatum. Greek forces thrust deep into Albania. As a member of the Nationalist Youth Organization, Theodorakis cares for the wounded in the town hospital.

5 April 1941 The Germans come to the aid of their Italian allies and invade Greece.

27 April 1941 The Germans reach Athens. The country is divided into three zones of occupation: German, Bulgarian and Italian. Tripolis is in the Italian zone.

31 May 1941 Manolis Glezos and Apostolos Santas tear down the swastika from the Acropolis, a symbolic act calling for resistance to the occupation forces.

27 September 1941 The EAM[1]—'National Liberation Front' —is set up. Later the Front sets up an armed organisation: ELAS.[2]

28 October 1941 On the anniversary of the Greek 'No' to Mussolini the three letters EAM blaze on Mount Hymettus, near Athens.

Winter 1941–2 Greece is hit by famine: hundreds of thousands die of hunger.

25 March 1942 Theodoros Kolokotronis (1770–1843), the hero of the war of Greek independence, lies buried in the town of his birth, Tripolis: during a demonstration at his tomb on the first anniversary of the beginning of the present war of independence, Theodorakis is arrested for striking an Italian officer. In prison he is tortured for the first time. His fellow prisoners introduce him to communism. On his release he sees his duty as being to join the resistance.

Summer 1943—summer 1944 Theodorakis is arrested again, this time by Festuccio, the Italian police chief in Tripolis. Festuccio warns him: the Italians are soon going to capitulate. In a few days the Germans will take control of the region and then Theodorakis and many others will be arrested. The following day his family send him to stay with an uncle who lives in the Nea Smyrni district of Athens. Immediately afterwards the Germans arrive in Tripolis. They search for Theodorakis in vain. Half a dozen of his comrades are arrested and executed. In Athens Theodorakis becomes a member of EPON,[3] the youth movement of the National Liberation Front, EAM. The director of the Athens Conservatoire, F. Ekonomidis, takes Theodorakis on as a student.

Theodorakis is arrested while carrying clandestine documents. His friend, who was helping, is tortured and killed before his eyes, but miraculously Theodorakis is freed. (Although he was still only a student he had written in his identity card 'composer' and this title had impressed the Germans.)

Theodorakis meets Myrto Altinoglou in her parents' house, where he goes to listen to the BBC's Greek broadcasts (1943).

He becomes a member of ELAS, the military organisation of EAM. In the summer of 1944 the Greek partisans control over three quarters of the country: in the liberated zones peace is being prepared—a democratic structure and a new system of education are established. After over a hundred years of so-called independence the partisans see a chance for the Greek people themselves to conquer Greece. But Greece's English allies, the Greek government in exile and the collaborationist régime have other views.

12 October 1944   Churchill and Stalin agree to Greece belonging to the British 'sphere of interest'. The same day the Germans leave Athens and Piraeus. Theodorakis meets Vasilis Zanos, the head of a department in the EAM, at Falirou Square in Piraeus; together they disarm the staff of the Luftwaffe and hand the arms over to the 'Lord Byron' student group. (One member of this group was Yannis Xenakis, now a world-famous composer.)

14 October 1944   The British 'liberation army' lands at Piraeus. The British commander and the old politicians demand that the partisans obey their orders, but the partisans do not want a return to the conditions which prevailed before the war.

3 December 1944   Theodorakis and his Nea Smyrni group take part in a demonstration against the new 'occupation force'. The British troops open fire on the unarmed crowd: there are dead and wounded. Theodorakis soaks a Greek flag in the blood of a dead comrade and walks forward to the barricades. He is felled by the butt of a British rifle.

4 December 1944   The order is given by the British to wipe out the Greek partisans. ELAS sends its forces to Athens. Six hard weeks of struggle for the Greek capital follow; 7,500 members of the resistance are arrested by the British and sent to the El Daba camp in Libya. This arouses the strong and united indignation of the free world. 'Most of my comrades were killed by a bullet in the back of the neck,' says Theodorakis.

13 February 1945 In the town of Varkiza the Greek government and the EAM agree to the disarmament of all the resistance groups and to try those who betrayed the country during the occupation. Very soon it becomes clear that the agreement is simply a unilateral attempt to disarm the popular army so as to brush aside its political demands. In the spring Theodorakis is attacked in the street by a group of 'indignant citizens', one of the many terrorist bands used by the government, and some weeks later he is arrested following the discovery of a clandestine printing press at a friend's house. Influential friends save him from a long term of imprisonment; many of his comrades arrested at the same time were to spend twenty years inside.

1 June 1945 The trials come to an end with three collaborators being sentenced to death; not one of the sentences is carried out. Yannis Rallis, the head of the Greek puppet government during the German occupation and as such directly responsible for the deaths of dozens of Greeks, does not receive the death sentence. Political life is taken over by the Nationalists: the partisans *are* communists, in other words, they are considered to be agents of the Devil. The Greek security battalions, organised by the Germans during the war to fight against the resistance, are now looked upon by the government as allies in the struggle against 'the enemies of the nation'. After all, Hitler, too, was an anti-communist.

January 1946 Theodorakis expounds his ideas on a cultural resistance policy at a congress of EPON.

26 March 1946 Demonstration in Athens connected with the forthcoming parliamentary elections (31 March). The crowd sings 'The Song of Captain Zacharias'; Theodorakis is at their head. Before they reach Syntagma (Constitution) Square the demonstrators are arrested by a large detachment of police. Theodorakis is suddenly surrounded by soldiers; they hurl themselves at him and beat him up; he faints and falls to the ground and is taken away in an ambulance. When he comes round, he is lying on a marble slab, surrounded by corpses—in a hospital morgue.

27 March 1946 A morning paper prints a brief report that the demonstrations had suffered one victim—Theodorakis. His friends get him transferred to a clinic, where he is operated on for a fractured skull. He is in hospital for two months and when he leaves he has reduced vision in one eye.

1 September 1946 The Royalists organise a plebiscite for the return of the king. In spite of great pressure, only a slender majority vote for his return.

27 September 1946 George II returns to Greece as king of the royalist minority. The hunt for the 'reds' continues.

12 March 1947 Declaration of the Truman Doctrine.[4] Great Britain has to give up her interest in the internal struggle in Greece; her allies on the ground have been shown to be too weak and the task is too great for the former world power. The United States assumes 'responsibility' for keeping Greece in the Western world (in the hallowed phrase), pouring millions of dollars into the country, intended mainly for military purposes. From this date on the United States determines the development of Greece's domestic politics.

July 1947 In the space of a single week ten thousand members of the resistance are arrested in Athens: Theodorakis is one of them. After two weeks the internees are transported, with much suffering, to Psitalia, a parched island in the Aegean between Athens and Corinth. Although it is extremely hot the prisoners are given no water. Two weeks later they are taken to Ikaria, an island near the Turkish coast. There Theodorakis meets up again with Vasilis Zanos, with whom he had disarmed the Luftwaffe staff three years before. There is a little more freedom on Ikaria. Theodorakis sees a lot of Zanos, and composes and copies popular songs and teaches them to his comrades.

7 September 1947 A coalition government is formed under Sofoulis. It adopts a conciliatory attitude towards the 'reds' and is therefore doomed to fall. Nevertheless, a large proportion of the internees are to benefit from its amnesty decree. Theodorakis and Zanos return to Athens in the same boat. Shortly afterwards the manhunt gets under way again and the assassinations and executions continue.

24 December 1947 A partisan government is set up in the mountains under the leadership of Markos Vafiadis. The civil war is now official. Theodorakis receives orders from the Communist Party to join the armed partisans. But the roads round Athens are blocked; he has to spend the winter in the capital. Being a wanted man, he cannot go to see his parents or his friends. He spends nights among the rocks and at building sites with his friend Pavlos (Papamerkouriou). Theodorakis contracts a lung disease. He then finds work in the theatre at Piraeus; the leading role is being played by Melina Merkouri. He makes secret trips to the Conservatoire to play the piano and for choir rehearsals. Every Wednesday he meets Myrto Altinoglou in a café and they go out to the cinema; in the cinema Theodorakis retires to the toilet with a parcel of clean clothes and returns with the dirty ones. He can no longer resist the temptation and one day he visits his parents at Nea Smyrni; a few hours later the police are knocking at the door—but this time it is Pavlos's turn to be arrested and tortured: they fracture his vertebra. He is condemned to death and has to be carried to the firing squad. Theodorakis later writes 'Song of the Dead Brother' in his memory.

June 1948 After being interrogated by the police at Nea Smyrni, Theodorakis is taken on a Liberty ship back to Ikaria, where he learns of the death of Vasilis Zanos. He also learns of the death of Makis Karlis, one of his Tripolis friends, a soldier on the government side, who had fallen victim to the partisans. Theodorakis writes a symphonic work and dedicates it to these two victims of the fraticidal war.

December 1948 Those deported to Ikaria who are still young enough not to have done their military service are taken to the island of Makronisos, south-east of Attica, where the government has set up a 're-education centre' for those who have been contaminated by the 'red virus'. A radical re-education. The thirty thousand internees on the island are government hostages from the anti-partisan struggle and at the slightest opportunity hatred unleashes massacres of prisoners. One evening, after a day of arduous forced labour on roads which will never be used, Theodorakis gives the first performance of the 'Elegy of Zanos and Karlis'. One of the prisoners on Makronisos is the poet, Yannis Ritsos, and his tuberculosis, like Theodorakis's, goes back to this period.

29 February 1949 Some five thousand detainees are assembled in a gorge which opens out into the sea. The re-education can begin: they are fired on and hundreds are killed or wounded. The survivors are invited to sign a declaration of citizen's allegiance to the government—a formality which is required for entry into the Royal Army. This continues until there are only thirty-five survivors left. Fifteen are later executed. Among the twenty is the future editor of the Left-wing daily *Avgi*, Potis Paraskevopoulos (deported to Leros in 1967). A future EDA[5] deputy, Leonidas Kyrkos, also refused to sign: he is put in a bag and plunged several times into the sea until he loses consciousness. (Kyrkos was imprisoned in the Averof on 21 April 1967.) Each day Theodorakis bears witness to what being 'called to active military service' means.

300

25 March 1949   On the anniversary of the outbreak of the war of independence the 'lost' prisoners of Makronisos receive a visit from Queen Frederika, a former member of the Hitler Youth. (George II, who died in March 1947, was succeeded by his brother, Paul, Frederika's husband.)

26 March 1949   The following day the authorities come to 'enrol' Theodorakis's class in the Army: three hundred men, including Theodorakis, have decided not to sign on. They are gathered together and maltreated for ten hours, with baton blows; Theodorakis collapses, exhausted. A soldier dances on his chest until he loses consciousness. That same evening Theodorakis is taken in hand by the notorious executioner, Loris, who specialises in torturing his victims' bones. Theodorakis is bound to a table and Loris begins twisting his leg with great professional dexterity. The 'treatment' ends with Loris's speciality : he breaks Theodorakis's right leg. A Cretan friend guides Theodorakis's hand—he is still unconscious—and he makes a cross on a piece of paper. A doctor orders that Theodorakis be transferred immediately to Military Hospital 401 in Athens, where dying prisoners are usually taken (Makronisos is only rarely a place of death). By chance Theodorakis's father learns that his son is in hospital and goes to see him; each time he passes his son's stretcher without recognising him and Theodorakis sees him but cannot speak because of his dislocated jaw. Theodorakis leaves Military Hospital 401 two months later.

September 1949   The last engagements of the civil war; the government is victorious.

Summer 1950   Despite these trying and troubled years, Theodorakis passes his finals and graduates from the Athens Conservatoire. He continues his 'military service'. He is sent to Alexandropolis with a group of musicians. Fifteen days later, when his captain finds out about his list of crimes he orders him to be cropped and put in a cell; he threatens to send him back to Makronisos. In desperation Theodorakis tries to commit suicide by eating gunpowder. He is transferred to a hospital in Thessalonika, where he is stomach-pumped and put in the mental patient's ward. It is almost worse than Makronisos. Here too the only language they know is that of the club: they hit the mental patients to keep them quiet. Theodorakis's father comes to his aid. He is transferred first to Athens and then to Crete, where he continues his military service in charge of a depot.

August 1951   EDA—the United Democratic Left—is formed.

Summer 1952   Theodorakis leaves the Army: he has finished his military service. He becomes a music critic in Athens, first for *Prodeftiki Allagi*[6] and then for *Avgi*.[7] Among other things, he writes the music for the ballet 'Orpheus'.

1953   Theodorakis writes his first film score. Armed with fifteen thousand drachmas he marries Myrto Altinoglou, who has meanwhile finished her medical studies. Theodorakis becomes her first patient. Ten years of suffering have left their mark; 'Makronisos fever' is the worst and for several years the mere memory of his stay in the concentration camp is enough to start a palsy which confines him to his sick bed.

1954   Theodorakis receives a bursary and goes to study in Paris; he becomes a student of Eugène Bigot at the Conservatoire.

1955   Six months after arriving in Paris, Theodorakis presents the École Normale with his Sonatina for piano.

5 October 1955   Brushing aside all the party leaders, King Paul appoints a comparatively unknown young politician called Konstantin Karamanlis as the new Premier. The next eight years under Karamanlis were to seem calm, but the islands and prisons were still crammed with political prisoners. The seeming democracy is mercilessly crushing all its opponents.

1956   Theodorakis's first commission for a foreign film: he writes the music for Powell and Pressburger's 'Night on Crete'. He can now buy his first car, an Opel.

1957   Theodorakis is a member of the Greek delegation to the Moscow youth festival and in Moscow receives a gold medal for his First Suite for Orchestra and Piano.

1958   Theodorakis is sitting in his Opel one evening, reading 'Epitafios', a collection of poems by Yannis Ritsos; he is waiting while Myrto does the shopping. By the time she gets back he has written music for eight of the poems. This is to be the turning point: his international prestige grows. He is commissioned to do three ballets: 'Antigone' for Margot Fonteyn in London, and 'Les Amants de Téruel' and 'Le Feu aux Poudres' for Ludmilla Tcherina in Paris. They achieve great success at Covent Garden and the Théâtre Sarah Bernhardt in 1959.

1959   His daughter, Margarita, is born in November. The family visits Greece, where Theodorakis renews old contacts and makes new ones.

1960   The composer Manos Hadjidakis records 'Epitafios', he directs his own orchestra and Nana Mouskouri is the soloist. The record is an enormous success and, despite Theodorakis's past, the songs are broadcast on Greek radio. But Theodorakis is not satisfied; he starts his own orchestra, featuring the bouzouki. He presents his own version of 'Epitafios' with Grigoris Bithikotsis as soloist: his interpretation is based wholly on popular tradition, which although much scorned is still very much alive. Theodorakis sparks off a national polemic: people are either pro-Hadjidakis or pro-Theodorakis. The two factions confront one another at meetings, in cafés and in the columns of the press. But behind the musical exterior there are hidden the deep political conflicts of the thirties and forties: in the controversy between the two composers the oppressed people see an opportunity to make their voices heard. Theodorakis decides to return to Greece to join the fray: this decision coincides with the development of political consciousness among the

303

young. By continually bringing out new songs and operas to add fuel to the debate, Theodorakis becomes a representative of this trend. 'My people have been told that they are nothing,' Theodorakis says. 'Through my music I tell them that our country is great and beautiful, and that we can do anything. Greece can live happily.'

May 1960 His son, Yorgos, is born in Paris. Theodorakis begins concert tours throughout Greece; the local gendarmerie often try to prevent the concerts from taking place. They forbid people to go to them, they break the instruments, and they send along their own agents provocateurs. When trouble starts at a concert in Naousa, Theodorakis goes to the microphone and announces: 'I have just finished writing 'Song of the Dead Brother'. It's about the civil war. At the end the enemies become friends. What unites us is stronger than what separates us.' Greece is preparing for elections. The fall of the Karamanlis régime is imminent. During a performance of 'Antigone' at the Stuttgart Opera Theodorakis speaks out against the régime's use of terror against the Greek people as a way of holding on to power. He is threatened: 'If you come back to Greece, you'll be killed!' Theodorakis replies by giving the date and the time of his arrival at Athens airport: he is met by a group of students singing his songs.

29 October 1961 Karamanlis 'wins' the elections. It was revealed later that this was one of the most scandalous cases of election rigging in the history of modern Greece. The *Pericles Plan* (of which George Papadopoulos was the special secretary) meant that officers and ordinary soldiers voted in thirty different places and that people who had been dead for years were put on electoral registers. George Papandreou brings the opposition together for its 'unrelenting struggle' against the régime. In years to come Greece was to be the scene of students' and workers' demonstrations and frequent abuse of power.

March 1962 During a student demonstration to get more

money (15 per cent more) for education, Theodorakis throws himself between the students and the police and is beaten. That evening he writes the song which a year later was to become the hymn of the Lambrakis Youth.

Summer 1962 Theodorakis's tuberculosis breaks out and he spends two months in King Edward VII's Hospital for Officers in London and another two months in a sanatorium near Athens. On leaving hospital he forms the thirty-man Athens Little Symphony Orchestra, MOA.

December 1962 The resistance hero Manolis Glezos is freed; he had been in prison since 1958 accused of espionage. (On 21 April 1967 he was deported to Leros.)

21 April 1963 The peace movement organises the first Marathon march. It is banned by the authorities. Several thousand people are arrested, including Theodorakis. Only the EDA deputy, Grigoris Lambrakis, goes on marching to the end, protected by his parliamentary immunity. Lambrakis is a well-known sportsman, having been champion at the Balkan Games several times; he is also a doctor and professor at Athens University.

22 May 1963 After a peace meeting in Thessalonika Grigoris Lambrakis is run down in the middle of the street, in full view of police and gendarmes. He is fatally wounded. Another EDA deputy, George Tsaroukhas, is hit and his skull is fractured.

27 May 1963 Lambrakis dies at dawn. Consternation and despair, especially among the young, develops into hatred of the authorities. The people had already guessed what was eventually to be discovered : the régime was behind the assassination. (Some of those responsible, including the 'small fry', were found guilty and condemned. In September 1969 the junta rehabilitated the two gendarmerie officers who were the main culprits.)

28 May 1963 Athens. Half a million people accompany Lambrakis to his grave, crying : 'Lambrakis lives' ('Lambrakis zi' = 'Z'), 'Democracy!', 'Every young person must become a Lambrakis!'

31 May 1963 'It's a law that assassins drown in the blood of their victims. The Mafia who are behind this syndicate of crime and who are drinking the blood of our people have made a fatal mistake. By picking on Lambrakis as their victim they have chosen their judge and their avenger. A single Lambrakis is more than enough to send them all to their graves. Lambrakis is lost but thousands of Lambrakides have been won—thousands of suns which will keep him alive and illuminate his memory.' (Article by Theodorakis in the daily, *Athinaïki*.)

1 June 1963 As a result of growing political agitation—and chiefly because of the murder of Lambrakis—Konstantin Karamanlis retires.

8 June 1963 Twenty Greek scientists, artists, workers, students and journalists meet to set up the 'Lambrakis Youth', the 'Lambrakides'. Theodorakis is later elected president.

3 November 1963 Parliamentary elections. George Papandreou's Centre Union[8] emerges as the strongest party but does not get an absolute majority. Papandreou refuses the support of EDA because he wants to fight both Left and Right at the same time. This means there has to be a second election.

16 February 1964 Parliamentary elections. Theodorakis is elected for the second ward of Piraeus. The Centre Union gets 53 per cent of the vote and forms a government, but the Papandreou government is a government in name only. Although it manages to get several reforms through—in education, for example—and to free the majority of political prisoners, real power is still in the hands of royalist reactionaries in the Army and the civil service. Soon after the elections King Paul dies; he is succeeded by his son, Constantine.

October 1964 Première of Theodorakis's grand oratorio,

306

'Axion Esti' (Dignum est).[9] Theodorakis divides his time between his artistic and political activities.

15 December 1964   Letter to Theodorakis: 'If the police haven't told you already—we're going to get you. You'll meet the same end as Lambrakis. KKK.' (Ku Klux Klan)

15 July 1965   When Papandreou tries to take control of the Army and become the real head of the government in Greece, he is dismissed by the young King Constantine. Only a few months later the king manages to get a parliamentary majority behind his new Premier. By breaking the rules of the parliamentary game in this way the king is paving the way for the political crisis which is to be used to justify the military's seizure of power on 21 April 1967. The violent demonstrations of the following weeks are strongly supported by the Lambrakides, whose effectiveness is increasing markedly.

19 July 1965   The Greek Army is put on alert. So as to avoid provoking any reaction, George Papandreou has not appeared in public since his fall, but now he announces that he is going from his house outside Athens to his office in the city. On the way he is cheered by about a million people.

21 July 1965   Theodorakis is to make a speech. He is carried through the crowd by a Lambrakides, Sotiris Petroulas, a 23-year-old economics student. Later the same evening Petroulas is killed by a tear gas grenade which explodes above his head; the police whisk the body away.

22 July 1965   In the morning some Lambrakides catch a group of agents in the act of burying Petroulas at Kokkinia. Theodorakis is told. With the help of the local people, they are made to hand over the body, and next day hundreds of thousands of people accompany it from Athens Cathedral to the cemetery. Theodorakis has written a song to the memory of his dead friend; it is sung by the cortège. After Constantine's coup de force against democracy the Lambrakis Youth grows enor-

307

mously in strength: over two hundred Lambrakis clubs spring up and there are more than fifty thousand members. Theodorakis suddenly finds himself the president of the biggest political organisation in Greece. The Lambrakides undertake political and social work; they plant trees, restore churches, give their blood, open houses of culture and libraries, and organise concerts. There are to be many attempts to dynamite their projects; the police and the gendarmerie are behind them. Members of the Lambrakis Youth are arrested on the slightest pretext and pressure is put on their bosses to sack them.

1 January 1966   King Constantine gives his New Year address. 'During the year just passed I have, to my great regret, witnessed the transformation of healthy and constructive political discussion into passions which are violent and which distort the truth.' He says the communists are responsible for the political agitation. He is accusing at least 70 per cent of the population of being communist—from the Centre Union (53 per cent) to the extreme Left. As a direct consequence of the king's speech Theodorakis's music is banned on Greek radio. The sale of his records increases despite attempts by the police to get the names of the purchasers. The unions organise concerts of Theodorakis's music which generally end in political demonstrations. January sees the appearance of the 'Manifesto of the Lambrakides—Who are we? What do we want? Why do they fight us'. It is written by Theodorakis. The book makes a violent attack on the royal family. The main target is the administration of the queen's funds; there is no obligation to publish the accounts. The queen's funds come from a number of indirect taxes and are a hangover from the period of reconstruction after the civil war. In order to make the royal family popular it was given the role of 'social ministry', to hand out alms. Now it was being asked whether all the funds had been handed out.

22 May 1966   Thousands of Greeks and foreigners take part in the peace march from Marathon to Athens to commemorate the third anniversary of the assassination of Lambrakis.

10 July 1966 Peasants in the north of Greece are unhappy about the price of cereals. They march to Thessalonika. The military stop them. The result: 140 wounded. Demonstrations against the king's anti-parliamentary actions become more and more frequent over the next eight months. In the end the king bows to the pressure of the opposition and promises new parliamentary elections for 28 May 1967.

19 April 1967 Theodorakis approaches Papandreou with a view to forming a united patriotic front against the fascist threat.

20 April 1967 Theodorakis spends the day at home in Nea Smyrni. Myrto is preparing for her husband's trip to Holland, where he has been invited by Philips, the recording company.

21 April 1967 A friend on the Right telephones Theodorakis at four in the morning to tell him that the military *coup d'état*, which had been feared for a long time, has taken place. Theodorakis goes underground. At six o'clock he and a friend make the first appeal for resistance. It later transpires that it is the secret service officer, George Papadopoulos, and some other colonels who have carried out the *coup*—and not the king's generals. Their *coup* was planned for the 23rd...An emergency state of martial law is proclaimed and thousands of people are arrested and deported to island prisons, among them several who had been in prison in the forties and fifties. What amounts to a police state is set up and 30 per cent of national revenue is set aside for defence and security. The Ministry of Public Order is the most important ministry in the administration: it takes up eleven columns in the telephone directory, compared with the Ministry of Education's two and a half. Censorship and torture become the noblest expressions of the new régime. The junta's seizure of power took place in accordance

309

with NATO's Prometheus Plan (mobilisation against the enemy within in the event of conflict with an enemy without). The junta's collaboration with NATO staff is to become total.

23 April 1967 Theodorakis publishes his second statement; it is roneoed.

28 April 1967 Greek Good Friday. The colonels prepare the 'feast of the resurrection' of Greek Orthodox civilisation with speeches and Te Deums. Theodorakis comes out of hiding and into town for a first meeting with the Lambrakides who have escaped the first wave of arrests. They decide to publish a resistance newspaper, *Nea Ellada (New Greece)*.

12 May 1967 The régime publishes its first list of banned works. There are several hundred titles, among them classical tragedies and a Bulgarian-Greek dictionary.

1 June 1967 Army Order No. 13 : 1. We have decided and we order that throughout the country it is forbidden (a) to reproduce or play the music and songs of the composer Mikis Theodorakis, the former leader of the now dissolved communist organisation, the Lambrakis Youth, because this music is in the service of communism; (b) to sing any songs used by the communist youth movement which was dissolved under Paragraph Eight of the Decree of 6 May 1967, since these songs arouse passions and cause strife among the people. 2. Citizens who contravene this Order will be brought immediately before the military tribunal and judged under martial law.

General Odysseas Angelis

(The German composer Paul Dessau has set this document to music—for narrator, mixed choir and nine instruments—in honour of Theodorakis.)

12 July 1967 'Athanassia Panagopolou, 23, has been arrested and brought before the tribunal in Athens accused of having contravened the law. At her house, 37 Evelpidon, she had put a Mikis Theodorakis record on her record-

310

player and turned the volume full up. Twelve records in her possession have been seized.' *(Eleftheros Kosmos)*[10]

21 August 1967   Theodorakis is arrested. He is taken to the headquarters of the Security Police at 18 Bouboulinas Street. The next morning he is transferred to Cell No. 4 on the fourth floor.

2 November 1967   Theodorakis begins a hunger strike in protest at not having been accepted as a witness in the trial of his Patriotic Front friends who have been arrested. Ten days later he is taken unconscious to the Averof prison hospital. The authorities refuse to allow Theodorakis to take part in the trial because they are seeking to create the impression that his arrest is due to the betrayal of his friends and that he himself has betrayed the organisation.

9 November 1967   'A military tribunal in Thessalonika last Wednesday condemned Konstantinos Daoutis, a 24-year-old shopkeeper, to four years' imprisonment for having sold a record of Mikis Theodorakis, whose music is banned.' (Agence France Presse)

15 November 1967   The trial begins at the Athens military tribunal of 31 people—15 men and 16 women—members of the Patriotic Front accused of acts of sabotage. It is like a trial of Theodorakis without Theodorakis being present. Captain Lambrou of the Security Police pretends in his testimony that Theodorakis is not the real head of the organisation, despite the fact that he founded it. Lambrou says Theodorakis has simply been exploited by the extremists in the Greek Communist Party who very quickly removed all powers of decision-making from him. It is clear from the cross-examination of the accused that they have all been tortured.

17 November 1967   Theodorakis writes 'The Sun and Time'.[11]

13 December 1967   King Constantine, who has never been able to accept that the April *coup d'état* was the work of the colonels and not of his generals, tries to effect a *coup d'état* in order to establish a distance between himself and the junta. In his message to 'his Hellenes' he says: 'Over the past twenty-five years the communist minority has tried, by treacherous and violent means, to overthrow our social and political institutions. This has brought us destruction and ruin, has contaminated the youth of the country and has put at risk the very existence of our race.' King Constantine's 'Hellenes' do not follow him: they know from experience that they do not accept his definition of communism. Theodorakis is in the Averof prison at the time of this *'coup d'état'*. When it is found out who the instigator of the *coup* is, panic spreads among the prisoners: they fear a large-scale massacre.

24 December 1967   The prisoners are allowed to spend Christmas Eve together. 'Averof University'—the name given by the prisoners to their society—sends out an invitation to the 'world premiére' of songs written by Theodorakis in his cell in Bouboulinas Street. Then the prisoners move on to Greek folk dances to keep out the cold. Papadopoulos (Premier since 14 December 1967) grants a Christmas amnesty for a few hundred prisoners; Theodorakis is one, but he is not freed.

22 January 1968   At the Athens Appeal Court Theodorakis's counsel, Khristoforos Argyropoulos, demands that his client be freed in accordance with the Christmas amnesty. It appears that the amnesty applies only to prisoners with sentences of less than six months; however the Court quashes one of Theodorakis's three sentences and reduces the other two, which are both of eight months, to four months and fifteen days respectively. There was now a chance of his being freed; apparently the régime had given in to international pressure. But at the same time it is made clear that after being freed Theodorakis will be transferred to the concentration camp on Leros, which is not considered to be a prison but an internment camp

312

for citizens who constitute a 'threat to society'. A court decision is not necessary for such a transfer.

27 January 1968   After a series of legal complications Theodorakis is freed. 'If he renounces all involvement in politics the ban on his music will be lifted,' says Sideratos, director-general of the Ministry of Information. He implies that an agreement has already been reached. 'I accept no compromises,' Theodorakis tells a Reuter correspondent.

28 January 1968   After five months' imprisonment without trial Theodorakis receives the world press at his house. His 'freedom' becomes residence under surveillance for the next few months. Captain Lambrou calls on him constantly, and telephones him at all hours of the day and night.

12 May 1968   The deputy George Tsaroukhas (the second victim in the Lambrakis murder of 22 May 1963) is killed by the Security Police outside Thessalonika, after being in hiding for over a year.

12 June 1968   The director-general of the Ministry of Information announces at a press conference that the ban on Theodorakis's music is in force again. It has never been lifted.

13 August 1968   A young student, Alekos Panagoulis, fails in an attempt on Premier Papadopoulos's life.

21 August 1968   The Security Police come for Theodorakis and his family in their summer residence at Vrakhati; they are transferred to the mountain village of Zatouna.

29 September 1968   A '92 per cent' vote for the new Greek Constitution confirms the dictatorship *de facto*.

3 November 1968   Half a million people accompany George Papandreou to the cemetery, shouting 'Down with the junta!', 'Democracy!' and 'NO to the Constitution!'

There are scuffles with the police but in the end the authorities get the situation under control.

November 1968 A German television team returns from Zatouna with tape recordings by Theodorakis.

16 March 1969 John Barry discloses in the *Sunday Times* that he has been to Zatouna and has succeeded in smuggling out several tapes recorded by Theodorakis and letters, some of which are addressed to U Thant, Secretary-General of the United Nations. On the tapes Theodorakis has recorded some new songs and describes the conditions of his internment.

21 April 1969 The junta celebrates the second anniversary of its seizure of power with dignified processions and chauvinist speeches. Theodorakis writes a song attacking Marc Marceau, the *Le Monde* correspondent in Athens and author of *La Grèce des Colonels* (1967).

19 October 1969 It is officially announced that Theodorakis has been transferred to the Oropos prison, north of Athens. The reason given is that it will be easier to look after him there.

26 March 1970 A Scandinavian parliamentary delegation goes to Greece with a Danish lung specialist with the aim of giving Theodorakis medical help, but they get no further than Athens airport.

9 April 1970 Theodorakis is admitted to the Sotira prison hospital after a recurrence of tuberculosis.

13 April 1970 The French politician Jean-Jacques Servan-Schreiber lands at Paris-Le Bourget at 17.30—accompanied by Theodorakis. Servan-Schreiber had been in Greece making representations on behalf of members of the 'Democratic Defence' league who had been condemned, when he suddenly had the unexpected chance of getting Theodorakis out, thanks to the personal intervention of Premier Papadopoulos. It transpired later

314

that Theodorakis's name had been on a list of 322 prisoners whom the junta was intending to free on its third anniversary in power, 21 April 1970. Freeing Theodorakis prematurely was doubtless an attempt to influence the ministers of the Council of Europe who were to meet on 15 April in Strasbourg to decide whether the 1,200 page report of the Human Rights Commission on the use of torture in Greek prisons should be published. Publication of the report was approved by seventeen member countries in spite of the junta's efforts to bribe delegates. When Theodorakis had left Le Bourget airport in an ambulance, Servan-Schreiber read a statement he had drafted in the aircraft: 'I still cannot understand that I am a free man. A few hours ago I was completely isolated. Now, after three tragic years, I can breathe free air again. But the taste of freedom is still bitter, for I have left my wife and two little children in Athens, and many of my comrades are still suffering. The fact that I am here this evening is due to international solidarity and many European friends.'

11 May 1970   Myrto Theodorakis and the two children, Margarita and Yorgos, arrive in Paris while Theodorakis is speaking at a public meeting in the Salle de la Mutualité. They had managed to escape from the Greek police with the help of three young Frenchmen. For more than twenty hours they had fought storms and seasickness in a small boat before landing safe and sound in Sicily.

(Note: This chronology is by Ole Wahl Olsen, and taken from Mikis Theodorakis, *Fem meter fra min celle* [Five Yards From My Cell], published by Sigvaldis Forlag, Denmark.)

References

1 Ethniko Apeleftherotiko Metopo.
2 Ethnikos Laikos Apeleftherotikos Stratos: National Popular Liberation Army.
3 Ethniki Panelliniki Organosi Neon: National Panhellenic Youth Organisation.

4 In his 12 March speech to Congress, President Truman described Greece as one of the 'free peoples' which it 'must be the policy of the United States to support'. Both Greece and Turkey, the President said, were 'still free countries' but were 'being challenged by communist threats from within and without'; they were now valiantly struggling to preserve their liberties and independence. The speech sought military and economic aid for Greece, Britain having informed the United States on 24 February that she could no longer pay for her troops in Greece. It was the civil war in Greece which gave President Truman the opportunity to declare that the world was divided between two alternative ways of life and to proclaim an ideological crusade against the 'un-American' way. 'One way of life is based upon the will of the majority and is distinguished by free institutions, representative government, free elections, guarantees of individual liberty, freedom of speech and religion and freedom from political repression. The second way of life is based upon the will of a minority forcibly imposed upon the majority. It relies upon terror and oppression, a controlled press and radio, fixed elections and the suppression of personal freedoms...' (Translator's Note.)

5 Enosis Dimokratikis Aristeras: United Democratic Left.

6 'Progressive Change'.

7 *Dawn,* daily of the United Democratic Left, EDA.

9 EK: Enosis Kentrou.

9 Oratorio composed to the verse text of Odysseas Elytis. Elytis (pen name of Alepoudelis) was born in Crete in 1911 and comes from a well known industrial family from Lesbos. He is now a businessman. 'Axion Esti' is perhaps his greatest work and certainly the most complex; it is modelled on a Byzantine liturgy and verse and prose alternate to describe the genesis and growth of a poet's consciousness. The title is the first two words of a liturgical hymn to the Virgin, 'It is meet to bless thee'. (Translator's Note.)

10 'Free world'.

11 'O Ilios ke o Khronos', a cycle composing of sixteen songs—words and music both written by Theodorakis—and thirty-two poems.

DICTIONARY OF THE GREEK RESISTANCE

Amnesty International: International organisation having consultative status at the Council of Europe and concerning itself with the problems of political detention in different countries throughout the world. Following an enquiry in Greece in December 1967 it drew up a crushing report proving that torture was systematically used by the junta's police.

Andreas Papandreou: The son of the former Premier is usually known in Greece by his first name. He was a refugee in the United States during the war and made a university career, becoming professor of political economics at Harvard. He supported the liberal cause which brought John F. Kennedy to the White House. He returned to Greece in 1961 and played a decisive role before the putsch: the manifestly progressive positions he took up and the establishment under his aegis of a dynamic Centre-Left, which went beyond and embarrassed his father's traditional party, nudged the country's political equilibrium firmly to the Left. He became the target of attacks by the Palace and the Right wing, who attempted to destroy his prestige by accusing him of having organised a republican plot within the Army (cf. Aspida). He was arrested by the junta on 21 April 1967 but was released the following year after numerous representations from American political and university circles. He sought refuge in Sweden and then Canada; he now holds a chair at Toronto University. He founded a resistance movement, the PAK, which advocated armed struggle and which

319

to this day has refused to join the National Council of the Resistance.

Asfalia: General Security Police, in charge of security throughout the country, the cracking of clandestine networks and the suppression of all so-called 'subversive' activities.

Aspida ('shield' in Greek): Plot denounced by the Right under the Centre government. Rumours of its activity led to the trial, in January and February 1967 (three months before the putsch), of twenty-eight officers who supported Papandreou and who were accused of having constituted a Nasserite junta whose plan was to bring Andreas Papandreou back to power and reverse Greece's alliances. This tumultuous trial was undertaken *in camera* and very quickly without the guilt of the accused being established and the role played by Andreas Papandreou demonstrated. In fact it served to set in motion a vast purge of Centrist elements in the Army.

Assassinations: Despite the official myth of a 'clean revolution', the junta has several times resorted to assassination to liquidate its opponents. Among the most notorious was the assassination in Rhodes in 1967 of the lawyer Mandilaras, who had defended the officers accused in the Aspida affair. His body, which had been thrown into the sea so his death would appear to have been an accident, was washed up and found on an island. George Tsaroukhas, the EDA deputy who had been at Lambrakis's side when he was murdered, was arrested on 8 May 1968 and some hours later was beaten to death by the Salonika security police. The police told his family he had had a heart attack and refused to allow them to open the coffin. On the day of the burial Tsaroukhas's daughter threw herself at the coffin, managed to open it and saw her father's battered and bloodstained face. Maria Kalabrou was killed in the middle of an Athens street on the day of the putsch and Panayotis Ellis, a former member of the resistance, was summarily executed at the Athens racecourse two days later for refusing to shout nationalist slogans.

Avgi: *Dawn*, the daily newspaper of the EDA party, banned since 21 April 1967.

Babalis: Well-known torturer for the Athens Security.

Bleaching: Procedure which makes it possible for a Greek citizen no longer to be taken for a 'red' and to have his dossier filed with the police. It consists essentially of 'Dilosis' (q.v.).

Bouboulinas Street: Headquarters of the Athens Security Police until 1971, and where opponents of the régime were 'welcomed' after their arrest. This building, with its famous 'terrace', is the symbol of a medieval terror. The brutalities committed there take up a large part of the report of the Council of Europe's Commission on Human Rights.

Bridge: An idea put forward by Averof, the Foreign Minister in the Karamanlis government, according to which the men of the *ancien régime* should build a bridge between themselves and the junta with a view to leading the latter to become more liberal and 'civilised'. This was the old idea of collaborating with the oppressor in disguise.

Bulgarians: The name the Right-wing Greeks give to the communists.

Certificate: The *passe-partout* of the Greek citizen, without which he is powerless and cannot get work. The most important certificate is the Citizen's Certificate, which has been required of all candidates for public or semi-public posts since the civil war and without which it is impossible to enrol at a university, obtain a driving licence, etc.

Communist: For the thirty years in which the Right has been in power in Greece this term has vaguely included everything which is not connected with the most lunatic reaction, so that one has always been a 'communist' in someone's eyes.

Coups d'État: In contemporary political mythology a distinction must be made between several types of *coup d'état*. The *electoral coup d'état* of 1961, and the atmosphere of terror created by the Army and the Karamanlis government in order that the election should be won. The *constitutional coup d'état* of July 1965 when King Constantine accepted Papandreou's resignation (which had not been formally offered) although he had been carried to power by 53 per cent of the electorate. The *colonels' coup d'état* which brought the present régime to power. The *generals' coup d'état* which would have taken place some days later, with the king's consent. Finally, the *counter-coup d'état* of King Constantine which was intended to re-capture power from the colonels and which ended in a complete fiasco.

Cruiser 'Elli': Royal Greek Navy ship on which political prisoners were tortured after the putsch.

Democratic Defence: Centre-Left resistance organisation founded in the summer of 1967. The arrest of Professor Karayorgas as he was handling an explosive device in his house led to the cracking of one of its most important networks and the trial of the thirty-four in April 1970.

Dilosis Metanoias: 'Declaration of repentance'. Plays the same role in contemporary Greek history as recantation did under the Inquisition. Under this declaration, any suspect person officially repudiates communism and can thereby be freed and reinte-grated into the 'national community'. Since 1936 thousands of progressive leaders and militants have remained interned for years, refusing to sign this declaration. It has often divided the Left into 'signatories' and 'non-signatories'.

Dionysos: Military camp about twenty kilometres north-east of Athens and under the command of Major Manousakis. It special-ises in the 're-education' of the young, especially the Lambrakis Youth, who were subjected to daily brutality and systematic brainwashing. The camp's existence was only brought to the attention of world public opinion at the beginning of 1968. Colonel Vasilios Ioannidis, the head of the military police, per-sonally conducted the interrogations.

EAM: National Liberation Front (Ethniko Apeleftherotiko Metopo). A clandestine organisation founded in 1941 on the initiative of the Greek Communist Party. It rapidly became the main strength of the resistance to the Nazi occupation. In 1944 EAM had, in effect, liberated the entire country single-handedly, and it had then to confront the British intervention.

EDA: United Democratic Left (Enosis Dimokratikis Aristeras).
A legal party founded in 1951, the Greek Communist Party—
banned since the civil war—having only a clandestine organisation. EDA attracted a part of the Communist Party's former
support while, at the same time, being open to all progressive
forces with a very moderate and flexible programme. It was
banned after the 1967 putsch.

EK: Centre Union (Enosis Kentrou), George Papandreou's
party.

ELAS: National Popular Liberation Army (Ethnikos Laikos
Apeleftherotikos Stratos), the military organisation of EAM under
the occupation.

Elytis, Odysseas: Greek poet, born in Crete in 1911, author of
'Axion Esti', on which Mikis Theodorakis wrote an oratorio
(see Note 9 on p. 32).

EPON: National Panhellenic Youth Organisation (Ethniki
Panelliniki Organosi Neon), set up in 1943 on the initiative of
EAM.

ERE: Radical National Union (Ethniki Rizospastiki Enosis),
Rightist party founded in 1956 by Konstantin Karamanlis. The
party was in power without a break until the elections of 1963,
which brought in the Centre Union. After Karamanlis's exile
to Paris in December 1963, the party was led by Panayiotis
Kanellopoulos, who was Premier at the time of the 1967 *coup
d'état*.

Esso-Pappas: Standard Oil's petroleum complex set up in
Greece and run by a Bostonian businessman of Greek origin, Tom
Pappas. Pappas, who financed the Nixon election campaign and
heads an industrial empire, symbolises for the Greek people the
hold which the American economy has on Greece. In an interview published in 1967 Pappas admitted that he worked for the
CIA.

Estia: Newspaper of the extreme Right which specialises in anti-communism and anti-semitism. It belongs to the Kyrou family.

Falanga: A kind of torture which is peculiar to the Greek police. As reported by Amnesty International and the Human Rights Commission, the technique is to tie the prisoner to a bench and hit the soles of his feet with a baton or a lead pipe. The treatment lasts anything from one to four hours. Often the victim's shoes are kept on, with the result that the resonance in the brain is stronger and his feet swell. The next stage is to untie the prisoner and make him run around the bench, while being beaten all over his body. The wounds on the feet take about four months to scar over and heal. Fractures of the metatarsus are not uncommon and the victim may limp for the rest of his days.

Funerals: National funerals are decisive moments in contemporary Greek history at which passions that have been contained too long by oppression explode. Like the chorus of the old, the crowd engages in a dialogue with the dead person which is truly overwhelming as it is taken up by thousands of voices all the way down the funeral cortège: 'Athanatos!', 'Immortal!' Such a funeral was that of the poet, Palamas, under the Occupation, at which Sikelianos, by way of a funeral eulogy, recited to the crowd a poem full of blazing patriotism, and that of the former head of ELAS, General Sarafis, which became the pretext for a demonstration against the Anglo-American intervention. In 1963 half a million people accompanied the assassinated deputy, Grigoris Lambrakis, to his grave. These funerals marked a turning point in post-war Greek history, initiating a process of liberalisation which was to bring the Centre Union to power. After Papandreou's fall there was the funeral of Sotiris Petroulas, who had been killed by the police during a demonstration against the royal *coup de force,* and that of George Papandreou, on 3 November 1968, which took place in an atmosphere of terror created by the junta and which turned into a real riot: over 400,000 people—the figure estimated by foreign correspondents—escorted the remains of the former Premier with cries of 'Liberty!', 'Down with the junta!', and 'Today we're voting!' Because of its size, and because it happened only a month after the referendum imposed by the régime, this first mass demonstration against the junta marked a psychological turning point and destroyed once and for all the myths of 'acceptance' and 'passivity' of the Greek people.

Glezos, Manolis: Resistance hero, known throughout the world for having torn down the Nazi flag from the Acropolis on 31 May 1941, one month after the Germans had entered Athens. In 1959 he was condemned for espionage by the Karamanlis government. In 1961 he was elected deputy for Athens while still in prison; his election was quashed. He was freed in December 1962 as a result of an international campaign. He was arrested again on 21 April 1967 and deported to Leros. He was released in July 1971.

Graeco-Christian Civilisation: This glorious expression neatly covers the confused ideology of the military régime. There is also the slogan which is found everywhere: 'Greece of the Christian Greeks'.

Grammos: A mountain in the Pindhos range, in the north-west of the country, near the Albanian border, where the last action of the civil war took place in August 1949. Surrounded, cut off and under attack from vastly superior numbers of royalist forces fighting with American equipment, the partisans of the Democratic Army—those who were not killed—had a choice between exile in the East and the White terror.

Hadjidakis, Manos: Composer of, among other things, 'The Children of Piraeus'; very famous in the 1950s. The success of Theodorakis's 'Epitafios' in 1959 established a rivalry between himself and Hadjidakis, and split Greece into two musical camps.

Halikarnassos: Camp on Crete where women were deported; closed in 1970.

Ioannidis, Lieutenant-colonel: Chief of the military police, and one of the régime's hardliners.

Justice: 'Greek justice is and always will be the best justice that has ever existed in human society' (Colonel Papadopoulos).

Kanellopoulos, Panayotis: Uncle by marriage of Karamanlis and his successor as leader of the ERE Party in 1963. Much more liberal than Karamanlis and university-educated, he enjoyed a certain intellectual prestige. He was Premier in April 1967 and was arrested in his home on the night of the putsch. Since then he has increasingly defied the régime by making appeals to world public opinion and giving evidence for the defence before military courts.

Karamanlis, Konstantin: Premier from 1955 to 1963. Leader of the Rightist party, ERE. His period in power came to an end with the Lambrakis affair, his difference with the Palace, and the arrival in the United States of the Kennedy Administration, which favoured a Centrist government in Greece. His prestige was damaged by various scandals and he exiled himself to Paris, where he dreamed of making a de Gaulle-like return to 'save' Greece; however, the 1967 putsch, by putting the former political class in the shadows, reduced his chances of making a saviour's comeback. Karamanlis has broken his silence only twice to condemn the junta: in 1967, on the eve of the king's counter-*coup d'état,* and in 1969, just before the Council of Europe's condemnation of the colonels' régime.

Karapanayotis: Notorious torturer for the Athens Security.

Kioupis: A 'doctor' highly valued by the Security torturers. He gives on-the-spot advice so that they do not go too far and kill their victims, thereby attracting trouble.

KKE: Initials of the Greek Communist Party (Kommounistiko Komma Elladas).

Kokkinia: Suburb of Piraeus. At dawn on 17 August 1944 Kokkinia was sealed off by the SS and the population assembled in the square and ordered to kneel down. Members of the resistance in their midst were then denounced by hooded informers and publicly tortured and executed. By the end of the day over 150 patriots had been martyred and 6,000 deported to Germany, most of them never to return.

Koliyannis: Secretary of the Communist Party. At the 12th plenum, held abroad in August 1968, he provoked a split by refusing to accept responsibility for the reverses suffered by the movement in Greece in connection with Partsalidis and other Politburo members who had fallen from their posts and had been thrown out. The latter, who belonged to the 'Interior Bureau' within Greece, then decided to take over responsibility for the direction of all the Party's organisations. This was how the final split came about between the Koliyannis faction, which was obedient to Moscow and supported the intervention in Czechoslovakia, and the Interior Bureau, which stood for the autonomy and independence of Greek communists within the international movement. After attempting to reunite the two sides, Theodorakis eventually threw in his lot with the latter in the spring of 1970.

Kollias, Konstantin: Supreme Court Prosecutor at the time of the Lambrakis affair, and a man who had the confidence of Queen Frederika. He was suspended by the Papandreou government for having put pressure on the magistrate during the preliminary investigation of the Lambrakis case. He was reinstated after Papandreou's fall in July 1965 and in the hours which followed the putsch, when the junta needed a 'civilian cover', he was put forward for the post of Premier, which he held until the king's counter-*coup d'état* in December 1967, whereupon he went into exile.

Kolonaki Square: A square in the centre of the 'chic' part of Athens; it is a rendezvous for artists, intellectuals and the cosmopolitan bourgeoisie.

Koukoue: 'Coco', or communist.

KYP; Central Intelligence Service (Kentriki Ypiresia Pliroforion), where Colonel Papadopoulos worked for a long time; its activities are closely linked with and subordinate to the American intelligence services.

Ladas, Colonel: Secretary-General in the Ministry of Security and later Minister of the Interior. Ladas is one of the junta's hardliners, a passionate anti-communist whose brutality is legendary.

327

Lambrakides: Members of the Lambrakis Youth, an organisation founded in 1964 following the assassination of the deputy, Lambrakis; the founder and president of the Lambrakis Youth is Mikis Theodorakis. Under his impetus it started a vast cultural renaissance movement: libraries and clubs, scholarships, the development of popular song, etc. The organisation, which had more than fifty thousand members and three hundred branches all over Greece, very soon provoked a hysterical reaction from the Right which clamoured for its dissolution. After the *coup d'état* the Lambrakides were relentlessly hunted down and tortured by the Security because they represented the strength and dynamism of a new political generation which had decided not to accept the *fait accompli* and to reject the 'prudence' of the old militants.

Lambrou, Vasilios: The junta's most celebrated torturer, the deputy director of Security, whom Theodorakis in one of his poems calls 'Suleyman the Magnificent'. Elegant, affable and with a polished vocabulary, Lambrou is in charge of all that goes on at Bouboulinas Street. He often pretends to his detainees that he is profoundly grieved to have to deliver them into the sadistic hands of his subordinates; however, he does not disdain to take part himself in the 'performances'.

Law 509: Emergency law applied from 1947 to the end of the civil war, and in force under all governments ever since. It sets outside the law any movement which is related, however loosely, to the Communist Party and any organism which 'has as its aim the overthrow by violence of the state system and the existing social order'. This law permits of any number of interpretations and serves to discourage the holding of oppositional views. It was made complete by another device inherited from the Metaxas dictatorship (1936) which provided for sentence of death for any espionage offence. The notion of espionage also gives rise to the most diverse interpretations and this procedure of exception which has been perpetrated for more than thirty years has been responsible for the execution of Beloyannis, for the solitary confinement of Glezos and for the very heavy sentencing of the majority of the régime's opponents.

Leros: Island in the Dodecanese where two deportation camps were opened at the end of 1967 to take the detainees from Youra. The camps were closed in 1971.

Liapis: Procurator at military tribunals. A sinister silhouette figure encountered in all the big trials: the Fouquier-Tinville of the 'National Revolution'.

Makarezos, Colonel: Minister of Co-ordination since April 1967 and the only member of the junta with any competence in economic matters.

Makronisos: Small, rocky, uninhabited island in the Aegean, near Cape Sounion. In 1948 Makronisos became a camp for 'national re-education' and all Greeks suspected of holding progressive views were deported there. Barely three years after the revelations about Nazi camps the 'free world' had shut its eyes to this resurgence of horror. The entire élite of the Resistance and the Democratic Army were liquidated on Makronisos as a result of innumerable experiments: bludgeonings, drownings, summary executions, 'falanga', sham burials, and deprivation of water. Makronisos was at the end of the chain of island prisons of Youra, Lemnos, Ikaria and Ayios Efstratios. In all, more than a hundred thousand men were to follow this path to their Calvary. But can one speak of Makronisos? As Ritsos, who, like Theodorakis, survived it, said, 'Makronisos, like hell, has no stories to tell. There is nothing to say about it.'

Mallios: Famous torturer, Lambrou's assistant at the Athens Security.

Massacres: There were about a dozen in Greece under the Occupation. Among the most horrifyingly famous are Kalavrita, a village in the Peloponnese, where, on 11 December 1943, the Germans locked the women and children in the church and set fire to it, then took the men and boys over fourteen to the cemetery and machine-gunned them to the ground—death toll 1,100; Kommeno-Arta, where, on 15 August 1943, 317 villagers, among them 97 children under fifteen, were killed; Distomo, near Levadia, where, on 10 June 1944, 296 villagers were massacred by the SS in a sadistic outburst; Klisoura, where, on 6 April 1944, 233 peasants were executed. And so on.

329

Metaxes, General: Premier under King George II in 1936. At the king's request and taking a general strike as a pretext, Metaxas established a dictatorship known as the '4th August régime', which lasted until the German intervention of 1941. The Metaxas régime was in many respects—the exception procedure, police terror, deportations, fascist-like ideology—a forerunner of the one which came to power on 21 April 1967.

Mountain, The: Synonym for the Maquis in Greece; the 'government of the Mountain' is that of the Resistance, and later of the insurgent communists during the civil war.

Nation: This concept is linked in the Greek mind with a constant anxiety with regard to a national independence which has always been threatened by the Great Powers. This is why the word 'nation' is so frequently encountered in the vocabulary of the Left, and notably in the writings and statements of Theodorakis.

National Council of the Resistance: Formed in 1971 by the most important resistance organisations, which were anxious to co-ordinate their action—the Patriotic Front, Democratic Defence, Free Greeks and the Defenders of Liberty.

Oropos: Deportation camp in Attica, opposite the largest of the Greek islands, Euboea. The final place of detention for Theodorakis.

Oxi: 'No'—the Greek people's reply to Mussolini's ultimatum of 28 October 1940, the commemoration of which became a national holiday.

PAM: Patriotic Anti-Dictatorship Front (q.v.).

PAK: Panhellenic Liberation Movement (Panelliniko Apeleftherotiko Kinima), of the Centre-Left, founded by Andreas Papandreou.

Panagoulis, Alekos: Responsible for a failed attempt on the life of Colonel Papadopoulos on 13 August 1968; it took place in conditions which, in the junta's official version, are scarcely credible and which the ensuing trial made no clearer. The important thing is that Panagoulis claimed responsiblity for the assassination attempt with such courage and idealism that his personal defeat became the first decisive act of resistance to the dictatorship. Panagoulis was condemned to death in November 1968 and because of the indignation the sentence aroused throughout the world the junta gave way and suspended the execution, at the cost of causing a grave crisis within the Revolutionary Council. Panagoulis is still detained in inhuman conditions.

Papadopoulos, George : The organiser and inspiration behind the plot which led to the *coup d'état* of 21 April 1967. He is a born conspirator who is only at ease in secret and likes power too much to be satisfied with anything but the real thing. This instinct for intrigue, allied with a consuming ambition, doubtless explains his dominance of his equals which has enabled him to overcome several internal crises without difficulty. He likes people in Greece and abroad to think there is a subtle distance between himself and the other colonels, to give credence to the thesis that he is leading a 'liberal' group against a group of 'hardliners'—men like Ladas and Ioannidis. His aim is to appear to be the lesser evil on all occasions; but he is gambling on the patience of the Greek people.

Papandreou, George: Papandreou the Elder. Premier from November 1963 to July 1965. These twenty months are the only liberal interlude the country has enjoyed since 1936. A political animal *par excellence* and a brilliant orator who knew how to establish emotional links with the people, Papandreou's political activity summed up thirty years of Greek history, with his equivocations, wild impulses and concessions to the parliamentary game. The disappointment he caused was in proportion to the hope he had embodied. Perhaps he was only really great in defeat, when he provoked an almost desperate fervour around himself. In this sense his death (1968) allowed him to take his most beautiful political revenge.

Patriotic Anti-Dictatorship Front: PAM (Patriotiko Anti-diktatoriko Metopo), resistance organisation found in May 1967 by Mikis Theodorakis and embracing most former members of EDA. In August 1967 the Theodorakis-Filinis network was

331

cracked and Theodorakis was arrested. The official split in the Greek Communist Party in February 1968 had its repercussions in the Patriotic Front, which drew closer to the interior Communist Party as opposed to the Koliyannis faction, which tended towards Moscow.

Pattakos, Stylianos: General and one of the triumvirate, the other two being Papadopoulos and Makarezos. His contribution to the success of the putsch was decisive for he commanded the training centre for the armoured divisions of the Athens region. He brought himself immediately to the attention of the public with his coarse frankness; his gaffes have become famous: 'We undertook the *coup d'état* in order to avoid the elections', 'Youra is an idyllic spot', 'There are no political prisoners in Greece', 'The Council of Europe is just a mosquito attacking an ox's horn', etc. Thanks to this picturesque soldier's talk, Pattakos is the only member of the junta to enjoy some measure of popularity. His political role is relatively unobtrusive.

Petroulas, Sotiris: Student and member of the Lambrakis Youth, killed by the police at the demonstration in the centre of Athens during the summer crisis of 1965.

Plans: Although the Plans bear the prestigious names of Greek heroes of antiquity, these names do nothing to remove their evil nature. The *Pericles Plan* was put into effect by the Greek Army in 1961 to enable it to intervene directly in the electoral consultations on behalf of Karamanlis's government party; the aim was achieved but the electoral *coup d'état* brought about a grave crisis, angered the opposition and led to the defeat of the Right in 1963. The *Prometheus Plan* was drawn up by the NATO staff for use in the event of a communist *coup* in Greece; it was implemented in full on 21 April 1967 just when the country was preparing to vote the Papandreou party back into power. The *Poseidon Plan* is known only by a leak of information; it was intended, in the minds of the Greek intelligence services, to control and eliminate Greek political exiles in Europe in 1969.

Rigas Ferraios: Clandestine Greek student organisation, bearing the name of an Independence hero.

Ritsos, Yannis: Poet, born in Momemvasia in 1909. 'The greatest living poet' (Louis Aragon, April 1971). Deported from 1948 to 1952 for his progressive ideas, he was arrested again on 21 April 1967 and sent to Youra and Leros. After eighteen months' detention he was sent to live on the island of Samos. His poor state of health necessitated his being freed at the end of 1970. His collection of poems, 'Epitafios', which appeared in 1936, was set to music by Mikis Theodorakis in 1959 and gave the composer his first great popular success. Another collection 'Greekness' (Romiosini), was set to music in 1965.

Seferis, George: Poet, born in Smyrna in 1900. Nobel Prize for Literature, 1963. Several of his poems have been set to music by Theodorakis, among them 'Mythology', 'Epiphany' and 'Raven'. In March 1969, Seferis, who had remained silent since the *coup d'état,* publicly adopted a position against the régime: 'It is a state of enforced torpor in which all the intellectual values we have made such efforts to keep alive are gradually submerged in a bog, in stagnant waters.'

Sixth Fleet: American Mediterranean squadron which is seen dropping anchor each time a crisis looms on the Greek political horizon.

Spanos: Notorious torturer for the Security Police.

TEA: National Guard Regiments (Tagmata Ethnofylakis Amynis) which go back to the time of the civil war. They are paramilitary formations made up of armed peasants and led by serving officers. They have often intervened during elections—notably in 1961—to create an atmosphere of terror and to influence the outcome of the vote.

Terrace: The terrace of the Security Police headquarters in Bouboulinas Street became the main place of torture. Beneath it a motor cycle was started up to drown the victims' cries.

Vlachou, Helen: Owner of a chain of Rightist newspapers, *Mesimvrini* (Meridian), *Kathimerini* (Daily News) and *Ikones* (Pictures), which she stopped publishing as a protest against the new régime. She now lives in London.

333

Zakhariadis, Nikos: General Secretary of the Greek Communist Party before the war. Deported to Dachau during the Occupation. On his return to Greece in May 1945 he resumed the leadership of the Communist Party and led it into armed struggle with the monarcho-fascist régime. In spite of the defeat of the Democratic Army in 1949 and the complete isolation of the movement, Zakhariadis got his dogmatic Stalinist line approved at the Party's Third Conference in 1950. The Twentieth Congress of the Communist Party of the Soviet Union in March 1956 led the Sixth Plenum of the Greek Communist Party Central Committee, meeting abroad, to agree to a severe charge being made against the Stalinist régime which had been imposed on the Party by Zakhariadis and against the errors committed during the civil war.

Gérard Pierrat